Born in the U.S.A.

A Volume in the Series
Public History in Historical Perspective
Edited by Marla R. Miller

Born in the U.S.A.

BIRTH, COMMEMORATION, AND AMERICAN PUBLIC MEMORY

★ ★ ★ ★ ★ ★ ★ ★ ★ ★ ★ ★

EDITED BY

Seth C. Bruggeman

University of Massachusetts Press

Amherst and Boston

LC 2012007992
ISBN 978-1-55849-938-6 (paper); 937-9 (library cloth)

Designed by Sally Nichols
Set in Scala Family
Printed and bound by Thomson-Shore, Inc.

Library of Congress Cataloging-in-Publication Data

Born in the U.S.A : birth, commemoration, and American public memory / edited
by Seth C. Bruggeman.
   p. cm. — (Public history in historical perspective)
Includes bibliographical references and index.
ISBN 978-1-55849-938-6 (pbk. : alk. paper) — ISBN 978-1-55849-937-9 (library
cloth : alk. paper) 1. Historic sites—United States. 2. Birthplaces—United States.
I. Bruggeman, Seth C., 1975–
E159.B745 2012
973—dc23
                                                        2012007992

British Library Cataloguing in Publication data are available.

Contents

Acknowledgments

Every edited collection relies for its success on the countless lifelines that buoy each of its contributors, and so I reserve these acknowledgments for those folks who helped our shared enterprise along. First thanks on that account go to Brian Horrigan of the Minnesota Historical Society whose session at the 2007 meeting of the National Council on Public History in Santa Fe got me thinking that a book about birthplaces might not be a bad idea. Next up, of course, are the contributors. I'm grateful to all of them for sharing their wisdom and enduring my constant fussing. In particular, I thank Kris Myers for managing an impossible deadline. Paul Lewis wrote a fantastic essay *and* helped offset production costs. Pat West and David Glassberg deserve special thanks too for lending their time and their considerable presence to this project.

A number of people filled gaps along the way in my understanding of birthplace commemoration. At Temple University, Wilbert L. Jenkins helped me plumb the problem of Barak Obama's birthplace controversy, and Travis Glason reminded me early on that people are born in Britain too. Devin Thomas, of Temple's public history program, spent long hours on the phone surveying birthplace stewards about visitation numbers and funding sources. I want to thank the Alice Paul Institute's Barbara Irvine too for keeping this project on track at the last minute, and for giving us an opportunity to recognize her important work.

I count myself incredibly fortunate that Marla Miller, who edits the University of Massachusetts Press's Public History in Perspective series, agreed that a birthplace book might be interesting and, better yet, worthy of her series. Her close reading and careful guidance makes us all seem a lot smarter. I am grateful too for support from the rest of the UMass team, including Clark Dougan, Kay Scheuer, Bruce Wilcox, and everyone else including our anonymous reviewers who have a hand in getting books made. The making of this one also benefited from a generous gift from Temple University's College of Liberal Arts Research Council.

It's wholly a matter of happenstance that while writing about birthplaces, I've had cause to dwell on one in particular. My daughter, Juniata Gladys Bruggeman, was born just as this volume went to press. Although I've refrained from erecting a monument, I can't help but think that this place will always hold special meanings for both of us.

Born in the U.S.A.

Actress Claire Luce, photographed by Bob Landry in 1945, stands beside a sign that directs tourists to the birthplace of William Shakespeare on Henley Street, Stratford-upon-Avon, Warwickshire, England. Photo courtesy of Getty Images.

INTRODUCTION
Locating the Birthplace in American Public Memory
SETH C. BRUGGEMAN

Does it matter where we are born? Does "the accent of one's birthplace," as the early modern pundit François de La Rochefoucauld put it, "[persist] in the mind and heart as much as in one's speech?" Or does our obsession with origins amount to a fool's quest? Are we, like Herman Melville's wayward patriot, Israel Potter, condemned to discover that the birthplaces we cherish exist in memory alone?[1] The essayists in this volume neither test La Rochefoucauld's maxim nor tend Potter's homesickness. Rather our purpose here is to suggest that both typify a preoccupation with birthplaces that has figured prominently in the American commemorative landscape. That it has is evident in the phalanx of bronze placards, granite obelisks, and historic homes that preside over the nation's hallowed birth sites. For nearly two hundred years in some cases, birthplace monuments have enshrined nativity alongside patriotism and valor as among the key pillars of America's historical imagination. Our task, then, is to ask why this is and to inquire after the cultural significance of the birthplace monument in American memory.

One need not look much further than the world of American electoral politics to understand why ours is a task worth undertaking. Consider, for instance, Jerome R. Corsi's *Where's the Birth Certificate?: The Case That Barack Obama Is Not Eligible to Be President* (2011), which in June 2011 ranked sixth on the *New York Times*'s list of best-selling hardcover nonfiction. Corsi's book is, at its core, a book about birthplaces. It contends that persistent doubts concerning the site of President Obama's birth and the legality of his citizenship demand that his presidency be invalidated. But Corsi's screed is only the latest in a battle first joined during the heady run-up to the 2008 presidential election. Readers now may be surprised to recall that the presidential birthplace wars did not at first concern Obama alone, but also entangled his Republican opponent, Senator John McCain. Starting in 2008, bloggers claimed that McCain was not a natural-born citizen because he was born in a small town just outside the U.S.-controlled Panama Canal Zone, where the Navy stationed his father in 1936. His birthplace, they argued, disqualified McCain for the American presidency. A bipartisan spate of agitated senators responded swiftly to these charges by signing a joint resolution declaring their full confidence that McCain was a perfectly natural American and, given his impressive record of national service, perhaps even more so than most. Thus defended, John McCain cast his birthplace controversy into the wake of an otherwise ill-fated campaign.[2]

Obama was not so fortunate. Questions about his birthplace drew a considerably more virulent attack by those among his detractors who sought to leverage racism and xenophobia against the possibility of an African American president. Conspiracy theorists argued throughout 2008 that Obama had fabricated evidence of his 1961 birth in Honolulu, Hawaii. These so-called Birthers, for whom Corsi has become a prominent mouthpiece, alleged that Obama was actually born near his father's home in what is now Kenya, but which was then still a British colony. The Birthers still propose that Obama is doubly disqualified for the presidency on account of geography and British nationality laws. For its part, the Obama campaign stifled any reasonable doubt by circulating a copy of his birth certificate online in June 2008. And yet the controversy persisted well into Obama's presidency. As late as July 2009, mainstream news outlets including CNN, MSNBC, and NBC *Nightly News* continued to entertain the possibility of Obama's *un*natural citizenship. The Obama administration relented in April 2011 and, despite criticism from supporters who warned against bowing to the fringe, published the president's long-form birth certificate. Corsi's book appeared on shelves less than a month later.[3]

Partisan muckraking on both ends of the political spectrum has been a matter of course in American history. The dogged persistence of Obama's birth debate, however, signals something different. It demonstrates just how obsessed Americans are with origins. Where a person is born concerns us. Our preoccupation with presidential nativity is particularly telling because it reveals just how much authority we grant birthplaces in determining who is and who is not properly American. Both McCain's and Obama's birthplace controversies show that, despite important incentives everywhere to think globally, we still reckon our identities against prevailing political geographies. Where one is born—and, consequently, one's nationality—can often be, as in

McCain's case, a matter of mere political exigency and a handful of miles (or kilometers). The persistence of the awkward Constitutional proposition that a "natural" American can only be born within the nation's political boundaries, is striking in a supposed country of immigrants. Unfortunately, and more importantly, the suggestion that there is a right way to be born American necessarily implies the possibility of the opposite. This explains, in part, why racist invective achieved such remarkable ground during the 2008 election and why debates over immigration have dogged the nation more or less since its own birth.[4]

It also explains why presidential candidates so carefully narrate the circumstances of their early lives. From a campaign's standpoint, the actualities of one's birth hardly matter in a culture where public memory can be written in bylines and blogs. Presidential candidates have known this for a long time, at least since William Henry Harrison's famous 1840 campaign. Harrison, who was born in a Virginia mansion, rode to victory on a log cabin slogan twisted from an opponent's jab about how the old man should retire to a log cabin and a barrel of hard cider. Being born in a log cabin has since become a key strategy for presidential aspirants. It worked most famously for Abraham Lincoln, who actually was born in a log cabin. James Garfield used it in 1880 to dodge accusations of corruption and graft. Conversely, Adlai Stevenson decided against issuing a campaign biography during his 1952 campaign seeing as how "I wasn't born in a log cabin."[5] Even in the post–log cabin era, presidential candidates including Jimmy Carter and Bill Clinton—famously born in "a place called Hope" (Hope, Arkansas, that is)—have staked presidential aspirations on humble beginnings. In this volume, Christine Arato tells us that Rose Kennedy reminded visitors to her son's birthplace monument that "Jack thought being born at home was almost as good as being born in a log cabin like Lincoln."

Being born in a log cabin, however, does not ensure history's approbation. Enter the birthplace monument. Americans of all stripes have, especially during the last century, created birthplace monuments to safeguard uplifting memories of presidential births. Some of these, like Abraham Lincoln's century-old birthplace monument—which attracts nearly 180,000 visitors to Hogdenville, Kentucky, every year—are elaborate affairs with visitor centers and shrines. Others are more esoteric, like the simple stone pyramid that has marked James Buchanan's remote

Pennsylvanian birthplace since 1907. In either case, birthplace monuments cater to and most certainly reinforce our shared desire for true stories about great people born, as is often the case, in not-so-great circumstances. As Hilary Iris Lowe shows us in her essay, Mark Twain personally advocated for the preservation of Lincoln's birthplace, reasoning that since Lincoln "was marked by Providence as the one to bind up the Nation's wounds," it must have been, "no accident that planted [him] on a Kentucky farm." "The association there," Twain argued, "had substance in it." As evidenced by the scores of birthplace monuments, presidential and otherwise, that dot the American landscape today, the "substance" of that connection has proven among the most enduring themes in American public memory. This volume is partly intended to explore what precisely that substance has been and how it has changed over time.

The following essays demonstrate, however, that birthplace commemoration is not just about remembering. Rather, these monuments bear persistent influence on American political culture. Their quiet influence is so great in fact that we've come to believe that a presidential candidate's commemorative potential is itself a prequalification for office. Consider Drew Zahn's *WorldNetDaily* exclusive, "Born in the USA? Where's Monument for Obama's Birthplace?" Zahn proposes that the uncertainty surrounding Obama's birthplace, combined with the uninteresting circumstances of a hospital birth and the bureaucratic challenge of creating *any* national monument, spells doom for an Obama birthplace marker.[6] Writing alongside the Birthers, Zahn implies that the inability to commemorate Obama's birth renders him somehow less presidential than past worthies like John Adams and Ronald Reagan. Weak though it may be, Zahn's argument reminds us that Americans place remarkable faith in the testimony of simple old-fashioned historical markers. Even today, as our notions of authenticity are constantly redefined by new digital horizons, we still assent to the authority of cast bronze signs that boldly declare, like the one in Delaware, Ohio, that "this tablet marks the birthplace of Rutherford B. Hayes."

It is the birthplace monument's peculiar persistence in the nation's commemorative landscape that motivates this collection of essays. Certainly the golden age of birthplace commemoration has come and gone. Many of the campaigns to commemorate famous American births trace their origins to the first half of the twentieth century. Birth sites marked since the 1960s have often aimed to redress the cultural myopia of those earlier generations who failed to recall that women, workers, and people of color have been born here too. An even more recent spate of birthplace commemoration sought to stave off economic collapse by attracting tourist dollars to cash-strapped communities. So, how many birthplace markers and monuments are there in the United States? Because memory gets packaged in countless ways, tallying historic sites is a notoriously tricky business. The National Register of Historic Places, which eschews birthplaces unless they are of unparalleled historical significance, lists twenty-seven.[7] A quick Internet search turns up at least sixty more, ranging from simple plaques to historic homes. Arriving at an exact number would require a careful accounting too of state historical markers like the one erected recently in my hometown of Philadelphia, Pennsylvania, to honor the birthplace of pioneering bee keeper Lorenzo Langstroth. And what about the scads of unregistered local markers like the one in Kosciusko, Mississippi, that celebrates the birth in 1954 of Oprah Winfrey, "the world's foremost TV talk show host [who] never forgot . . . her heritage and has been a regular supporter of folks back home"? Though perhaps not so ubiquitous as war monuments, birthplace markers are indeed everywhere.

If, as it seems, birthplace monuments still clamor for our attention, what is it, then, that they are trying to tell us? The Obama birthplace wars suggest that the question may be more pressing than it seems on first glance. Wondering what it is that has compelled Americans to recall and often embellish birth stories is an important step toward understanding how commemoration plays an active and ongoing role in national culture. Public historians have known for some time that we trust museums and historic sites more than almost any other institutional source of historical knowledge.[8] What we cannot forget, however, and what Zahn makes painfully clear, is that the process by which memory is made at public monuments is always political. Our task here is to identify what is at stake and who is at play in the politics of remembering birth.

A Brief History of Birthplace Commemoration

As commonsensical as they might seem now, birthplace monuments have only made sense for as long as we have been used to believing that how and where we are born shapes who we become. This belief is so powerful that it's easy to forget that the idea has a history of its own. In the Western tradition, at least, the presumed link between birthplaces and adult character can be traced to the seventeenth century, during which Enlightenment musings about the origins of distinctive personality traits trickled into the itineraries of early European literary tourists who increasingly sought out places with biographical relevance to famous authors. John Milton's birthplace on London's Bread Street ranked among the earliest of these must-see destinations. William Shakespeare's Stratford-upon-Avon has been attracting tourists since at least 1769, including Thomas Jefferson and John Adams, all eager for a glimpse of the bard's birthplace. Its popular allure prompted Henry James's satirical short story "The Birthplace" (1903), wherein the keeper of a historic home wrestles with the possibility of its disingenuousness.[9] Patricia West shows us in our closing essay that James's lampoon still holds wisdom for those who manage historic house museums today.

Caroline E. Levander argues that, by the late eighteenth century, the frequent rhetorical admixture of childhood with emergent states—democracies, in particular—prefigured a kind of "natal nationalism."[10] Were we to write a history of American birthplace monuments, it might be no surprise that the early stirrings of natal nationalism on this side of the Atlantic concerned George Washington. First marked in 1815 about seventy miles south of Washington, DC, on Virginia's rural Northern Neck Peninsula, Washington's is likely the first birthplace monument in the United States. Washington's adopted grandson, George Washington Parke Custis, initially marked the spot in a fit of filiopietistic national pride right after the War of 1812. It was not until the 1920s, however, that a patriotic women's organization called the Wakefield Association began the serious commemorative work of building a replica of Washington's birth home. The site became a national monument, indeed one of the very first of the National Park Service's historical parks, just in time for the nationwide celebration of Washington's two hundredth birthday in 1932. That the "memorial house" turned out to be wholly inauthentic, and built on the wrong spot at that, didn't keep visitors away. About 100,000 people still come to see it every year.[11]

The history of Washington's birthplace suggests two stages in the evolution of American birth memory. First, Custis's errand into the Northern Neck reveals that the old Enlightenment association of origins with adult character had survived in North America, even as Americans struggled to navigate the inconsistencies of a new democratic republic. His meager birthplace marker would have resonated, for instance, with the politicians, clergy, and pundits of all sorts who encouraged the politically powerless wives of upwardly mobile white men to make their patriotic contribution by cultivating republican virtue in children. That any young boy might grow to be like Washington if raised appropriately was, after all, the lesson of Mason Locke Weems's *Life of Washington* (1800) and its notorious cherry tree fable. These early appeals to women would fundamentally shape how subsequent generations of preservationists remembered birth. The ideal of republican motherhood spread through advice manuals that instructed women how to cook, clean, and decorate in precisely the right ways to encourage moral character among impressionable children. This outpouring of what historian Sarah Robbins calls "domestic literacy narrative" persisted throughout the nineteenth century and colored the sensibilities of women like those at Washington's birthplace who sought to extend the didactic possibilities of republican motherhood to historic sites across the nation.[12] Even today, the recommendations of nineteenth-century domestic advice writers like Lydia Maria Child echo in the interpretive schema of birth shrines, childhood homes, and house museums of all kinds. Visitors to Harriet Beecher Stowe's preserved home in Hartford, Connecticut, for example, can tour a kitchen arranged according to the advice that Stowe and her sister Catharine doled out in their immensely popular *The American Woman's Home* (1869).

If the intellectual seeds of birthplace commemoration were sown during the first half of the nineteenth century, then the proliferation of birthplace monuments following the Civil War—including the expansion of Washington's during the 1920s—signaled a second stage, really the high tide, of American birthplace memory. Americans were never more fascinated by famous births than during the decades straddling the turn of the twentieth century. If we were to graph the frequency with which the word "birthplace" appears in books published in the United States between 1800 and 2000, a significant increase would be evident until about 1890, after which appearances would decline gradually by half.[13] Granted, readers in those years bracketed by the Civil War and World War I may have been as interested in books like William H. Roose's *Indiana's Birthplace* (1911), which celebrated the origins of a place, as they were in Henry Fitz-Gilbert Waters's *Birthplace of Roger Williams* (1889), but the point stands that origins mattered a great deal to America's reading public. They mattered enough at least to spawn some of the earliest birthplace monuments in this country, which recalled the origins of a motley bunch including Benjamin Thompson (1876), who invented Rumford Baking Powder; the Quaker poet John Greenleaf Whittier (1893); and President Grover Cleveland (1913).

This is not to say that there weren't other commemorative hot spots during those years. On the contrary, the birthplace craze paralleled a national preoccupation with secular shrines and historical pilgrimage of all sorts. Students of tourism and the heritage industry have used the language of ritual and pilgrimage at least since the 1970s to explain the various cultural activities associated with modern historic sites.[14] Well before that, however, the builders of America's public historical landscape understood their work as akin to temple building. Ann Pamela Cunningham and her Mount Vernon Ladies Association, who are typically credited for initiating the nation's love affair with historic preservation by saving Washington's adult home in 1858, wanted to create a "shrine where at least the mothers of the land and their innocent children might make their offering in the cause of the greatness, goodness and prosperity of their country." By 1930, preservationists at Washington's birthplace still thought in these terms when they described their own monument as a "great American shrine."[15] Even today, as Cynthia Miller shows us in her essay on Bill Monroe's birthplace, historic site promoters encourage visitors to think of themselves as pilgrims bound to "holy ground."

How birth got mixed up with historical places and shrines, however, is not immediately evident. A birthplace after all is not the same kind of historic place as a battlefield or the site of a great discovery. Suggesting that a birthplace is significant because it produced someone who eventually went on to do great things pushed the acceptable limits of cause and effect, even during the early years of historical professionalism. We know, though, that commemoration relies for its power on much more than research and analysis, the usual stuff of history. Historians attribute the shrinification of the American landscape following the Civil

War—characterized by a proliferation of monuments, historical associations, and preservationists—to a complicated mix of fears and aspirations spawned by radical changes in the nation's social and cultural fabric at the turn of the century. This modernity crisis owed its intensity to the war's ravages, rampant industrialization, savage class conflict, and a sudden onslaught of new immigrants and shifting domestic populations. Any number of centennial anniversaries marking everything from the nation's birth to Washington's death provided the grist for America's memory mill. Civic boosters, politicians, and other denizens of the nation's rising tourism industry kept that mill turning by rediscovering a stunning array of "historic" homes, in most of which George Washington had somehow spent a night.[16]

In this vein, birthplace reverence may have served a special anxiety concerning the fate of the American home. Beginning in the mid-nineteenth century, many Americans suffered from what historian Susan J. Matt describes as a "cultural preoccupation with home." Concerned by modernity's dislocations, consumers turned once again to domestic advice manuals and even popular songs like Stephen Foster's "Old Folks at Home" (1851) for memories of a cozy yesteryear that, by and large, had never actually existed. Matt argues that the Civil War elevated this preoccupation into a full-blown diagnosis. Doctors increasingly referred to the symptoms of homesickness as evidence of "nostalgia," which they blamed for no less than thirteen deaths during the war's first two years.

Over time, however, the medical establishment grew less sympathetic to nostalgia sufferers as the impossibility of returning to any home became increasingly evident. New Englanders drawn home by "old home week" festivals during the new century's first decade barely recognized their childhood homes amid landscapes radically transformed by new class regimes and even newer technologies.[17] In their absence, commemorative birthplaces could serve as metaphorical substitutes for real lost homes. It turned out that the spurious replica at Washington's birthplace, for instance, actually replicated the birth home of Josephine Wheelright Rust, the Wakefield Association's founding president. In New York City, the Women's Roosevelt Memorial Association constructed a replica of Theodore Roosevelt's birth home in 1919 on the very spot where the original house had been demolished only three years earlier. And it appears that not even presidents themselves are immune from homesickness. President Lyndon Johnson had a replica of his own Texas birthplace built in 1964, while he was still in office.[18]

Although birthplace commemoration may have satisfied a desire to reclaim lost homes, they were not the homes of all Americans. As Levander suggests, natal nationalism obscures our memory of ethnic and racial conflict by presenting difference as simply constitutive of the American experience, an unproblematic and largely innocent happenstance.[19] In reality, however, collisions between new and old immigrants intensified conversations about birthplace and character. Charles Darwin's theory of evolution, and Herbert Spencer's sloppy translation of it, placed origins at the center of immigration debates and fueled American nativism after the Civil War. By the turn of the twentieth century, origins—and, really, birth itself—had suddenly, in the most literal sense, come to mean more than ever before thanks to new methods of statistical and social scientific data analysis. The U.S. Bureau of the Census, for instance, issued its first standards for the registration of births and deaths in 1900.[20] Where keeping birth records had been an informal undertaking, usually managed if at all by churches, local governments, or families, it was now a matter of federal law. Perhaps more significant at the time, however, birth meant more as more people vied for a claim on American memory. A new generation of freeborn African Americans struggled to square their birthright with white America. Waves of new immigrants faced a similar struggle tinged by long-standing strains of anti-Catholicism and xenophobia. The Ku Klux Klan's resurgence during the 1920s, and its campaign of terror against both groups, made the victims of hate crime understand all too well how significantly the facts of one's birth could figure in daily life.

On the other hand, a generation of Progressive social reform in schools, hospitals, and charitable organizations also focused new interest on birth and childhood, which since the late nineteenth century had grown increasingly less tied to economic productivity at home and on the farm.[21] Just as children figured as vessels of republican virtue during the nineteenth century, their welfare became increasingly entwined with nationalist aspirations during the twentieth. As Arato demonstrates, for instance, Rose Kennedy's hopes for her famous son were born not only of her family's privileged station, but of the *Ladies'*

Home Journal too. What's more, the scientific study of child development emerged during these years alongside other trends in the social sciences, such as anthropologists' fascination with the "primitive" mind and Sigmund Freud's pioneering work in psychoanalysis that, as any daytime television watcher knows, has long since convinced us that adult behavior reflects early life experiences buried deep within the subconscious. All of this is to say that the popularization of birthplace monuments in this country by the 1920s accompanied a perfect storm of cultural and historical intersections that all but ensured that we would come to accept, as one late-century cultural theorist claimed, that "the house we were born in is physically inscribed in us."[22]

Birthplace reverence had grown so ubiquitous, in fact, that it continued to shape the nation's commemorative landscape even as Americans became less preoccupied with origins. If we recall our hypothetical graph of the word's appearance in print over time, it appears that interest in birthplaces among the American reading public gradually declined throughout the twentieth century. And yet, at the same time, birthplace monuments proliferated. During the 1930s, '40s, and '50s, monument builders celebrated birth en masse. Writers and politicians enjoyed most of the fanfare, though a few military leaders appeared in the mix as did a monument for Mormon leader Brigham Young, whose birthplace blurred the lines between memory and hagiography. Juliette Gordon Low, who founded the Girl Scouts of America, and Clara Barton, who is most recognized for beginning the Red Cross, stand out among the few women whose births were commemorated prior to the 1960s. The mounting political power of black Americans and the persistent hypocrisies of a segregated nation fighting fascism abroad compelled the U.S. Congress in 1943 to designate the George Washington Carver National Monument at his birthplace in Diamond, Missouri. And yet, confronting segregation head on proved too much. The Department of the Interior refused to commemorate radical abolitionist Frederick Douglass, for example, but agreed to establish a national monument in 1956 at the birthplace of the decidedly less radical Booker T. Washington.[23] David Glassberg and Robert Paynter's essay in this volume explores how the complicated interplay of race and memory lingers on in recent efforts to commemorate W. E. B. Du Bois's childhood home in Great Barrington, Massachusetts.

The primacy of white male politicians and writers during those decades, beyond revealing the chauvinisms of the time, recalls the interplay between birth memory and nationalism. Despite declining popular interest, birthplace commemoration flourished in practice because the federal and state governments struggled against a succession of crises—the Great Depression, World War II, and the Cold War—by encouraging patriotic nationalism alongside labor relief programs. The National Park Service (NPS) led on both fronts. Although the NPS emerged earlier in the century to protect the nation's natural splendor, its leaders envisioned an expanded system of parks designed to bolster patriotism by interpreting the full scope of American experience. Franklin Roosevelt's New Deal provided the labor to build it. The creation of the Civilian Conservation Corps (CCC) in 1933 coincided that year with Roosevelt's Executive Order 6166, which shifted management of natural *and* cultural resources to the NPS. This confluence of policy triggered a glut of park building throughout the decade and created the bedrock on which federal stewardship of the nation's public memory expanded throughout the twentieth century.[24]

Washington's birthplace heralded the shift. NPS Director Horace Albright had acquired the site in 1930 in his lobbying efforts for the expansion of the park system. Although the birthplace didn't turn out to be the best model on which to build a national system of history parks, it did demonstrate how park building could create jobs. Hundreds of CCC men worked there throughout the decade. Most built recreational facilities and park infrastructure. Many contributed to the park's earliest archaeological and historical research. It was CCC men, in fact, who excavated the foundations of Washington's real birth home, thereby casting the Memorial House into a decades-long dispute about the meaning of authenticity. State governments also invested in patriotic memory projects with the aim of attracting federal jobs. As Lowe points out in her essay, much of what is interesting about the history of commemoration at the state of Missouri's Mark Twain's birthplace (1931) results from the CCC's time there and its own policy of racial segregation. And even as Depression-era reforms yielded to wartime concerns, birthplace commemoration continued to serve memory and nation. Birth memorials to Dwight Eisenhower (1946) and Harry Truman (1959) celebrated the wellspring of American global power while others to Carl Sandburg (1946), Walt Whitman (1957), and Will Rogers (1961) honored the modern authors of American exceptionalism.

This is not to say, however, that Americans accepted the commemorative claims of birthplace monuments without question. Henry James's 1903 riff on Shakespeare's birthplace anticipated a similar skepticism, at least in arts and letters, among American commemorative circles. Historian Karal Ann Marling describes how the painter Grant Wood, for instance, chipped away at birthplace mythology in his *The Birthplace of Herbert Hoover* (1931). Supporters of President Hoover commissioned a painting to link him rhetorically with George Washington, whose own birthplace was grabbing headlines in the run-up to the 1932 bicentennial birthday celebration. Wood, however, exposed the myth by caricaturing it. He rendered Hoover's birthplace as too good to be true, "a kind of Iowan [Colonial] Williamsburg . . . a manufactured, fully modernized birthplace mythos."[25] Hoover, unsurprisingly, demurred. Decades later, in his chronicle of a cross-country ramble, John Steinbeck made light of small towns that "proudly announce their celebrated sons." "Myth wipes out the fact," he observed, in places like Sauk Centre, Minnesota, where Sinclair Lewis was born and which inspired his snarky portrayal of fictional Gopher Prairie, made infamous in *Main Street* (1920). Although the town once derided Lewis and his satiric novel, Steinbeck grumbled that "today Sauk Centre celebrates itself for having produced him."[26]

Steinbeck's critique mirrored a growing dissatisfaction during the 1960s with the nation's long-standing historical tunnel vision. Motivated first by the civil rights movements and increasingly by campaigns for equal rights across the spectrum of American difference, historians turned their attention to topics such as class and gender history that spurred seismic shifts in American museums and historic sites. The change filtered immediately into the designation of birthplace monuments. The National Register for Historic Places (NRHP), established under NPS supervision in 1966 to create national standards for historical preservation, recognized the birthplaces of Amelia Earhart (1971), Martin Luther King, Jr. (1977), and Queen Kamehameka III (1978), among others associated with previously unrepresented Americans. And yet, at the same time, the NRHP's systematization of birthplace commemoration demonstrated that the old days of passionate birthplace reverence had long subsided. In response to the preponderance of ill-conceived birth markers and monuments, the NRHP's guidelines specifically prohibited designation of birthplaces as historic places save for those cases where no other site or building remained that might do justice to a historically significant individual's "productive life."[27] By the late twentieth century, the nation's obsession with origins met with the bureaucratic logic of state-regulated public memory.

Making Meaning at American Birthplace Monuments

But just because the heyday of birthplace commemoration is long gone doesn't mean that the birthplace markers, monuments, and historic homes that remain have lost their audience. On the contrary, an informal survey suggests that hundreds of thousands of people visit birthplace monuments in the United Sates every year and that these places still get funding from public and private sources.[28] What sense visitors make of birthplaces, however, is unclear. Short of surveying them, we can guess that people today still recognize that birthplace memorials reinforce the old idea—passed down from the Puritans, Alexis de Tocqueville, Frederick Jackson Turner, and no end of presidential stump speeches—that Americans are special because they come from a special place. This meaning at least is still perceptible in the lingua franca of birthplace commemoration, which invariably—like the commemorative marker in Lancaster County, South Carolina, that reminds us that Andrew Jackson was born "on Southern soil"—reinforces our belief in birthright exceptionalism.

As harmless as that notion may seem, though, history tells us that its persistence in public memory should give us reason for pause. Obama's birthplace fracas, as we have seen, is a case in point. The story of Virginia Dare is another. Since 1587, Virginia Dare has been remembered in histories and folklore as the first English person born in the New World. Hers is the first modern American birth memory. Though more legend than fact, since Dare was born into Virginia's ill-fated Roanoke Colony, her memory has lived on especially in the service of white nationalism. Memories of Dare have, from the beginning, been about race and nation. In the first fictional account of Dare's saga, written in 1840, she is as one literary scholar puts it, "preserved by the savages out of an uncontrollable love for her pure white beauty." Nearly a century later, she had evolved into a symbol of a powerful young America, an "unabashed priestess of the post-Freudian cult of primitivism."[29] North Carolina firmed up the memory with a birthplace monument in 1896. Along the way, Dare had become a symbol particularly of southern womanhood and often of white supremacy. During the 1920s, for example, North Carolinians opposed suffrage for black women "in the name of Virginia Dare." As recently as 2002, former *Forbes Magazine* editor Peter Brimelow created the VDARE foundation and its conservative website to advocate against immigration into the United States.[30]

In this light, the story of how Americans have remembered Virginia Dare's birth is a cautionary tale about the power of birthplace memories to perpetuate, even if unwittingly, proprietary histories. And Dare's story is not unique. Celebrating the first white child born in any given locality had become a matter of course in communities across the nation by the early twentieth century. A Philadelphia tour book produced by the Federal Writers' Project in 1937, for example, directed tourists to the corner of 2nd and Walnut Streets, where in 1680 John Drinker supposedly became "the first white child . . . born in Philadelphia."[31] Framing memory with whiteness has long served to mask the diversity of our shared heritage. But it can also, in the case of birthplace monuments, assert ownership. Remembering Drinker's white birth posits Philadelphia as one chapter in a bigger story about the success of European colonization in North America. That success, of course, came at the expense of people whose births we usually do not choose to remember. If the NRHP is any guide, then the vast majority of birthplace monuments in this country still honor white men who achieved artistic, political, military, scientific, or financial success. Although birthplace commemoration has become significantly more inclusive in recent decades, one might still infer from our public memory of birth that the best way to be born an American is to be born a white male. Even the contents of this volume reflects the trend.

The examples of Dare and Drinker show us how birth monuments can convey meanings not immediately evident in the rough prose of commemorative placards. Teasing these out, however, is a challenge, especially since scholars have not had much to say about what birthplaces mean or, perhaps more important, what they tell us about the production of historical meaning.[32] We are fortunate, though, that recent decades have been remarkably fertile for the study of memory in public spaces. We know now, for instance, that monuments tell us much more about the people who sponsor them than the people, places, and events that they commemorate. We also know that memory and history are very different beasts. Doing good history means undertaking a careful investigative process that asks questions of the past aimed at making sense of the present. Memory, on the other hand, tends to abhor questions and rather seeks to caress the competing claims of history into a singular narrative that reaffirms our supposed core beliefs about the past. Memory speaks loudest where history is most conflicted. This is why war monuments outnumber all others. The authority with which monuments speak about the past is often intended to obscure the possibility of competing memories. In other words, because we are so impressed by the timelessness of these places, it is easy to forget (or, not to care) that each one was born of the fear that its story about the past might be eclipsed by a competing narrative. A generation of case studies shows us that the memories that monuments preserve for us are always selected by the few for the many. Discovering whose voices prevail in our nation's mnemonic landscape is a study in the history of social power.[33]

Understanding what those voices have to say, and why they still demand our notice, has also been a favorite project of memory scholars. In this vein, we benefit from landmark studies of war monuments, house museums, pageantry, historical associations, and a host of other venues where public memory is shaped and reshaped over time. We even have studies of grave markers, death monuments, and the significance of loss in American memory.[34] This group in particular provides an interesting point of comparison with birthplace monuments since, in obvious ways, they are *the* mnemonic counterpoint. Michael Kammen's recent examination of American reburials, for instance, suggests that the motivations for editing our memory of significant deaths have been frequently rooted in state, regional, and sectional pride.[35] On this count, birthplace monuments hold much in common. We learn in Lowe's essay, for instance, that long-standing uncertainties concerning the authenticity of Mark Twain's various birth cabins result from and, in some ways, explain the failed efforts by residents of Florida, Missouri, to assert their community's identity in a radically altered landscape. Similarly, we learn from Paul Reber and Laura Lawfer Orr that the impulse to commemorate Robert E.

Lee's birth in Virginia originated in Connecticut, of all places, among displaced southerners hoping to reconcile their regional pride with the memory of sectional discord.

And, yet, comparing birthplace monuments with death memorials reminds us too that the meaning of commemoration varies in important ways with its form. Because death monuments typically pivot on the greatness of the deceased, and not usually on a particular death site, our memory of death and its significance is transferable to whoever hosts the internment. This is why, at the very beginning of the twentieth century, Missouri and Kentucky could reasonably, as unreasonable as it may seem in hindsight, argue over which state had greatest claim to Daniel Boone's remains. Although Boone died in Missouri, Kentucky boosters argued that their state owned his memory.[36] Memories of births, however, presume a necessary and significant correlation between the *place* of an individual's birth and his or her adult character. As Angela Phelps notes in her essay concerning John Muir, "there will be many places associated with later life, but there can only be one birthplace." Freeman Tilden, the father of American heritage interpretation, understood that the "replica" house at Washington's birthplace was really a fake, but he still sensed that "the spirit of our great whole man is *there;* and [that] in these lovely and provoking *surroundings,* the staunch character of our hero comes to the imagination."[37] By its very definition, the significance of a birthplace cannot, like a grave, be transported to another place unless by mistake or historical shenanigans. Rather, the place itself, in the usual birthplace narrative, somehow begets greatness. As Zachary J. Lechner explains in his study of the Jimmy Carter birthplace in Plains, Georgia, the presumed constancy of a birth*place* and its qualities appeal powerfully to political leaders whose legacies are otherwise clouded by inconsistent policymaking. Carter, by living in Plains to this day, casts himself as a living link between his public legacy and the southern rural community to which the Jimmy Carter National Historic Site and Preservation District attributes his adult character.

It is this link that explains in part why so many Americans visit birthplace monuments year after year. Birthplace commemoration is distinctive for its ability to convince us that something of our essential American character is retrievable from the presumably hardscrabble places in which our heroes were born. The problem for birthplace

stewards, however, is that conjuring an acceptable picture of historical hard times requires a degree of narrative and physical intervention
that renders any historic site fundamentally inauthentic, if authentic
is taken to mean "unchanged." Debates about authenticity, although
ubiquitous at historic sites, have long been intensified at birthplaces
by the combined power of the humble origins myth and the possibility
of sharing in the greatness of people born into circumstances like our
own. Seventeenth-century visitors to Milton's birthplace on London's
Bread Street, for instance, could not believe that the famously reserved
author took his first breaths in such a hectic urban place. As Aaron
Santesso puts it, "it is as if Thoreau had been born in Times Square."[38]
Christine Arato shows us in this volume how Rose Kennedy's vision
for John F. Kennedy's birthplace in Brookline, Massachusetts, recycled
popular beliefs about Kennedy's greatness in ways that mitigated the
National Park Service's ability to demonstrate just how uncommon
Kennedy's birthplace really was.

Examining how these places have been edited to better correspond with our contrived memories of heroic births is a useful step
toward mapping out the layers of meaning birthplace monuments have
accrued over time. We've already seen how race and nation figure into
the equation. Other themes are similarly prevalent and even covalent.
Take class consciousness, for instance. Social class and memory are
intimately entwined in the United States where, recalling Harrison's
log cabin campaign, humble births pass as political and cultural cur-
rency. We look to them for models of upward mobility. We want our
leaders' births to have been humble enough to guarantee their good
character, but not so humble as to render them pathetic. The difference
has usually been a matter of entwined chauvinisms that, themselves,
illuminate the changing face of public memory. At Washington's birthplace, for instance, the Wakefield Association demanded that the "replica" birth house be built of brick rather than wood—the more likely
option—so that nobody would mistake it for the home of a pauper.

The story of Washington's birthplace also demonstrates how gender and motherhood have figured in the various meanings ascribed to
these monuments by their makers. It's easy to dismiss the Wakefield
Association's Memorial House as a fraud. Closer examination, however,
reveals that its members did not limit their notion of authenticity to

architectural verisimilitude alone. Rather the Association sought to replicate the social and cultural conditions that it presumed had been responsible for Washington's greatness. It conceived of the Memorial House
as a stage on which to perform a new brand of republican motherhood
fine-tuned for the twentieth century. In this way, the Association recognized early on that birthplace monuments are ideal places to laud the
accomplishments of mothers. And redeeming Mary Ball Washington,
who during the 1920s was derided by guides at her restored home in
nearby Fredericksburg as a "Tory who denounced her son," would have
certainly cheered those members of the Wakefield Association who perceived themselves as inheritors of her legacy.[39] Women, at least, who visited Washington's birthplace during those early days would have most
certainly understood the message: good moms make a powerful nation.

At the same time, the Association defined positive motherhood
in decidedly narrow terms. Good moms, in the Association's model,
exerted control over their families by creating orderly domestic spaces,
preserving familial memory, and insulating their sons from the corro-
sive influence of the world beyond the home. For Washington, who was
born on an eighteenth-century Virginia plantation, that world was predominately black. And he most certainly enjoyed the care of surrogate
mothers drawn from his family's slaves. Those moms, however, did not
figure in the Wakefield Association's vision. Indeed, the preponderance
of white mothers at American birthplace monuments reminds us once
again that whose births we've chosen to remember has always been an
index of prevailing beliefs about nation and citizenship.

Remembering Birth in the New Order

The following essays confirm that these themes—nation, citizenship,
motherhood—have suffused birthplace commemoration throughout
the last century. And if recent years are any indication, they will continue to for some time. New birthplace monuments appear around the
globe every year. Only a year after Michael Jackson's death in 2009, for
instance, officials in Gary, Indiana, announced plans to open a museum
complex honoring his birth there. Cuba declared Fidel Castro's birthplace a national monument in February 2009 and, more recently, the
sale of Adolf Hitler's birthplace in Braunau am Inn, Austria, has raised

concerns about its power to commemorate evil.[40] Women have fared particularly well during the last decade. Visitors can now enjoy birthplace museums that commemorate Judy Garland (2003) and Susan B. Anthony (2010). A 2010 management plan suggests that the birthplace of the women's rights advocate Lucy Stone may soon open to the public as well. In this volume, Kris Myers tells us the story of suffragist Alice Paul's birthplace, Paulsdale, whose founders decided early on to make the house into an educational center particularly for young girls, rather than a typical house museum.

Working more women into the mix will help to engage a new generation of museum goers that promises to be statistically more female than ever before. In fact, the Paulsdale model, which recalls the Clara Barton birthplace in North Oxford, Massachusetts, where childhood diabetes education has been a priority since 1932, suggests that the commemoration of women's births has prompted particularly innovative uses of the past to engage diverse publics.[41] But the next generation of visitors, we are told, will also be older and more ethnically diverse than museums and historic sites have grown accustomed to. Their lives will have been fundamentally shaped by economic instability and a growing energy crisis. Will the old patriotic themes undergirding twentieth-century birthplace commemoration still speak to them? How can institutions that interpret birthplace monuments remain vital even as museum professionals openly debate whether house museums are still a worthwhile enterprise?[42] Will we always, as Henry James suggested over a century ago, be duped by commemorative hyperbole, or is there an opportunity in birthplace commemoration to do serious history? Judging by the essays in this volume, it appears that answers to these questions are in fact taking shape alongside new strategies for conveying the significance of birthplace commemoration within the nation's ever evolving mnemonic landscape

Two of our contributors, for example, demonstrate how recent appeals to heritage tourism have yielded mixed results for birthplace commemoration. Although it has been largely discredited as an unsustainable model for most historic sites, the old practice of blending tourism and history experienced a sharp revival during the 1990s in the United States as towns and communities of all stripes struggled to thrive in a postindustrial economy.[43] The NRHP added several birthplaces to its list during the '90s, including sites relating to U. S. Grant, J. E. B. Stuart, and the Kukaniloko birthstones on Hawaii's island of O'ahu. Anna Thompson Hajdik chronicles the remarkable investment by Mason City, Iowa, during the 1990s in the public memory of composer Meredith Willson and his award-winning stage musical *The Music Man* (1957). We see how Mason City, by mingling its own identity with Willson's fictional River City, however, has risked marketing nostalgia for a cultural moment that means less to Americans all the time. As Hajdik points out, it's unclear what will remain of the "real" Mason City once reverence for Willson's birthplace vanishes. Similarly, since 2001, Rosine, Kentucky, has pinned its hopes for economic revival on the belief that tourists will always want to visit the birthplace of bluegrass legend Bill Monroe. Cynthia Miller shows us how Monroe's birthplace mingles the story of Monroe's birth with the birth of American bluegrass music. Metonymy of this sort— where the birth of a person stands in for a larger concept or phenomenon—is a common interpretive strategy for birthplace monuments and tourism bureaus alike. In the case of Rosine, however, we must wonder whether the town's celebratory investment in bluegrass interferes with its ability to examine Monroe's complicated journey from a small southern railroad town to global stardom.

Several of the following essays suggest that the peculiarities of birthplace monuments create unique opportunities to engage Americans who are struggling to make sense of the post-industrial and, increasingly, post-national order. While modern birthplace monuments can still inspire us with the accomplishments of great Americans, they can also empower visitors to make sense of complicated pasts by challenging us to examine why it is we remember famous births the way we do. In this regard, Paul Lewis and Dan Currie ask why, despite the proliferation of birthplace monuments in this country, we haven't commemorated Edgar Allan Poe's birthplace in Boston. Glassberg and Paynter reconstruct the intersections of race, memory, and global politics in Great Barrington, Massachusetts, where W. E. B. Du Bois was born. Both essays challenge us to find interpretive opportunities in the stories of unwanted birthplace memorials. Angela Phelps also pushes birthplace memorials into new analytical territory by showing how these places can cut across national borders. In Phelps's treatment, John Muir's historic homes—his birthplace in Dunbar, Scotland, and his adult home in

Martinez, California—suggest a possibility for using birthplace comemoration as a starting point for critical engagement with the politics of global memory. And, although we have typically understood twentieth-century commemoration as dominated by discourses of nation and power, Keith Erekson's history of Mormon leader Joseph Smith's birthplace shows us how the popularity of birthplace monuments reveals a less recognized tension between sacred and secular memory that clearly persist in today's cultural milieu.

All of these observations suggest that not only can birthplace monuments be relevant and viable in the new century, but that they are ready-made to engage a broad public since, as Patricia West points out in her afterword, "that someone was once a baby is a basis for substantial consensus." But, as West also observes, it's up to public historians to rethink the conventional birthplace narrative, to admit, as she puts it, "the constructed nature of historic houses," if we are to entice new visitors who've grown wary of old stories. Interpretation at historic house museums has labored too long to fulfill the aspirations of founders whose hopes for these places no longer correspond with the needs and capacities of modern visitors. This problem is especially pronounced at birthplace monuments where the one story that rarely gets told is the story of birth itself. Rather than emphasize the fixity of American values, as they so often do, birthplaces must highlight change. Change and choice, after all, are two themes—beyond, of course, birth itself—that resonate with any story about babies. A reflexive approach to interpretation, one that reveals why and how we remember birth in the first place, can demonstrate the remarkable power that common people have to change history by choosing what to remember and what to forget. It can remind us too that the great gift of life in America is the power to choose who we will be, no matter where we are born.

NOTES

1. La Rochefoucauld composed maxim no. 342 in 1678. This translation of it appears in François, duc de La Rochefoucauld, *Maximes*, trans. L. W. Tancock (Baltimore: Penguin Books, 1967), 77. Herman Melville, *Israel Potter: His Fifty Years of Exile* (New York: G. P. Putnam, 1855), 272–76.

2. See, for instance, Carl Hulse, "McCain's Canal Zone Birth Prompts Queries about Whether That Rules Him Out," *New York Times,* February 28, 2008.

3. For a sample of relevant news coverage, see Andrew Malcolm, "Barack Obama's birth certificate revealed here," *Los Angeles Times,* June 16, 2008; Andrew Malcolm, "Alan Keyes stokes Obama birth certificate controversy," *Los Angeles Times,* February 21, 2009; Scott Martelle, "Mystery solved: Barack Obama was American-born," *Los Angeles Times,* August 22, 2008; Brain Stelter, "A Dispute Over Obama's Birth Lives on in the Media," *New York Times,* July 25, 2009; and Brett Michael Dykes, "New infomercial revives 'birther' controversy," *Yahoo! News Blog,* September 29, 2009.

4. For a history of American immigration debate, see Peter Schrag, *Not Fit for Our Society: Immigration and Nativism in America* (Berkeley: University of California Press, 2010).

5. On presidential autobiographical revision, see Jill Lepore, "Bound for Glory: Writing Campaign Lives" *New Yorker,* October 20, 2008. For a broader treatment of the log cabin myth, see Edward Pessen, *The Log Cabin Myth: The Social Backgrounds of the Presidents* (New Haven: Yale University Press, 1984). For an overview of the 1840 election, see Paul F. Boller, Jr., *Presidential Campaigns: From George Washington to George W. Bush* (New York: Oxford University Press, 2004), especially chapter 14.

6. Drew Zahn, "Born in the USA? Where's Monument for Obama's Birthplace?" *WorldNetDaily,* August 3, 2009, www.wnd.com/index.php?pageId=105612.

7. Thanks to John P. Byrne, National Register Database Manager, for helping me navigate the NRHP's criteria exception C relating to birthplaces and graves.

8. See the ten-point scale of historical trustworthiness in Roy Rosenzweig and David Thelen, *The Presence of the Past: Popular Uses of History in American Life* (New York: Columbia University Press, 1998), 21.

9. On Milton, see Aaron Santesso, "Birth of the Birthplace: Bread Street and Literary Tourism before Stratford," *English Literary History* 71 (Summer 2004): 377–403. On Shakespeare, see Nicola J. Watson, *The Literary Tourist: Readers and Places in Romantic and Victorian Britain* (New York: Palgrave Macmillan, 2007), 56–60.

10. See the introduction to Caroline F. Levander, *Cradle of Liberty: Race, the Child, and National Belonging from Thomas Jefferson to W. E. B. Du Bois* (Durham: Duke University Press, 2006).

11. Seth C. Bruggeman, *Here, George Washington Was Born: Memory, Material Culture, and the Public History of a National Monument* (Athens: University of Georgia Press, 2008).

12. Sarah Robbins, "'The Future Good and Great of Our Land': Republican Mothers, Female Authors, and Domesticated Literacy in Antebellum New England," *New England Quarterly* 75 (December 2002): 562. A massive scholarship concerning republican motherhood and the role of women in the early republic traces its beginnings to Linda Kerber, *Women of the Republic: Intellect and Ideology in Revolutionary America* (Chapel Hill: University of North Carolina Press, 1980).

13. "Birthplace," Google Books Ngram viewer, accessed November 17, 2011, http://books .google.com/ngrams.

14. See, for instance, Dean MacCannell, *The Tourist: A New Theory of the Leisure Class* (New York: Schocken Books, 1976; Berkeley: University of California Press, 1999), 42–43; and Edith and Victor Turner, *Image and Pilgrimage in Christian Culture* (New York: Columbia University Press, 1978).

15. The Mount Vernon Ladies Association is cited in Mike Wallace, *Mickey Mouse History and Other Essays on American Memory* (Philadelphia: Temple University Press, 1996), 6. On Washington's birthplace, see Bruggeman, *Here, George Washington was Born,* 84.

16. The starting point for scholarship on American modernity crises is T. J. Jackson Lears, *No Place of Grace: Antimodernism and the Transformation of American Culture, 1880–1920* (Chicago: University of Chicago Press, 1981). On Washington tourism at the turn of the

century, see Edward G. Lengel, *Inventing George Washington: America's Founder, in Myth and Memory* (New York: HarperCollins, 2011), chapter 5.

17. Susan J. Matt, "You Can't Go Home Again: Homesickness and Nostalgia in U.S. History," *Journal of American History* (September 2007): 479–85, 491–92.

18. National Park Service, "Theodore Roosevelt Birthplace National Historic Site," in *The Presidents of the United States, Survey of Historic Sites and Buildings*, www.nps.gov/history /history/online_books/Presidents/site42.htm. Johnson built the replica as a guest-house and surrounded it with several heirloom trees including a sapling from George Washington's Mount Vernon. National Park Service, *Lyndon B. Johnson National Historical Park Final General Management Plan and Environmental Impact Statement* (Washington: U.S. Department of the Interior, 1999), 65.

19. Levander, *Cradle of Liberty*, 6–8.

20. National Center for Health Statistics, "Report of the Panel to Evaluate the U.S. Standard Certificates" (April 2000), www.cdc.gov/nchs/data/dvs/panelreport_acc.pdf, 9.

21. See, for example, Linda Gordon, "The Progressive-Era Transformation of Child Protection, 1900–1920," in Paula S. Fass and Mary Ann Mason, eds., *Childhood in America* (New York: New York University Press, 2000); and Steven Mintz, *Huck's Raft: A History of American Childhood* (Cambridge: The Belknap Press of Harvard University Press, 2004).

22. Gaston Bachelard, *The Poetics of Space* (Boston: Beacon Press, 1969), 14. On Freud and anthropology, see Ann Douglas, *Terrible Honesty: Mongrel Manhattan in the 1920s* (New York: The Noonday Press of Farrar, Straus and Giroux, 1995), 44–50.

23. West, *Domesticating History*, 136–54.

24. See Harlan D. Unrau and G. Frank Williss, *Administrative History: Expansion of the National Park Service in the 1930s* (Washington: Department of the Interior, 1983).

25. Karal Ann Marling, *George Washington Slept Here: Colonial Revivals and American Culture, 1876–1986* (Cambridge: Harvard University Press, 1988), 318.

26. John Steinbeck, *Travels with Charley: In Search of America* (New York: Penguin, 1997), 62–63, 103.

27. John H. Sprinkle, Jr., "'Of Exceptional Importance': The Origins of the 'Fifty-Year Rule' in Historic Preservation," *The Public Historian* 29 (Spring 2007): 90 n.22, 92, 98.

28. Of forty-four birthplace monuments and museums informally surveyed by telephone during summer 2011, eight welcomed more than 50,000 visitors each year, whereas fif-teen sites hosted between 10,000 and 50,000 visitors and twenty-one reported less than 10,000. Abraham Lincoln's birthplace counted 177,000 visitors during the previous year, making it the most popular of the group. These include nine state-operated sites, six units of the national park service, eighteen private monuments, and eleven hybrid institutions. Seven birthplaces reportedly earned a majority of their operational funding from competi-tive grants.

29. Robert D. Arner, "The Romance of Roanoke: Virginia Dare and the Lost Colony in American Literature," *Southern Literary Journal* 10 (Spring 1978): 5–45.

30. Anastatia Sims, *The Power of Femininity in the New South: Women's Organizations and Politics in North Carolina, 1880–1930* (Columbia: University of South Carolina Press, 1997), 139–40. The quote appears in Donald W. Patterson, "Time Hasn't Diminished the Image of Virginia Dare," *News and Record*, Piedmont Triad, NC, April 23, 2000, 12. Learn more about VDARE at www.vdare.com/why_vdare.htm.

31. Federal Writers' Project, *Philadelphia: A Guide to the Nation's Birthplace* (Philadelphia: William Penn Association of Philadelphia, 1937), 405. The New England Historic Genealogical Society, however, attributed this distinction to Edward Drinker, born in Philadelphia in 1680. See *The New England Historical and Genealogical Register, Volume 4* (Boston: Samuel G. Drake, 1850), 373.

32. The only book-length study of birthplace commemoration to my knowledge is Bruggeman,

Here, George Washington Was Born. Shorter treatments include a chapter on the Booker T. Washington birthplace in Patricia West, *Domesticating History: The Political Origins of America's House Museums* (Washington, DC: Smithsonian Institution Press, 1999); and Dwight T. Pitcaithley, "Abraham Lincoln's Birthplace Cabin: The Making of an American Icon," in *Myth, Memory, and the Making of the American Landscape,* ed. Paul A. Shackel (Gainesville: University Press of Florida, 2001). Aaron Santesso discusses birthplace commemoration in England in "The Birth of the Birthplace," *English Literary History* 71 (2004), as does Nicola J. Watson in *The Literary Tourist: Readers and Places in Romantic and Victorian Britain* (New York: Palgrave Macmillan, 2007), especially chapter 2. The National Park Service occasionally generates reports associated with its various birthplace monuments including, most recently, Alexander von Hoffman, *John F. Kennedy's Birthplace: A Presidential Home in History and Memory* (Historic Resource Study) (Washington, DC: National Park Service, U.S. Department of the Interior, August 2004). Brian Horrigan organized a lively conference session titled "Going Home Again: Birthplace and Childhood Homes as Historic Sites" at the 2007 annual meeting of the National Council on Public History, Santa Fe, NM.

33. For an excellent overview of scholarship concerning memory and commemoration, see Kirk Savage, "History, Memory, and Monuments: An Overview of the Scholarly Literature on Commemoration," online essay commissioned by the Organization of American Historians and the National Park Service, www.nps.gov/history/history/resedu/savage .htm. On war monuments and memory, see the introduction to Savage, *Monument Wars: Washington, D.C., the National Mall, and the Transformation of the Memorial Landscape* (University of California Press, 2009). The most significant recent contribution to memory studies is Erika Doss, *Memorial Mania: Public Feeling in America* (Chicago: University of Chicago Press, 2010).

34. On the latter, for instance, see Drew Gilpin Faust, *This Republic of Suffering: Death and the American Civil War* (New York: Knopf, 2008).

35. Michael Kammen, *Digging up the Dead: A History of Notable American Reburials* (Chicago: University of Chicago Press, 2010), 9.

36. Ibid., 129–33.

37. Freeman Tilden, *Interpreting Our Heritage* (Chapel Hill: University of North Carolina Press, 2007), 73. Italics are mine.

38. Santesso, "The Birth of the Birthplace," 392.

39. Lengel, *Inventing George Washington,* 111.

40. "Gary, Ind., Has High Hopes for Michael Jackson Museum," Associated Press, *USA Today Travel,* June 9, 2010, http://travel.usatoday.com/destinations/2010-06-08-gary-indiana-michael-jackson-museum_N.htm. "Cuba Declares Castro Birthplace a National Monument," Associated Press, *International Herald Tribune,* February 4, 2009, http://cuba-journal.blogspot.com/2009/02/cuba-declares-castro-birthplace.html. John Cummins, "Hitler House Sale Alarms Locals," BBC News, November 6, 2009, http://news.bbc.co .uk/2/hi/europe/8347438.stm.

41. Mary E. Tangney, "Diabetic Children at Clara Barton Camp," *American Journal of Nursing* 35 (April 4, 1935): 307–10.

42. Center for the Future of Museums with the American Association for Museums, "Museums & Society 2034: Trends and Potential Futures" (December 2008), http:// futureofmuseums.org/reading/publications/upload/MuseumsSociety2034.pdf. Carol B. Stapp and Kenneth C. Turino, "Does America Need Another House Museum?," *History News* 59 (Summer 2004): 7–11.

43. On the shortcomings of heritage tourism, see James Vaughan, "Introduction: The Call for a National Conversation" *Forum Journal* 22 (Spring 2008): 6.

John Muir's adult home on Alhambra Boulevard, Martinez, Contra Costa, California, as it appeared in 1900. Library of Congress, Prints and Photographs Division, Historic American Buildings Survey, HABS CAL,7-MART,1-1.

1

Odd as it may seem for a book concerned with American birthplace commemo-
ration to begin its query abroad, Angela Phelps's analysis of John Muir's historic
homes provides a perfect introduction to themes and issues that concern sites on
both sides of our Atlantic World. We discover that political boundaries are hardly
discrete in heritage contexts that concern immigrant lives. It turns out that
American tourists played a key role in encouraging commemoration of Muir's
birthplace in Scotland, where his legacy hadn't achieved such heights as in the
States. How to remember his birth, however, proved another question entirely. By
examining how various Muir devotees responded to that question, and how their
decisions compared with those made at Muir's adult home in California, Phelps
retrieves a history of alternative interpretive paths that reveal the intellectual
challenges and possibilities awaiting all birthplace stewards.

Remembering John Muir, the Trans-Atlantic "Father" of Wilderness Conservation

ANGELA PHELPS

John Muir's lifelong adventure began in 1838 in the town of Dunbar on the windswept east coast of Scotland and ended seventy-six years later and five thousand miles away in California. A love of the outdoors nurtured in the land of his birth blossomed with his experiences in America, culminating when he became the founding president of the Sierra Club, now one of the most renowned environmental organizations in the world. Despite his being little known in his native land, his fame in his adopted country became such that in 1964 the United States Congress commemorated his home in Martinez by declaring it a National Historic Site. That same decade Muir's bibliographers Bill and Maymie Kimes retraced his journey back to Dunbar, turning a slow trickle of American admirers into a pilgrimage that underpinned both the identification of places familiar from his stories and protection of the house where he was born. Established by a small number of enthusiasts, the Dunbar John Muir Association started a process that now finds the birthplace presented as a modern museum of environmental awareness, attracting some fifteen thousand museum visits a year, in addition to the varied educational workshops and cultural activities.[1]

Many people rise to national distinction through political and economic achievement, or through their contribution to cultural life and society. But why do some individuals excite such fervor that interest in their personal life supersedes that in their achievements? In particular, why should their *birthplace* become a focus of fascination, sometimes eclipsing sites associated with their later life? There is a long tradition drawn from religious pilgrimage that invests location with spiritual significance, but does a visit to the birthplace of a secular hero or heroine create a "cultural moment" of similar status, distinguishing such properties from other types of heritage attraction? How important to the experience is the presence of personal belongings and authentic fittings? Last, but by no means of least importance to this chapter, how does the interaction of local interest groups and professional organizations determine what is conserved and how it is presented?

The project to celebrate the life of John Muir offers an opportunity to explore these questions in an international context. This essay examines the discovery of the heritage of Muir in his native Dunbar and the home of his later life in Martinez, California. Concepts of authenticity and voice will be explored through a comparison of re-creations based on Muir's writings, contemporary reminiscence, and local historical research. Within the comparison, we find different paths to conservation and presentation reflected in an uneasy alliance between the John Muir Birthplace Museum and the Muir Family Home National Historic Site. The project to save, conserve, and present the properties associated with John Muir provide an opportunity to explore the choice between a focus on historic authenticity and the introduction of new interpretative themes to provide contemporary relevance.

Laurajane Smith argues that heritage should not be defined simply through the physical environment, but more in the way people *use* places; she argues that heritage meanings are constructed by cultural activities, particularly those supporting memory work.[2] If this is the case, then the importance of a birthplace rests not in the building, but in the opportunity it provides for visitors to consolidate their interest through their physical presence at a location with unique meaning in time and space. There will be many places associated with later life, but there can only be one birthplace.

The Birthplace as Heritage Site

A *birthplace* museum is a property open to the public for the sole purpose of presenting the story of one individual, housed in the building where he or she was born or very near the site. Although the great houses of Britain have provided the birthplaces of many famous people, their stories are usually but one thread in a continuity of history. Thus Blenheim Palace exhibits the life and achievements of generations of Churchills, not just Sir Winston Churchill, who was born there in 1874. The 1987 inscription of Blenheim on the UNESCO World Heritage list records the tangible heritage of its architectural importance as "a perfect example of eighteenth century princely dwelling," not the intangible heritage that may be experienced at a birthplace.[3]

Birthplace museums usually celebrate the life and work of someone who is regarded as a "national treasure," so the selection of personality provides an interesting reflection on local and national identity at any given time. In the United Kingdom most current birthplace museums present cultural celebrity, particularly in the literary field.[4] Heroes (and one heroine[5]) of military and other expeditionary feats are also commemorated, while political and social endeavor is represented but infrequently. These museums are the antithesis of the "footloose" tourist attractions that arise wherever a concentration of potential visitors is found. Birthplace museums are by definition located by the origin of their namesake; inevitably many are in obscure locations, requiring a higher level of intent among their visitors. The managers of most birthplace museums claim that the majority of their visitors have been motivated by a particular desire to explore the origin of the revered personality, although in reality some entertain a considerable proportion of "general interest" visitors who are either local residents or tourists when chance has provided a location with other attractions. Thus literary pilgrims visiting Dickens's birthplace in Portsmouth may

rub shoulders with tourists who have little knowledge of Victorian literature, but have been prompted to visit the nearby Historic Dockyard
where attractions include the remains of Henry VIII's flagship the
Mary Rose. The need for authenticated location presents a geographical
imperative but may also provide an explanation for the best represented
period. In the United Kingdom formal records of birth started in 1837.
For births prior to that, baptismal records, commercial records, street
indexes, wills, legal proceedings, military recruitment, and many other
sources used in tracing family history may provide a general location
but rarely a specific address tied to the actual event. Birthplace museums from earlier periods tend to be those of individuals who continued
to live in the family home or wrote autobiographical accounts allowing the property to be identified. By the twentieth century the rise of
the medical profession moved most births into hospitals or nursing
homes, so the opportunity for creating a modern birthplace museum
in a private house has declined.

The geographical distribution of birthplace museums in the United
Kingdom shows many are rural and none are in major cities. Inevitably
many early buildings have been lost in modernizing development or in
the urban devastation of the Second World War. However, redevelopment
does not necessarily preclude a birthplace museum being established.
The successful Captain Cook Museum in Stewart Park Middlesbrough
has an urn in the grounds marking what is thought to have been the
site of the humble cottage in which the famous explorer was born in
1758. The cottage was lost in the landscaping of Marton Hall in 1858,
providing artistic freedom for subsequent impressions displaying a
Victorian image of rural idyll. The local authority chose to venerate the
site by building a new museum to house their ethnography collection,
opened for the two hundred and fiftieth anniversary of Cook's birth.[6] In
Nottingham the William Booth Birthplace Museum has been rescued by
the Salvation Army from a comprehensive area redevelopment; the former terrace is now reduced to just three houses surrounded by a modern complex giving a completely different environment to the property.

One of the earliest recorded tourist attractions in the United Kingdom
is the birthplace of the best-known playwright of the English language.
William Shakespeare became famous in his own time through the popularity of his plays, performed largely in London; the revered location

of his birth in Stratford-upon-Avon was not identified publicly until one hundred and fifty years after his death, by David Garrick, an actor who courted fame through his stage performances of Shakespearean heroes. It was indeed David Garrick who set the birth date for William Shakespeare as April 23; this was a guess based on a tradition of baptizing infants at three days of age, as the only record is his baptism on April 26, 1564. Garrick also identified the "birth room" within the house, which conveniently offered a window at the front from which a banner could be supported to publicize the Jubilee event he organized in 1769. As Aaron Santesso comments, the tradition of visiting this celebrated birthplace was so well established by the nineteenth century that Henry James could use it as the thinly disguised subject for his comic novella "The Birthplace," in which he lampoons the desire of ardent visitors for spurious "facts" to embellish the story.[7]

In Scotland, underpinned by a history of depopulation, there are three birthplace museums remembering men who migrated in their youth and achieved greatness in their adopted country. The John Paul Jones Museum celebrates the life of the American Revolution naval hero, presented with contemporary naval support as the "Father of the American Navy." In 1895 Louise Carnegie bought the cottage where her husband Andrew was born, opening it as a museum after his death in 1919. John Muir's birthplace in Dunbar is also dedicated to the life of a youthful migrant, rediscovered by the intervention of overseas interest. It is a powerful devotion that reaches across the ocean to recover the origins of such men, but is it a coincidence that all are presented as having risen from humble beginnings to fulfill the American dream? James Loewen argues that the selection of *whom* to memorialize may be unduly influenced by an interest in promoting people who reflect how a community or nation wants to see itself, rather than how it actually is.[8] Perhaps a contemporary upsurge in interest in the lifework of John Muir is timely as communities on both sides of the Atlantic struggle to come to terms with environmental degradation and seek more sustainable futures.

John Muir: "Father" of the National Park Service?

John Muir was a remarkable man and could as well be remembered for his technological inventions, his contribution to glacial or botanical science, or indeed his success in commercializing fruit production. The focus on environmentalism marks the way his story is told, by himself and others, and is reflected in the way properties associated with him are now used. John Muir is celebrated today as a forerunner of the modern environmental movement. He is credited with generating such interest to protect wild landscape through his writing and lobbying that he almost single-handedly brought about what has been dubbed "America's best idea" of national parks.[9] Muir is particularly associated with Yosemite Valley due to his wonderful descriptions of experiencing wild nature there, although Senator John Conness presented the valley as the first state park in California before Muir ever came across it. John Muir's influence is more properly attributed to arguing the case for dedicated, professional, management—hence he is more accurately remembered as "father of the National Park *Service*."

John Muir was born on April 21, 1838, in Dunbar, East Lothian, a small port south of Edinburgh. It was here that he undertook the formal schooling and religious instruction that would shape his outlook on life. His father, Daniel Muir, came to Dunbar as a recruiting sergeant for the British Army but then settled there, marrying Ann Gilrye, the daughter of a local butcher. He developed a successful business trading corn and grain, becoming a person of some note in the town. The Muirs started their family life living in cramped accommodation above their store in Dunbar High Street. John was their third child. Soon after he was born Daniel moved his expanding business and family into a much larger premises next door. Through astute trading Daniel achieved an enviable level of prosperity, but he was uninterested in the comforts of life and maintained a strict regime of work and prayer for his family.

In January 1849, in search of religious freedom, Daniel abruptly resigned his role as town councilor and moved his family to the United States.[10] John Muir had already shown an adventurous spirit that was ill suited to his constrained upbringing and, by his own account, relished the adventure offered by migration. The reality was somewhat less exciting, as he was destined to spend the greater part of his youth in hard manual labor as his family broke ground in Wisconsin, not once, but twice, creating productive farms. It wasn't until 1860, as a young man, that John Muir eventually broke free of his father's influence and moved first to university study and then to start his life of travels. Although he only returned to Dunbar once, for a brief visit in 1893, he would retain his Scottish identity through accent and influence, his personal possessions including works of celebrated Scottish writers such as Robert Burns, Walter Scott, and Robert Louis Stevenson.

John Muir's fame is based on his writings about nature and the legacy of his campaigning efforts to protect wild lands. Hailed as a "wilderness prophet," Muir is a familiar figure in North America. He spent many years exploring the Sierra Nevada range in California, particularly the Yosemite Valley.[11] While there he became known for guiding visitors and started to publish stories of his experiences. These writings were aimed at armchair readers of the urbanized coast, but through evocative phrasing Muir engaged his distant audience in virtual visits. Even after he had moved to live in the Alhambra Valley, he returned periodically to renew his personal commitment to wildness. As he became more aware of the damaging impact of lumbering and grazing, he sought to draw his readers into supporting conservation.

Muir corresponded with others of similar interest, including Ralph Waldo Emerson, entertaining them with fireside stories when opportunities arose. Although dubbing him a "publicizer," Roderick Nash accepts that his celebrated camping trip in the Yosemite Valley with Theodore Roosevelt in 1903 provides one of the grand narratives of landscape conservation. An ostentatious welcome with banquet and fireworks had been arranged for the president, but he preferred to bypass the waiting dignitaries and spent the night under the stars with Muir. At that time they shared a common interest in creating a legislative context for landscape preservation, but this was not to last, as the national interest in development and resource use presented ever greater threats to the land so loved by Muir.[12]

The face of this "great" old man is used to indicate wise counsel on Sierra Club publications, but also figures as the popular face of conservation. Muir's name is attached to landmarks from California to Alaska. Woods, parks, and trails remember him, and plants have been named after him. His fascination with the giant redwood trees of the Sierras pervades his work. His writing evokes a unique eyewitness, his enthusiasm for all things wild inspiring generations of readers to value wildness. His final campaign was to save the Hetch Hetchy Valley in the newly formed Yosemite Park from flooding as a reservoir. He campaigned vigorously, although increasingly alone as the argument for preservation declined and conservation, allowing the "wise use" of natural resources, won the day:

> Everybody needs beauty as well as bread, places to play in and pray in, where nature may heal and cheer and give strength to body and soul alike . . . ever since the establishment of the Yosemite National Park, strife has been going on around its borders and I suppose this will go on as part of the universal battle between right and wrong, however much its boundaries may be shorn or its wild beauty destroyed . . . These temple destroyers, devotees of ravaging commercialisation, seem to have a perfect contempt for nature, and instead of lifting up their eyes to the God of the mountains, lift them to the Almighty Dollar. Dam Hetch Hetchy! As well dam for water-tanks the people's cathedrals and churches, for no holier temple has ever been consecrated by the heart of man.[13]

John Muir's campaign for the preservation of Hetch Hetchy exposed the weakness of the piecemeal management of protected areas and demonstrated the need for more effective *national* recognition and management of protected areas.

In a recent biography Donald Worster describes Muir as "the greatest forerunner of modern environmentalism, a powerful influence on people far beyond the West Coast, and even beyond America's shores."[14] However, such acclaim came relatively late in life for a man whose origins are found thousands of miles away. Indeed, perhaps it is because his fame is based largely on his writings that in the United States his Scottish origins have been largely ignored. John Muir is so fundamentally associated with Yosemite that he appears a primeval "mountain man." Yet those who met him were in no doubt of his nationality, and descendants of other Scots migrants now rally to his name to celebrate a shared heritage.

Until quite recently in his native Scotland John Muir was forgotten, his family's fate caught up in the wider story of a migration stream that saw nearly a quarter of a million Scots settled in North America by the end of the nineteenth century. Although Muir traveled widely, his best-known publications focus on the mountains of the west coast of the

United States of America, and there his story rested until the fashion for literary pilgrimage brought his admirers to Dunbar in search of his origins.

John Muir Associations

The name of John Muir has been adopted by a confusing array of associations, spanning two continents and more than a century. Two distinct groups of motives underpin these associations, with examples of each on both sides of the Atlantic. In 1892 Muir was founder member and first president of the Sierra Club, consolidating the link between his name and wilderness preservation. The Sierra Club has gained international respect for its conservation work and grown into a substantial membership organization that, "since 1892 . . . has been working to protect communities, wild places, and the planet itself."[15] In 1956 the John Muir Memorial Association was founded in Martinez to rescue his home from dereliction and preserve the family gravesite. The property was added to the Register of National Historic Sites in 1966, and the National Park Service took over management. By 2004 the Association dropped "memorial" from its name and reasserted its mission to preserve John Muir's legacy through education and advocacy, particularly to "provide programs and activities that build understanding of the important legacy . . . of appreciation for nature and a desire to protect our planet's important natural resources."[16]

Inspired by the work of the Sierra Club, the Scottish John Muir Trust was established in 1983 with the aim of safeguarding the future of wild lands by stewardship of open land in Scotland. Since 1997 its annual John Muir Award has promoted exploration and outdoor challenges for young people. The Dunbar John Muir Association was formed in 1994 with a specific focus on Muir's legacy in the locale of his origin. Its stated aims were to "tell the world about Muir's life, his work, and his belief in the unique and irreplaceable value of wild places and wild creatures; and to implement his philosophy by conserving, restoring and enhancing landscape and wildlife in East Lothian and Scotland."[17] It published a town trail map to identify sites relevant to John Muir's story and opened the first museum at the birthplace, but did not have the resources to sustain the project alone.

In Scotland two government agencies have been involved in the story. East Lothian District Council is the local authority responsible for maintaining public services. Its interest in John Muir has focused on the economic potential for attracting tourists to a bypassed area of the Scottish lowlands. Historic Scotland is the central government agency responsible for identifying and protecting the built heritage. Under a system that prioritizes architecture, Historic Scotland listed much of the High Street of Dunbar in 1971. It included the tenement building where John Muir was born in Category B (regional or local importance). This recognizes that although the building is not of sufficient architectural merit to justify listing in the first category, its local heritage value supports conservation. The John Muir Birthplace Trust was formed in 1998 as a partnership project linking the John Muir Trust, the Dunbar John Muir Association, and Dunbar Community Council. A central feature of their work has been securing funding and planning permissions for the development of the birthplace building, through the agency of the East Lothian Council and the National Lottery. When the current birthplace museum was opened in 2006 under the management of East Lothian Museum Service, the Dunbar John Muir Association changed its name to Friends of John Muir's Birthplace.[18]

Although these associations have worked separately and together to ensure the enduring legacy of John Muir, it is not surprising that with so many involved some variation in priorities and process may be observed. In both countries the earlier associations expressed the widest conservation aspirations inspired by the later work of John Muir. Subsequent associations were more concerned to preserve properties associated with Muir himself. For one group the most significant achievement is the perpetuation of the ideals of wildlife and landscape conservation, while for others preserving artifacts and authentic structures representing the essence of the man himself takes priority. All the organizations now have mission statements emphasizing the contemporary relevance of John Muir's work, as environmental sustainability has become a worldwide concern. The organizations dedicated to the preservation of the tangible heritage disagree on the importance of the structure of buildings, their furnishings, and how best to present their cultural heritage to the public. The shifting balance of interest between preservation and conservation, historic accuracy and contemporary educational activity is reflected in the treatment of both tangible and intangible heritage. On both sides of the Atlantic the practical management of the buildings has moved into professional hands, in Scotland through East Lothian District Council and in the United States with the National Park Service. Both agencies have a wider purpose that now underpins management decisions, broadening their aims for the sites beyond a strict adherence to the story of John Muir.

Muir's Homes: From Dunbar to Martinez

Given the emphasis John Muir placed on experiencing the wonders of the natural world outdoors, it is perhaps surprising to find two buildings in urban areas now under government protection in the name of his legacy. In Dunbar a modest tenement building is preserved as his birthplace. In Martinez the elegant Italianate mansion the Muir family lived in for thirty years is presented as his home. The emphasis on built heritage would have surprised Muir himself, but it attunes with the desire of many visitors to engage with tangible relics. Both properties offer visitors an opportunity to learn about the life of John Muir, but the choices made between re-creation and museum presentation influence the visit experience. In Dunbar a modern museum educates visitors about his life and work but with little physical reminder of lifestyle, whereas in Martinez period room settings evoke the era and allow visitors to envisage the man at work. The different presentation illustrates both a difference in style and concerns about visitor engagement, and underpinning professional approaches to dealing with authenticity.

John Muir was born in Dunbar in a small tenement typical of Scottish towns. It fronts directly onto the main street and originally accommodated separate apartments on each of the three floors with shared stairs to a rear courtyard.[19] The Historic Scotland building record notes a three-story, three-bay, sandstone rubble harled tenement building with contrasting painted cement margins. The windows are described as "regular fenestration 12-pane glazed pattern, shutters remain." The record indicates that the building had undergone alteration and restoration.[20] When John Muir was born the family business occupied the lower ground level. His family was one of several living on the upper floors, shared occupancy being typical of the tenement system.

This modest building has survived, but with successive renovations and alterations that substantially changed both its external appearance and its internal arrangement. In the early decades of the twentieth century the front door was moved to fit large shop windows appropriate for its use as a drapery store. By the 1970s the interior floors were moved to accommodate the machinery of a dry cleaning business that occupied the building for many years. When interest arose in rediscovering John Muir's origins, the building was changed again with a restoration of the front and reinstatement of interior floors, accommodating a small period room setting museum above commercial use. In 2000 the whole building was acquired for a heritage center; this provided the opportunity to re-evaluate the approach to presentation and interpretation. A radical restoration was proposed: all features subsequent to the period associated with John Muir would be stripped out, leaving just the exterior walls and back stairs as an authentic shell to provide housing for a new "state of the art" museum. When a dispute arose regarding this decision, the designers employed by the John Muir Birthplace Trust turned to the Scottish Heritage architectural assessment to endorse their strategy, which verified that only features subsequent to the Muir residence would be removed. Thus the later cultural heritage of this part of Dunbar High Street was sacrificed to recover the early nineteenth-century appearance of this one building. However, the building next door, which is the one John Muir would have remembered as a child, retains the additional story added to accommodate a temperance hotel in the later nineteenth century.

In Martinez the preserved site includes the large mansion that John Muir inherited from his father-in-law, Dr. John Strentzel, along with an older adobe building standing in the grounds.[21] Dr. John Strentzel was an eminent horticulturalist who had established a substantial fruit farm in the Alhambra Valley. In 1882 he built his dream house on a rise overlooking the estate, a suitable property to reflect the achievements of a successful life. The timber frame house was designed by architects Wolfe & Son of San Francisco. Seventeen rooms on two floors with enclosed porch, basement, and a substantial attic capped by ornate cupola provide ten thousand square feet of usable space. Louie and John Muir moved into the house when her father died. Muir not only labored on the estate but built up its commercial value so successfully that within a decade he had achieved financial independence for his family. Although he traveled extensively in the latter years of the nineteenth century, with his wife's help he maintained the estate for the rest of his life.

The property may surprise visitors who expect to find a humble dwelling fitting the outdoor life advocated by Muir and described in his most popular tales. Instead the house offers impressive reception rooms with high ceilings and imported Italian marble fireplaces. The house also provided all modern conveniences, including water closets and bathroom, indoor plumbing and gas lighting (a telephone was available from 1884, and electricity was connected shortly before his death in 1914). In 1906 the San Francisco earthquake shook the Alhambra Valley and damaged the house. While making repairs Muir added a three-story extension and knocked through two first-floor parlors. In the downstairs family room he replaced a damaged fireplace with a large "mission style" brick structure and redecorated in a more austere style. John Muir's two daughters married and moved away, so family use ceased with his death. After a period of near dereliction, the building was saved by local entrepreneurs, and through the attention of the John Muir Memorial Association and subsequently the National Park Service, recreated to its appearance in Muir's lifetime with the help of his daughter Wanda Muir and surviving family friends.

Creating a Birthplace Museum: Divergent Approaches

These two buildings reflect both the enduring importance of presenting a tangible sense of place in relation to a celebrated personality, and opposing views on how best to achieve this. The explanation for the divergence may be found in the complex interaction of the associations and agencies involved in their conservation. Toward the end of his life Muir was encouraged to write an autobiographical account of his early years to satisfy the curiosity of his many admirers. He recounted memories of life in Dunbar but made light of the troubles of his family's emigration, choosing to edit much of the difficulty and labor from the account that was eventually published as *The Story of My Boyhood and Youth* (1913).

In one of his best-loved tales he recounts a youthful escapade in which he climbed out of the dormer window of his bedroom to escape into the night. But which window was this? American visitors seeking to locate this account were among the first to pace the High Street of Dunbar in search of his origins. Although John Muir's birthplace had been accurately identified as a modest tenement building, it was perhaps not always appreciated that his father's growing prosperity supported a move to the much larger building next door at 130–134 High Street. It was a dormer window on the top floor of what was at the time a two-story building that features in the oft quoted tale "Good Scootchers" from *The Story of My Boyhood and Youth*. Thus John Simpson's evocation of John Muir's own pilgrimage home in 1893 focuses on the house he would recollect as a child, rather than the building now celebrated as the birthplace.[22] Viewing the later roof extension chimes with Muir's gleeful description of the risk he took, but without it the reality would have been somewhat less hazardous.

The development of John Muir remembrance in Dunbar rests on the intervention of a few individuals and their relationship with the local authority. In an early act of commemoration in relation to land steward-ship, Frank Tindell, the director of the East Lothian planning department, was instrumental in naming the John Muir Country Park established in 1976 along the coastline west of Dunbar.[23] The identification and initial conservation of the building now housing the birthplace museum did not occur until interests focused on the built heritage decades later. The original birthplace museum was established on the top floor of the prop-erty, leased by the Dunbar John Muir Association, thus in a space that John Muir would never have occupied. For some years a stereotypical period room-setting portraying living conditions in the 1840s welcomed enquiring travelers and curious local visitors. None of the furnishings were authentic to either the building or the Muir family, but the museum evoked an impression of family life that satisfied many visitors. This low-key presentation was interrupted when the whole property came up for sale. The opportunities for developing local tourism interested the East Lothian Local Authority; the John Muir Birthplace Trust was established as a partnership to coordinate purchase and thus protect the tenement building where the Muir family lived when John was born. The build-ing was eventually purchased with funding from a number of sources, including public fundraising, Landfill Tax grant, and loans.[24]

The Trust faced a dilemma: did its desire to present the 1830s out-weigh retaining traces of the building's subsequent redevelopments?

Building, document, and archaeological research revealed the changes resulting from one hundred and seventy years of varied commercial use and residential occupation, leaving little link to the original space occupied by the Muir family.[25] A radical development proposal would restore the 1830s authentic fabric of the building and remove all subsequent additions. The Trust commissioned architects Richard Murphy, Bill Black, and Graeme Armet, with exhibition designers Campbell and Co. Edinburgh, to restore the shell of the building and create a structure within it to house the new museum. They designed a three-story steel-and-timber tower constructed to accommodate a museum to interpret the life of John Muir and engage the local community with environmental education fit for the twenty-first century. The innovative new design required gutting the building to remove the later alterations and constructing a free-standing exhibit space within the shell.

The proposal outraged some local people dedicated to the existing museum. The plan's apparent disregard for the integrity of the birthplace provoked an outcry, with a particularly intense campaign that eventually drew in the Architectural Heritage Society of Scotland, the Sierra Club, and Muir family descendants in debating the "desecration" of Muir heritage. A sustained campaign to retain the period room settings delayed planning permission for the renovation; it was argued that the suggestion that an "authentic" presentation of the "birth room" was being removed had misled more distant supporters who had never visited the site. The architects subsequently explained their surprise that the advantages of the new scheme were not immediately clear to all:

> The project hit enormous numbers of objections through massive misreporting in the press which purported that we were removing the original fabric of the house (exactly the opposite of the case). However after an inspection by Nicholas Gove Raines Architects for Historic Scotland confirmed that we were, as stated all along, simply removing what had been put into the house in the 1970s the sense of the project was widely understood and planning permission achieved.[26]

This statement is a good example of what Laurajane Smith calls the "authorised heritage discourse" at work.[27] The presumption is that the essence of heritage is found in the fabric of the building and that the best people to determine how this should be displayed are the experts—in this case the professional architects, backed by their colleagues working for the government agency tasked to advise the local planning authority on the appropriateness of any change. This strategy determined that authenticity was found in the 1830s structure; anything more recent was not considered of any importance. The plan not only required the removal of all trace of the subsequent life of the building, but also summarily disposed of the existing museum objects on the grounds that they were "inauthentic." The architects presumed that the protesters were simply ill informed and congratulated themselves that the wisdom of their project would be clear once everyone understood the intention. This seems to be the case, but there is little room here for prior consultation sensitive to the needs and expectations of a wider public who were more interested in atmosphere and experience.

An alternate approach is clearly displayed at Martinez. The property has been meticulously restored to the best representation possible of what it was thought to have looked like in John Muir's later life. Some period furnishings and fittings have been used, but much is recreated. The introductory film shown in a separate visitor center provides information about John Muir's life and orientation to the site. The house is left to speak for itself. Room settings have been created to resemble the 1890s appearance of the house as closely as memory and available materials will allow. The film presents a dramatization filmed in the recreated rooms which accentuates the idea that this is "how it was." If asked, rangers will explain that the furniture is "of the period," and point out the two objects thought to have survived from the original fittings. Crucially, one is John Muir's desk, allowing a reconstruction of the "scribble den" as though the great man was still working there, notes and correspondence strewn across the room.

Reproductions of paintings owned by Muir, including notable works by his friend William Keith, are hung in the reception rooms and the "scribble den." Although a National Park Service leaflet and notes on the website explain "period furniture and artefacts have been used wherever possible, with reproduction wall and floor coverings and paintings to reflect the historic period," visitors are encouraged to wander freely through the property, pausing to absorb the period atmosphere. Chairs and other ephemera are placed to encourage the impression that the great man has just "stepped out." Outside remnants of the fruit farm are being re-established, with attentive conservation of trees that John Muir may well have planted with his own hands. The family gravesite is also carefully conserved, although subsequent urban development on the intervening land has detached this from the accessible site. Visitors with more time are encouraged to hike the trail to Mount Wanda, the adjoining hillside Muir bought to share his enthusiasm for nature walks with his children.

Positioning Birthplace Museums in the Heritage Sector

The development of two sites associated with the same person, but separated by narrative time, physical space, and national interest, demonstrates how a similar initial motive can lead to quite different outcomes, depending on the varying balance between opportunity and constraint imposed by the available property, funding, and curatorial control. Visitors react to what they find, so comments elicited on-site at the time of a visit are usually complimentary. Indeed, where visitors are critical, their remarks focus on incidental circumstances, often beyond the control of the museum presentation staff. It is unusual to find a visitor who is able to envision an alternative presentation, so able to give a considered view on the choices made. Museum staff often become dedicated to a chosen pathway, acting to justify and perpetuate the style found without the opportunity to consider alternatives.

Thus it is informative to trace the origin of any birthplace museum. Frequently its discovery is preceded by the formation of an association researching the life and achievements of the individual, sometimes made up of just a few influential "friends." As most birthplaces celebrate lifetime achievement, there will usually be an interval of many decades, indeed in some cases centuries, before a museum is established. The first step is securing the property, often prompted by a pending sale or in some cases development threatening the integrity of the site. In major cities urban renewal is pressing, so fewer old buildings survive long enough to be identified and preserved. Consequently, a review of birthplace museums in the United Kingdom may suggest a spurious correlation between rural or small-town origin and great achievement.

A critical stage in the presentation of a birthplace rests on the adoption of the site by professional heritage management. Of the twenty-seven birthplace museums identified in the UK in 2010, four are operated by a local government department as part of their tourism presentation, six have been taken over by the National Trust (England) or the National Trust for Scotland.[28] Two are managed by national organizations as part of their institutional heritage, and the remainder are still presented by single-concern voluntary associations.[29] In many cases, the introduction of professional curatorial management has moved the presentation from a relaxed period representation to strict attention to authenticity, sometimes necessitating a shift from room settings to museum exhibits as is the case for the John Muir birthplace.

Another influential factor of recent years is the availability of funding from outside agencies. In the United Kingdom the National Lottery has been the source of significant capital resource, but meeting the exacting funding requirements of this agency places great emphasis on professional management, often prompting significant alteration in the approach to presentation. A contrary example is shown by the birthplace museum for the founder of the Salvation Army, William Booth, in Nottingham. Here, running against much contemporary practice, plans for refurbishment will add to the period presentation by opening the kitchen and front parlor of the house "dressed" with appropriate, if inauthentic, fittings. The museum that currently occupies this space will be redisplayed with improved facilities in an adjoining house. The work is both contracted and funded by the Salvation Army, giving greater curatorial freedom to meet the needs and expectations of their spiritual pilgrims.

In the United Kingdom the intervention of professional "authorising" staff is frequently followed by redisplay, removing objects and settings considered inauthentic. Although the "museum exhibit" approach provides a more flexible context in which to convey complex information, this does not necessarily best serve the needs of pilgrim visitors, many of whom will already know much about the subject. The presentation of properties associated with John Muir illustrates the choice. Few people in the United Kingdom have heard of him, so the Dunbar Birthplace Museum needs to provide an introduction to his life and work. However, in the future American visitors may be disappointed to find a glass case and text panel museum, even with its engaging use of interactive exhibit. Curiosity to experience the circumstances of John

Muir's childhood will no longer be satisfied. In Martinez the name of John Muir is much better known, so the "at home" presentation is perhaps more appropriate, even if the cultured reality comes as a surprise to many visitors.

The case of John Muir provides an opportunity to speculate on alternative narratives that could be employed. In both California and Scotland contemporary managers accentuate enthusiasm for wild places, although this has evolved out of earlier presentation of a simpler life narrative. In Scotland the purpose is more explicit, facilitated by interpretative media throughout the new museum and in the "expedition" out-reach work. The Dunbar museum uses the story of John Muir's travels around the world to open up wider concerns of global environmental conservation, leading visitors to consider personal action toward recycling and energy use. In California there is a more relaxed approach to the "message" of the site; the emphasis on period allows the visitor to dwell in nineteenth-century tranquillity, distanced from contemporary concerns, but its presentation by the National Park Service provides a wider contextual purpose.

The various John Muir associations share an interest in promoting the relevance of Muir's work to the contemporary audience. The properties provide both a physical and a virtual base from which to continue campaigns started by Muir's writings. In Martinez the National Park Service hosts events such as the annual John Muir Birthday/Earth Day celebration. While the John Muir Association celebrates the birthday with pipe band and cake, many local "green" associations join in advocating a more sustainable lifestyle. In Dunbar, the Birthplace Museum provides a base for environmental education work with local youth: inspired by Muir's example, young people are encouraged to explore, discover, and present their findings to encourage life-changing experiences through encounter with the natural world. Thus while John Muir lost his campaign to save the Hetch Hetchy Valley from flooding, his legacy is used to continue the battle between conservation and preservation he so eloquently identified in the wider interest of the twenty-first-century environment.

NOTES

My thanks to the rangers of the National Park Service at Martinez, to Tom Leatherman for taking time to show me John Muir's gravesite, and to Jo Moulin and her staff at the John Muir Birthplace Museum for the welcome they provided and their willingness to discuss their work. Nottingham Trent University provided a research grant to facilitate one visit, and the John Muir Association enabled me to attend a meeting in Martinez. I have learned much through many conversations with staff, visitors, and Muir enthusiasts, but the views expressed here are my own.

1. Learn more about the John Muir Birthplace Trust at www.jmbt.org.uk/content/pages/news -and-events.php.

2. See Laurajane Smith, *The Uses of Heritage* (London: Routledge, 2006).

3. Elizabeth McKellar describes the presentation of Blenheim Palace in a case study in *Understanding Heritage in Practice*, ed. Suzie West (Manchester: Manchester University Press, 2010), 180–99.

4. In 2010 there were 27 birthplace museums open to the public in the UK.

5. Sailors such as Robert Blake, James Cook, and John Paul Jones achieved fame for their explorations or military conquests. Grace Darling, the daughter of the Bamborough lighthouse keeper, was celebrated for her help in rowing an open boat through a storm to rescue survivors from the wreck of the SS *Forfarshire*.

6. The Birthplace Museum has been recently refurbished part-funded by the National Lottery and now houses the Middlesbrough Museum service ethnographic collection. See www .captcook-ne.co.uk/ccbm/index.htm.

7. Aaron Santesso "The Birth of the Birthplace: Bread Street and Literary Tourism before Stratford," *English Literary History* 71 (Summer 2004): 377–403. More detail about the Shakespeare Birthplace may be found in a case study researched by Nicola Watson in chapter 4 of West, ed., *Understanding Heritage in Practice*, 42–158.

8. James W. Loewen, *Lies Across America: What Our Historic Sites Get Wrong* (New York: Touchstone, 1999), 3.

9. Ken Burns and Dayton Duncan, *The National Parks: America's Best Idea* (New York: Borzoi Books, 2009).

10. Daniel Muir was a member of the Secession Church, a dissenting congregation from the established Protestant Church of Scotland. In time he rejected all organized religion and sought the freedom to become his own preacher, supported solely by bible reading.

11. Sierra Club, "The John Muir Exhibit," www.sierraclub.org/john_muir_exhibit/; and Peter Anderson, *John Muir: Wilderness Prophet* (London: Franklin Watts, 1995).

12. Roderick Nash, *Wilderness and the American Mind*, 3rd ed. (New Haven: Yale University Press, 1982), 122.

13. John Muir, *The Yosemite* (New York: The Century Company, 1912), chapter 15.

14. Donald Worster, *A Passion for Nature: The Life of John Muir* (New York: Oxford University Press, 2008), 3.

15. Sierra Club, "Welcome to the Sierra Club!" www.sierraclub.org/welcome/.

16. John Muir Association, "Our Mission," www.johnmuirassociation.org/php/about.php.

17. Dunbar's John Muir Association, "Dunbar's John Muir Association," www.djma.org.uk /djma/.

18. Friends of John Muir's Birthplace, "About," http://muirbirthplacefriends.org.uk/about/.

19. Notable buildings of Dunbar are described in Colin McWilliam, *The Buildings of Scotland: Lothian Except Edinburgh* (London: Penguin UK, 1978). Details of the birthplace are given in fact sheets available from the Museum.

20. Historic Scotland, Scottish Ministers' Statutory List, http://hsewsf.sedsh.gov.uk/hslive /hsstart?P_HBNUM=24825.

21. 4202 Alhambra Avenue was added to the National Register of Historic Places in 1966. Building no. 66000083 notes the builders as Martinez, Vicente, Wolf and Son. Area of significance: architecture, social history, agriculture, conservation, literature, science. The adobe building standing in the grounds was built in 1849.

22. John W. Simpson, *Yearning for the Land: A Search for the Importance of Place* (New York: Pantheon Books, 2002).

23. Legislation to enable local authorities to establish Country Parks in Scotland was passed in 1967. John Muir Country Park opened in 1976.

24. Jo Moulin, Manager, John Muir's Birthplace, personal communication with author, April 26, 2010. Landfill Tax is levied on companies disposing of waste in landfill sites. The intention is to reduce the amount of material deposited and adopt more environmentally friendly means of waste disposal, including recycling and composting. Money generated is allocated to environmental projects in the region.

25. *John Muir's Birthplace* East Lothian Council Museums Service fact sheet 1.03; McWilliam, *Buildings of Scotland.*

26. Richard Murphy Architects, "John Muir Birth Place Visitor Centre, Dunbar," www.richard murphyarchitects.com/projects/326/.

27. Smith, *The Uses of Heritage.*

28. Established in 1895 the National Trust (England) is a voluntary body dedicated to the preservation of countryside and places of historic value. Strangely, it does not operate the birthplace of one of its founders, Octavia Hill, which is managed by an independent trust.

29. Royal National Lifeboat Institution (Grace Darling) and the Salvation Army (William Booth).

Second-floor bedroom and nursery in the John Fitzgerald Kennedy Birthplace, 83 Beals Street, Brookline, Massachusetts, photographed by O. W. Carroll in 1970. Library of Congress, Prints and Photographs Division, Historic American Buildings Survey, HABS MASS,11-BROK,7-21.

2

A particularly ironic facet of birthplace commemoration has been its tendency to enshrine sons more often than their mothers, our "problem without a name" as Patricia West puts it later in this volume. Certainly members of organizations like the Mount Vernon Ladies Association imagined themselves as figurative mothers of the nation's republican heritage. But what if a "real" mom set out to commemorate the birth of her own son? Might motherhood figure differently in our memory of birth? Christine Arato explores this possibility in the fraught encounter between Rose Kennedy and the National Park Service at the Massachusetts birthplace of John F. Kennedy. Writing from the perspective of an agency insider, Arato uncovers a fascinating contest between Mrs. Kennedy, the NPS, and her son's admirers wherein President Kennedy's political legacy pivoted on competing performances of motherhood. The editing of an audio tour voiced by Mrs. Kennedy serves as a central metaphor for these negotiations while also demonstrating the practical challenges underlying collaborative practice at any historic site. At the same time, Arato's careful analysis of the tour's evolving script within its broader historical context demonstrates the power of multidisciplinary approaches to problems in public history.

This House Holds Many Memories

Constructions of a Presidential Birthplace at the John Fitzgerald Kennedy National Historic Site

CHRISTINE ARATO

In September 1960, in his address to the Greater Houston Ministerial Association, Senator John Fitzgerald Kennedy acknowledged the need to tackle the "so-called religious issue," which had until that moment overshadowed his presidential campaign. Kennedy's brief speech drew a clear line between Protestant America's anxiety over his Catholicism and what he believed were the real issues dominating the American political landscape: the spread of Communism, rural poverty, and the nation's reluctance to explore outer space. Kennedy elaborated upon this distinction between the secular and the sectarian, identifying himself not as "the Catholic candidate for President," but rather as the "Democratic Party's candidate for President who happens also to be Catholic." He went on to describe his ideal America, "where the separation of church and state is absolute," as a place where religious intolerance would someday end, and where there would be "no Catholic vote, no anti-Catholic vote, no voting bloc of any kind."[1]

Nine years later, as the tumultuous decade that Kennedy's campaign inaugurated drew to a close, the late president's mother, Rose Fitzgerald Kennedy, dedicated his restored birthplace in Brookline, Massachusetts, as a unit of the National Park System. Mrs. Kennedy related her understanding of the "historic value" of this three-story, eleven-room Colonial Revival style house at 83 Beals Street as both a "birthplace of a President of the United States" and as a window into "how people lived in 1917."[2] Members of Congress echoed her patriotic sentiment in the preparation and passage of legislation that established the birthplace as a national historic site, noting that it was "appropriate that the birthplace of John Fitzgerald Kennedy, who had such a sense of history, should be preserved by our nation."[3] Speaking from the front porch to a crowd of nearly 800 visitors, Mrs. Kennedy expressed in her dedicatory remarks the hope that young Americans who visited John Fitzgerald Kennedy National Historic Site would develop a sense of history and literature and that the adults who visited would be "imbued with the optimism" that she and her husband, Joseph P. Kennedy, shared.[4]

Whereas Kennedy confronted public fears of political, social, and cultural turmoil, his mother invoked what historians of public memory have labeled "official" culture, a "restatement of reality" that harnesses the abstraction of timeless sacredness to assert teleological certainties.[5] Consequently, a sense of nostalgia for a generalized past infused the birthplace restoration with a singular national narrative. Mrs. Kennedy's voice, captured in an eighteen-minute audio-tour, continues to guide thousands of visitors through the museum each year. The editing of Mrs. Kennedy's narrative—and, in fact, of the building itself—was the product of a complex exchange between her, the National Park Service, and the site's multiple audiences. All of them drew upon what David Lubin describes as "endlessly replicated and infinitely elastic chains of images" from Kennedy's life.[6] At the Kennedy birthplace museum, these "elastic chains of images" bind public memory and perception in spiraling temporal circles, dragging elements of the past into assessments of the present and, even, toward projections for the future.

This essay attempts to sift through these layered images by exploring the Kennedy birthplace as a site of multiple authors and audiences, of shared and contested narratives about the present and the past, and of overlapping and often contradictory commemorative functions. In short, it confirms that collective memory is an elusive product of historical and cultural imaginations, but also suggests that birthplaces provide a setting where the social act of speaking constitutes both collective reality and individual identity.

From Birthplace to Monument

In the past three decades, scholars have examined various ways in which collective memory is manufactured to organize societies, to validate or to challenge hierarchies and traditions, and to control or to inform public discourse.[7] A product of these multi-disciplinary efforts is the understanding that historical narratives represent the interplay between the authors and intended audiences that comprise interpretive communities.[8] In Brookline, popular recognition of the significance of the Kennedy family's Beals Street home preceded the president's assassination and the promulgation of an "official" narrative. In September 1961, just eight months after the American public thrilled to President Kennedy's heady inaugural exhortations, the Town of Brookline installed a commemorative bronze and granite monument to mark the site of his birthplace on what was then the front lawn of Martha Pollack. Local attention to the house where Rose and Joseph Kennedy began their family paid a fitting compliment to President Kennedy's entreaty to chart a new course at home and abroad. His clarion call of "let us begin" may have continued to sound in the minds of those who trod past the house during the daily course of events.

Yet, in just two years the public meaning of the house was transformed from a vision of the future—of a romance with the leader who ushered in the race to the moon—to the remembrance of his tragic assassination in Dallas, Texas, on November 22, 1963. In Brookline, hundreds of people converged on the president's birthplace to mourn locally. The Town of Brookline formed the John F. Kennedy Memorial Committee in an attempt to safeguard the powerful symbol of the presidential birthplace, but failed to acquire the Beals Street house. The National Park Service immediately began to monitor the property and, in 1964, dispatched a photographer to document the structure for the Historic American Buildings Survey.[9] The agency's initially unfavorable assessment of the site concluded that the association of Kennedy with Brookline "embraces not more than his first three and one-half years [and] does not hold much potential as an historic site to receive much visitation by the public without going to a good deal of expense."[10] Nonetheless, the Federal Advisory Board on National Parks recommended the birthplace for historic landmark status. Designation followed on July 19, 1964.[11]

Around this time the Brookline selectmen drafted a letter soliciting Rose Fitzgerald Kennedy's financial assistance for the proposed architectural documentation of the house. The unanswered letter suggests that the Kennedy family, too, initially did not intend to create a memorial at the birthplace. They had a very different notion of how to recapture the charisma of the martyred president. Mrs. Kennedy accompanied an exhibit of JFK memorabilia abroad in 1964–65, ostensibly as a fundraising activity for the family's primary civic monument to John F. Kennedy, the presidential library.[12] President Kennedy had already chosen the site and style of this building, a Georgian Revival structure on land contiguous to Harvard University, during the month before his death in 1963. By 1975, this very traditional tribute was abandoned for I. M. Pei's modernist design on the Boston waterfront.

Ultimately, however, both reluctant parties—Mrs. Kennedy and the National Park Service—were caught up in the events, exigencies, and effects of local storytelling.[13] Citing concern that the birthplace "shrine" would "fall into the wrong hands," a consortium of local attorneys signed a purchase agreement for the Beals Street property in August 1966 and immediately appealed to the Kennedy family through Mrs. Kennedy's nephew, Joseph F. Gargan. A second letter to the office of Senator Robert F. Kennedy finally obtained the desired response, and the attorneys transferred the purchase agreement to the Kennedy family on November 1, 1966.[14] That day a *Boston Globe* article reported that "Mrs. Rose Kennedy wants the 11-room home restored for future generations."[15] The partnership was sealed during the following spring when Mrs. Kennedy formally articulated her intentions for the birthplace:

> In recent years, I realized that this house, because it was the birthplace of a President of the United States, is of historic value to the American people . . . It is our intention and hope to make a gift of this home to the American people so that future generations will be able to visit it and see *how people lived in 1917* and thus get a better appreciation of the history of this wonderful country.[16]

In the May 1967 legislation to establish the Beals Street property as a unit of the National Park System, the United States Congress focused exclusively on the signal event of John F. Kennedy's birth. These slightly divergent narrative emphases presaged the vexed relationship that soon emerged between Mrs. Kennedy and the National Park Service, as well as between the respective "personal" and "official" narratives inscribed on the property, as their stories unfolded—and perhaps unwound—in the public domain of the birthplace.

Preserving a Mother's Memory

Work began on the birthplace soon after the Kennedy family purchased the property. Three families had occupied the house during the nearly five decades since the Kennedys had moved from their Beals Street home in 1920, and much of the household furnishings had been dispersed among the extended Kennedy family's primary and secondary residences. The family created a restoration account, and Mrs. Kennedy emerged as the principal agent in the project. She later recalled of the years following Kennedy's death that she "wanted to take part in and help . . . move along the memorials to Jack—the library, the cultural center, and so many others."[17] Why the birthplace restoration gained precedence over other memorial projects is unclear. Her expressed intentions to open the house to the public on May 29, 1967, the fiftieth anniversary of Kennedy's birth, however, certainly explains her

haste. Perhaps an explanation of Mrs. Kennedy's dedication to commemorative work at the birthplace lies in the relationship between collective memory and self-identification, in what one historian calls the
"everyday performance of self."[18] W. Fitzhugh Brundage describes this
performance as one in which "the narrative conventions of a group's
historical memory provide individuals with a framework within which
to articulate their experience, to explain their place, in the remembered
past" and, of course, in the unfolding present.[19]

In creating her own idealized version of the past for public consumption, Mrs. Kennedy worked closely with Robert Luddington, an
interior decorator at the Jordan Marsh department store who had
designed several "private" Kennedy interiors. The distinction between
"public" and "private" is somewhat undermined by Mrs. Kennedy's
demonstrated concern with public image made manifest in her family's homes. In her directions to the decorator working on the family's
Hyannisport home in 1948, for example, Mrs. Kennedy displayed family photographs along the alcove walls and composed four pages of cap-
tions that she directed to be printed in a small book accompanying the
gallery. The photographs featured Kennedy family members with notables such as Winston Churchill during Joseph P. Kennedy's tenure as
U.S. Ambassador to the Court of Saint James. Mrs. Kennedy employed
a similar design strategy at her Palm Beach home, where she specified
that the family photographs were to be hung chronologically. Her eli-
sion of public and private is most evident in the plaque she ordered
from Tiffany and Company to adorn a sofa sent from her Bronxville
home with the inscription: "Pope Pius XII Sat Here When, As Cardinal
Pacelli, He Visited Us In Bronxville On November 6, 1936."[20]

While it appears that Mrs. Kennedy designed most—if not all—of
her homes for public consumption, only the second iteration of the Beals
Street residence was not intended for "private" occupancy. Between late
1966, when Luddington took out a classified ad in a local newspaper
seeking several "50 year old" pieces of furniture, and May 1969, when
the birthplace museum finally opened to the public, Luddington and
Mrs. Kennedy assembled a collection of 946 objects to furnish the
birthplace.[21] The collection comprised a mixture of antiques and modern reproductions of items that Mrs. Kennedy recalled to have been in
the house during the family's time there. Luddington suggested during

a 1976 interview that Mrs. Kennedy gave him broad latitude in furnishing the house. To this day, however, he insists that Mrs. Kennedy personally chose or approved the acquisition and placement of all objects in the birthplace museum. His assertion jibes with how Mrs. Kennedy worked with other decorators. Moreover, receipts show that objects purchased by Luddington were later removed from the house because Mrs. Kennedy apparently did not approve of them.[22]

As the restoration project dragged on, NPS officials expressed concerns about the apparent lack of progress with the house interiors and with their lack of information concerning Luddington's preservation methodology. Luddington assured his partners that the work was well researched, using photographs as memory prompts for Mrs. Kennedy. The agency's project leader received "an encouraging report as to the methods and the content of the items that will be used in redecorating and furnishing the Beals Street house," and agency officials seemed further assuaged by visits with Luddington earlier in the year.[23] During a two-day visit to the Home of Franklin Delano Roosevelt, the presidential birthplace at Hyde Park administered by the National Park Service, Luddington apparently imbibed the agency's professional preservation methodologies and shared this knowledge with his employer, sending pamphlets and postcards from Roosevelt's birthplace to Mrs. Kennedy.[24] More important, it was at this NPS-run presidential site that Luddington first encountered Eleanor Roosevelt's taped tour of her husband's birthplace.

Decades later Luddington claimed that it was he who suggested that Mrs. Kennedy do the same for the Kennedy birthplace. And she, according to Luddington, wrote the text for the recordings.[25] It is unclear whether the decision to employ a narrative strategy that combined material culture and discursive interpretations of the birthplace originated exclusively with Luddington and Mrs. Kennedy or, more likely, derived from NPS promptings. However, NPS documentation does indicate that the audio-visual division of NPS's Harpers Ferry Center (HFC) created the recording scripts based on a November 1967 interview of Mrs. Kennedy conducted by Nan Rickey, the HFC's technical publications editor. According to Rickey, the interiors were nearly finished when Mrs. Kennedy accompanied the HFC staff through the birthplace.[26] That the *entire* project was nearly complete *in Mrs. Kennedy's mind* is supported by the fact that she had granted an interview at the house to

CBS News anchor Harry Reasoner in advance of her appointment with NPS staff. Reasoner's interview aired on October 31, 1967, and a similar segment appeared on the Merv Griffin show on Thanksgiving Day, close to the fourth anniversary of President Kennedy's assassination. With restoration delays having thwarted her original intention to dedicate the site on the fiftieth anniversary of her son's birth, Mrs. Kennedy tacitly, succinctly, and, perhaps subconsciously, interwove the beginning and ending of John F. Kennedy's life story in her commemorative interview at Beals Street near the anniversary of his death.

Narrating the Birthplace in the Age of Television

Perhaps more significant than the sense of narrative closure in Mrs. Kennedy's unveiling of her commemorative project to the public was the medium through which she chose to reveal her tribute to her son. Television was certainly one of the silent partners in the birthplace memorial project, and the Kennedy family had done more to seduce the media—and the viewing public—than any other American political dynasty to date. The conception of the Kennedy family as a dynasty was one to which Mrs. Kennedy aspired. On a visit to Brazil in the early 1950s, she confided to her diary that "the idea of a family serving in the government, generation after generation, as is the case with so many English families as well, is one we might do well to think about and encourage in our own country."[27] Nearly a decade before John F. Kennedy had become a household name with his victory over Nixon in the first televised presidential debate, his family had probed the potential of television as a campaign tool. In fact, the Kennedys' romance with communications technology dated to the early years of Mrs. Kennedy's marriage. Joseph Kennedy was an early investor in the "moving pictures" industry, buying up much of the Keith vaudeville empire and converting these venues into movie palaces for his own production companies.[28]

Technology was not just a business investment. Mrs. Kennedy recalled that she and her husband had a telephone and car "a little sooner than most of our friends." By the end of the second decade of their marriage, they had telephones "in nearly all the bedrooms and strategically placed in other areas [that] rang morning to night."[29] Moreover, radios and phonographs operated "morning, noon, and night around the house and grounds . . . each according to the taste of the person running the machinery."[30] That Mrs. Kennedy was keenly aware of the power of the media to confer political legitimacy is evident in a handwritten note added to the transcript of her tour of the birthplace in which she shared her memory that "Jack thought being born at home was almost as good as being born in a log cabin like Lincoln."[31] In late 1967, therefore, NPS staff revealed no sense of betrayal or chagrin with Mrs. Kennedy's preemptive appeal to the television public.

From the perspective of the agency, however, the task of storytelling remained incomplete. During the next eighteen months, NPS "professionals" labored arduously to shape the house interiors and the taped tour into an "authentic" depiction of the events of 1917. It is here that our story becomes most interesting because it is in the process of creating Mrs. Kennedy's taped tour of the Kennedy birthplace that the intertextuality of "her" narrative voice becomes most evident. In a summative evaluation of Rickey's 1967 interview, NPS Audio Production Specialist Bud Dutton observed the evocative value of Mrs. Kennedy's voice and anticipated the experience of its audience:

> Mrs. Kennedy's voice is of such quality that the visitor should get the feeling that he is being given a warm, personal tour. I like this intimate approach to interpreting the house. It's small—and in some ways—like the homes of the visitors so that a definite rapport can be attained between guest and hostess.[32]

Dutton explains that the tape contained "a wealth of information" and provided a "good *guideline* to making the final tape." Even so, he suggests improving the tour by eliminating irrelevant material, adding material "needed to *adequately* describe each room," composing a script to guide movement through the house, and including notes to help "retain the relaxed quality of a lady showing a guest through her home." While Dutton concludes that "Mrs. Kennedy will again do the talking," his memo communicates the agency's assumption that NPS professionals would approve and, ultimately, provide much of the content of the story.[33]

That Mrs. Kennedy brought a coherent narrative to the birthplace is evident in interviews she granted earlier that year. In her conversation with Rickey and the NPS team, she refers to an article she wrote in which she describes her strategies in supervising and educating a large family of nine children.[34] Transcripts from the CBS program earlier that autumn include Mrs. Kennedy's slightly self-deprecating depiction of herself as an efficient family manager, employing scientific techniques in the maintenance of a "card catalog" of all of the children's health histories.[35] Judging from the hundreds of responses that viewers of the Reasoner interview addressed personally to her, Mrs. Kennedy had well emphasized her role within the household as a intellectual and moral leader, at once a traditional and modern mother. One viewer confided that "I have tears in my eyes after watching the beautiful interview you gave on T.V. Oh how I wish I could be the type of mother you are."[36] Another assured Mrs. Kennedy that "they really should have you on another program—possibly one of your own—once a month talking of family life. We could all learn from you."[37]

Mrs. Kennedy's modern television persona played with an older iteration of modern motherhood. The trope of an efficient, organized, and scientific mother recalled Progressive Era proponents of home economics education for women. During the Rickey interview, Mrs. Kennedy alludes to her early training in the skills of modern motherhood—in contrast to those of her mother's generation—while describing one of the books displayed in the nursery: "I used to buy their books *carefully* at the Women's Exchange at school where they were demonstrated . . . but my mother bought this at Jordan's one day, and it doesn't fulfill any of the recommendations that they make for children's books."[38] Six years later, during the height of feminism's Second Wave, Mrs. Kennedy referred specifically to her "domestic science" training at the Sacred Heart Convent in Blumenthal, Holland, and to motherhood as a "work of love and duty" and "a profession that was fully as interesting and challenging as any honorable profession in the world." She said nothing about the campaign for woman's suffrage that made very different claims for American women during her early career as wife and mother.[39]

Despite this nod to her "honorable profession," a hint of defensive ambivalence is evident in the Rickey interview when Mrs. Kennedy describes the contents of the living room. She relates how she tried to stimulate children into "knowing, learning and being interested in helpful things and in Government," and lingers on descriptions of her own travels as a child to Europe and South America, when she accompanied her father, Boston Mayor John Fitzgerald, to meet with celebrities and dignitaries.[40] Even when Rickey redirects the conversation toward family life at Beals Street, Mrs. Kennedy returns to events and affinities outside of the home. While the children left little time for embroidery, for instance, she presided over the Ace of Clubs, a "current events club," the "highest, the best of all clubs" for young Catholic women in Boston. Mrs. Kennedy reiterates this assertion of worldliness in the study: "I didn't really do very much sewing, and as I said I really didn't have time, and I was always more interested in books and reading."[41]

The rather homeliness of the details of Mrs. Kennedy's 1967 narrative conceal not only the fundamental nature of her ambivalence toward the ideology of scientific motherhood, but also the foundational events of these contradictory impulses. At sixteen, she surrendered an opportunity to attend Wellesley College to the political imperatives of her father and his ally, Archbishop William O'Connell, who had set a priority for the advancement of Catholic education and the creation of an autonomous Catholic culture in the Boston archdiocese.[42] Her own life embodied the uneasy tensions between modernism and antimodernism that were so persistently latent in twentieth-century American culture and, consequently, in the domestic ideals invoked in American house museums. The full extent of Mrs. Kennedy's ambivalence toward the ideology of scientific motherhood was revealed two decades later, when she admitted during an interview with historian Doris Kearns Goodwin, "with a bitterness of tone which she did not often allow herself to betray," that her "greatest regret" was in not having gone to Wellesley College. "It is," she confided, "something I have felt a little sad about all my life."[43]

Making Rose's Memory Public Memory

That Mrs. Kennedy neglected to mention these ambitions and, moreover, that NPS staff failed to inquire about her experiences beyond motherhood, suggests that they were all focused on a shared "horizon of expectations" that referenced an idealized vision of home and the centrality of this concept to an idealized past. Of the 27 pages of transcribed notes from Mrs. Kennedy's interview, NPS staff reduced the script to less than a tenth of that size and incorporated even less of the "original" material. The central image in the revised story is a portrait of domestic bliss for the *nuclear* family. Not only did NPS staff eliminate all mention of the Fitzgerald family, they also reduced Mrs. Kennedy's reminiscences of her worldly youth to a single reference about the relevance of her past to the aesthetic education of her children.[44] Also excised were Mrs. Kennedy's comments about the servants whom she employed, the details of birthday parties, and first steps which "never made much of an impression." Her confused response—"well he wasn't away from home"—to queries about Joe Kennedy's work life suggests an inadvertent and defensive nod to his intimate relationship with the sultry film celebrity Gloria Swanson.[45] Even Mrs. Kennedy's uncertain references to the political events of 1917 wound up on the cutting-room floor, sacrificed to the timeless narrative of home life.

What remains is a rather charming and nostalgic portrait of quiet evenings at home:

> We spent a lot of time in this room in the evening. Mr. Kennedy was president of a bank and this was his one opportunity to read the newspaper or his favorite detective stories. He would sit in that red chair by the gate-leg table. We all read *The Boston Transcript* in the evenings in those days. Papers only cost a penny. Usually I would sit in the wing chair there by the table opposite him. I can't see that chair without remembering the holes in the children's stockings. They wore knickers then and the boys' knee stockings always had holes in them. They had to be darned once or twice a week.[46]

Given the agency's predilection toward factuality, it seems remarkable that this script flowed from the pen or, at the very least, escaped the knife of the technical publications editor. Despite Mrs. Kennedy's repeated and contradictory statements about her distaste for sewing, Rickey and her team integrated wholesale an idyllic domestic portrait which bears an uncanny resemblance to the illustrations found in prescriptive literature on interior decoration that appealed to middle-class housewives in the early decades of the twentieth century.

But why would the NPS accept such sloppy research methods? I suspect that a correlative statement in the depiction of the room appealed to the agency's commitment to accurate restorations based on careful documentary research. In her tour, Mrs. Kennedy describes her love and talent for playing the piano and her children's indifference to the instrument. The piano, frequently a symbol of women's roles as aesthetic and moral arbiters in the domestic sphere during the late nineteenth and early twentieth centuries, served Mrs. Kennedy's self-image as the intellectual and moral leader of the Kennedy home. She literally sat herself at the keyboard at the public dedication of the museum.[47] But for agency professionals, this piano was not merely a symbol, but also a specific object—a 1911 Ivers & Pond grand piano bestowed as a wedding gift by Mrs. Kennedy's uncles, James and Edward Fitzgerald— with a verifiable provenance. That one object could serve *at least* two overlapping, yet divergent notions of authenticity points to the elasticity of apparently simple images.

In her autobiography, Mrs. Kennedy describes the restored Beals Street home's "original furniture" as "good, solid, serviceable, conservative furniture in the taste of the time." The home's "muted color scheme," however, contrasted with her later taste for a "lot of bright colors."[48] The language here is redolent of early twentieth-century interior design manuals such as Elsie de Wolfe's 1913 treatise *The House in Good Taste,* which advocated a subdued palette, chintz window treatments, and historical styles, most notably the Colonial Revival style, for furniture.[49] This decorative agenda sought balance and harmony, refuge from the unsettling aspects of modern life, and the moral qualities of the nation's founding fathers and, more important, mothers. At the very least, Mrs. Kennedy's recreation of her early twentieth-century home depicted these domestic ideals. The beige grass wallpaper and mahogany suite in the restored dining room and the Martha Washington sewing table in Mrs. Kennedy's boudoir invoke the powers of a simple past to create a portrait of domestic calm amid the turmoil of contemporary streets. Mrs. Kennedy's invocations of the nation's colonial past exploited the ambiguities of the modern middle-class aestheticized "ancestral" home. Uncluttered rooms with "tasteful" reproductions of the "master" paintings imagine a privileged status for the family akin to contemporary design prescriptions and, ultimately, publicly realized in the Kennedy White House.[50] Such assertions of pedigree claimed social and cultural authority previously reserved to white Protestant elites.

Unlike the 1967 interview, which ended with Rickey and Mrs. Kennedy comparing their experiences as mothers, the tour scripted by the NPS provides a concerted conclusion to the visit: "I hope that you have enjoyed your visit to our home. We were very happy here and although we did not know about the days ahead we were enthusiastic and optimistic about the future."[51] It may not have been evident to NPS professionals or to the general public that Mrs. Kennedy's sunny farewell to her guests entailed a certain counter-factuality: namely, the suppression of a three-week episode in 1920 during which a discontented Mrs. Kennedy abandoned her husband and children and returned to her father's Dorchester home.[52] Yet, the overshadowing ending that could not be suppressed, but rather merely suspended, was the assassination of her sons. Mrs. Kennedy later admitted that the assassination of her seventh child, Robert F. Kennedy, in June 1968—while she was still involved in the birthplace restoration—was the kind of event "in fiction I would have put . . . aside as incredible."[53] In this instance, when the real-life events overthrew "the normal order of things," narrative memory entailed a social act that at once employed the capacity to remember and the capacity to forget. In the official birthplace narratives, "hidden things" are *not* "left for the hearer to discover," but rather willfully suspend "unpleasing" or discordant facts so that all can share in the redemptive ordering of both the present and the past.[54]

Hidden Things

One of the "hidden things" about which Mrs. Kennedy does not speak is the ethno-religious aspect of the Kennedy identity that proved divisive during the president's life. Whereas the aspiring president, John F. Kennedy, was forced to confront public doubts about the ability of a Catholic to lead a "Christian" country, Mrs. Kennedy could exploit her control over the birthplace museum to avoid such overt confrontations. Few signs of the family's Irish Catholicism appear in the birthplace restoration. Oblique references include an Irish linen bedspread, the shamrock motifs embroidered on a lace baby cap, and reproductions of religious images from Renaissance art that, at least in Mrs. Kennedy's taped description, reflect secular refinement and education. In the decades following the public dedication of the birthplace, NPS staff came to read the relative absence of religious iconography as a deficit of authenticity in Mrs. Kennedy's narrative strategy. The missing crucifix, documented in the Kennedy's wedding log and determined by professional historians to be essential in "creating the proper Christian domestic atmosphere," became an emblem of Mrs. Kennedy's selective memory.[55]

For Mrs. Kennedy, however, I suspect that the crucifix remained one of those "hidden things" that was, in turn, caught up in the more personally troubling valences of another related sign: motherhood. Throughout her life Mrs. Kennedy had frequent recourse to images of motherhood and mined the idea for its rich potential in depicting the often-troubling circumstances of her life. As a young woman at Sacred Heart Convent, she achieved a kind of identification with the paradigmatic mother of Catholic imagery, the Virgin Mary, in conceiving of motherhood as a calling for which she surrendered personal and professional ambition.[56] A decade later Mrs. Kennedy employed the trope of suffering forbearance to defend her dignity against Gloria Swanson.[57] Later she played an increasingly public role as the preternaturally youthful mother-of-nine and, paradoxically, as a Gold-Star Mother on Jack's campaign trails.[58] But by the late 1950s, another Mrs. Kennedy epitomized the new maternal paradigm. Jacqueline Kennedy personified the sophisticated, beautiful young mother, the Madonna who gathers her curly-headed child in her arms *and* invites 45 million Americans into her historically accurate refurbished home.[59] When the eyes of the world focused on Jacqueline Kennedy as a grieving widow and mother of two fatherless children, the president's mother remained in the background.

In the years following Kennedy's assassination, Jacqueline Kennedy did much to convince the public that "Jack's life had more to do with myth, magic, legend, saga and story than with political theory or political science."[60] She modeled his funeral after Abraham Lincoln's and, with Robert Kennedy, spearheaded the effort to design, fund, and construct the John F. Kennedy Presidential Library and Museum at Columbia Point. She also figuratively linked the Kennedy administration to the romanticized kingdom of Camelot and, in this regard, played a part in shaping the story at Beals Street. Rose Kennedy, who had given the draft script of the birthplace tour to Jacqueline Kennedy for review, prominently displayed a copy of *King Arthur and His Knights* in the nursery installation. She did not mention the book during the Reasoner interview, but made a passing reference to the Camelot myth—and Jacqueline Kennedy's role in promulgating it "afterwards"—in her walk-through with Rickey.[61] The recorded tour reduces the theme to an abbreviated nod to Mrs. Kennedy's scientific motherhood and her self-assertion as the presidential mother: "Probably Jack's favorite book was King Arthur and His Knights. I was very careful to select books which were recommended at school or by a children's bookshop."[62]

Across the hall, in the master bedroom, is where Mrs. Kennedy played out the full significance of motherhood as a profession, sacred duty, and archetypal identity. During the Rickey interview she offered relatively perfunctory replies to the team's queries:

> This is our bedroom and the President was born here and the other two children. And they [the doctor and nurse] always used the bed near the window in case the baby arrived in the daytime, and he did arrive at 3:00 in the afternoon. This again is the regular toilet set and Mr. Kennedy's toilet set. And these copies of famous paintings which I had seen in Rome.[63]

This matter-of-fact description of "the President's" birth contrasts with the monumental tone of the recorded tour:

> When you hold your baby in your arms for the first time and you think of all the things you can say and do to influence him it's a tremendous responsibility. What you do with him and for him can influence not only him, but everyone he meets and not for a day or a month or a year but for time and eternity. Years later, when Jack was elected president, I thought how fortunate I was out of all the millions of mothers in the United States to be one to have her son inaugurated president on that cold, cold day.[64]

It is tempting to attribute the mythic quality of the narrative to the nationalist tropes that are stock-in-trade in NPS interpretation, but Mrs. Kennedy employed the same wording in the Reasoner interview and during her dedicatory speech in May 1969.[65] Her use of the second-person pronoun, together with the mention of "eternity," gives Mrs. Kennedy's words the timeless air of allegory. She invokes the hardship of a log cabin birth alongside the powerful imagery of the emergence of fully formed gods in classical mythology. Mrs. Kennedy's presentation of self became decidedly more polished over the course of the birth-place rehabilitation project.

As in all of the rooms, the objects contribute to and often complicate the story. To the left of the doorway, a photograph of Rose Kennedy with her first son, Joseph P. Kennedy, Jr., typifies studio portraiture of the period. The image encourages the identification of "millions of mothers in the United States" with Mrs. Kennedy and plays on the home's allusions to an ordinary middle-class family. And certainly in this "elastic chain" of maternal images, the young Rose Kennedy of 1917 contrasts sharply with James McNeil Whistler's iconic portrait of his own mother, a copy of which hangs in the front hallway. Whistler's mother is a mere shadow of Mrs. Kennedy's glamour. But an oblique material reference suggests that Mrs. Kennedy did not see herself as merely *a* mother, but rather as *the* archetypal mother. Two reproduced Renaissance Madonnas hang above the twin beds in the master bedroom, a Botticelli above the birth bed and a Raphael above the other. In 1974, she confided to the BBC:

> I think of the Blessed Mother, when she watched her son being crucified . . . I thought of her so often at the crucifixion, when I saw Jack in the rotunda in Washington and Bobby in New York . . . I'm not going to be vanquished either, I'm going to carry on.[66]

In this light, the missing crucifix is troubling only if we forget that Mrs. Kennedy witnessed her sons' deaths second-hand, on television, with millions of other mothers. Mrs. Kennedy could only watch from a distance as the iconic image of Jacqueline Kennedy cradling the dying president replayed endlessly. Denied her appropriation of the image of the Pietà, Rose Kennedy inhabited the role of the young and nurturing "blessed mother."

Judging from visitor accounts and agency documentation, Mrs. Kennedy's identification with the archetypal Christian mother remained one of the "hidden things" *not* discovered by the American public and NPS professionals at Beals Street. Nor did Mrs. Kennedy's audiences realize that she was acting out the prescriptive literature of her early adulthood. Among the many objects of her commemorative project that somehow made their way to storage were a collection of women's magazines from 1917 and 1918. Visitors could not see how *House and Garden's*

"Little Portfolio of Good Interiors" (1918) might have influenced Mrs. Kennedy's conservative tastes, nor how this decidedly intellectual matron had eschewed her preference for politics and current events for sentimental bedtime stories nestled between the covers of *Smith's Magazine* or the *Ladies' Home Journal*. The National Park Service literally swept these objects under one of the twin beds in the master bedroom.

Hearing the Public Voice

However, visitors did seem to identify with the "spry, stoic Kennedy *matriarch who dominated*" the museum's dedication ceremony. As one account noted, "the throng, preponderantly women" were there to "welcome back Rose Kennedy, to hear her and to speak to her."[67] After the ceremony, Mrs. Kennedy led her guests through the museum, while "the throng" was only allowed through the first floor. According to the National Park Service, over 1,400 visitors toured the house during the first weekend and nearly 23,000 people filed through by the end of July 1969.[68] Initial reactions to the site were unanimously positive. Undersecretary of the Interior Russell Train remarked that "with great care and faithful attention to details that only she would know, she [Mrs. Kennedy] has restored it to the way it was at the time of President Kennedy's birth 52 years ago today."[69]

But a rift within the "public" soon divided the interpretive community along popular and professional lines. Journalists, echoing popular sentiment, reported on the special quality of Mrs. Kennedy's narrative voice. "Her presence is all around the house," remarked one, while another observed that "the quiet voice detailing the contents of the rooms brings back the happy, ordered world of childhood."[70] One visitor concluded that Mrs. Kennedy's "words are by far the most touching part of the tour, since they are clearly nostalgic and reflect a mother's fond recollection of the events that took place in she and her husband's first home."[71] But it was this "clearly nostalgic" tone that unsettled NPS professionals. Shortly after the site's opening, Rickey wrote:

> While this prospectus . . . will not recommend any revision of the refurnishing at the present time . . . it is strongly felt that preliminary work should be commenced now with a view to providing *authentic*

furnishing information for the future Service personnel who may, at
some time, believe that *a more accurate presentation* would better serve
the needs and purposes of the area.[72]

Curator Charles Dorman expressed a similar sentiment in 1970 when, in
a rather unorthodox move, he included evaluative comments in the site's
collection records. Dorman's comments were often vituperative, and
included a list of recommended improvements (replace "shamelessly
modern carpets" and the "French lamp in the nursery [that] is all wrong")
along with some complimentary remarks ("the tapes of Mrs. Kennedy's
voice . . . are a gem of interpretation" and "Mr. Luddington deserves a lot
of credit").[73] NPS Historical Architect Orvill Carroll, in his 1969 assessment of structural conditions, recommended that the agency "improve
upon the quality of the restoration" and correct "numerous errors."[74]

   While Rickey's 1969 report intimated that the passage of time would
permit the NPS to create a more accurate museum, the agency quickly
began retelling the past. At first, curators seemed content to remedy the
decorative record by replacing plastic talcum powder containers with
tin and altering photograph arrangements in Mrs. Kennedy's boudoir.
These "corrections" reflect the curators' preferences for the narrative
content of an idealized American home. In the hallway, staff undermined Mrs. Kennedy's depiction of the family's social and political lin-
eage by replacing photographs of Mayor John Fitzgerald with anachro-
nistic images of Jack as a childhood football hero and Mrs. Kennedy as
a demure debutante. In the boudoir, a darning egg joined the collection
of reading materials left on the Martha Washington sewing table. A
photographic portrait of the Fitzgerald women replaced an image of
Rose Kennedy with five of her children. The addition of a framed pin,
emblazoned with a shamrock and identified as a gift to Mrs. Kennedy
from Sir Thomas Lipton, perhaps recalled the family's ethnicity.

   Later, after extensive fire damage in 1975, NPS Associate Regional
Director Denis Galvin recommended changes to the "previous restoration" based on Luddington's admission that "Mrs. Kennedy probably
didn't have a complete recollection of [the kitchen]."[75] More recently,
curator Janice Hodson read Mrs. Kennedy's omission of a Victrola listed
in the Kennedys' wedding log as an illustration of the selectiveness of her
memory and suggested that these choices were purposive and, perhaps,

misleading.[76] Yet, while NPS curators questioned Mrs. Kennedy's rendering of the past, some of its rangers remained ensnared in sentimentalized, and often hagiographic, portrayals of the Kennedys' past. A recent bulletin referencing "no Irish need apply" signs, for example, linked the privileged Kennedys with nineteenth-century working-class Irish immigrants without noting the entitlement and exclusivity that separated Rose and Joseph Kennedy from their co-religionists at St. Aidan's Catholic Church.[77]

This impulse to correct mistakes may explain the agency's switch to ranger-led tours around 1990. The guided tours were intended to provide historical context, using excerpts from Mrs. Kennedy's tapes at short intervals. The public, however, would have none of it. A survey of visitors revealed their unanimous feeling that something vital had been removed from the house. One particularly irate visitor complained that the new format destroyed "the whole mystic flair of the Presidents [sic] Birthplace" because he "could not just stand there and admire the quiet reserve while the tapes of Mrs. Kennedy's remembrances filled the air."[78] Rather than information, the story they wanted was one that provided opportunity for contemplation and their own "performances of self."[79]

Despite attempts to limit the birthplace story to an "authentic" Kennedy past, the public's voice still prevails there. Over and over in the pages of comment books at the birthplace, visitors recall the specific moment of President Kennedy's death, but also the more general transition from memories of the "happy, ordered world of childhood" to a more staid accounting of the progression of lived experience. Historian of religion Mircea Eliade distinguishes the sacred from the profane both spatially and temporally, and in this light many visitors regard their experience of the site as sanctified, as a place to return to a break in time.[80] In the Kennedy birthplace, material culture manifests the rhetoric of civic religion. I would argue that both of these narratives play out in the ambiguities of the birthplace as both a sanctified space and home sweet home. And over and over again, the many publics who claim the social and narrative space of the Kennedy birthplace remind both the National Park Service and the Kennedy family that it was these audiences who first summoned the "official storytellers" to Beals Street. For this reason, the birthplace endures as a contested site for the performance, rather than the experience, of authenticity.

NOTES

1. Kennedy, "Address to Greater Houston Ministerial Association," September 12, 1960, www.americanrhetoric.com/speeches/jfkhoustonministers.html.
2. Mrs. Joseph P. Kennedy to Secretary of the Interior Stewart Udall, March 15, 1967, Resource Management Files, John Fitzgerald Kennedy National Historic Site, National Park Service (hereafter cited as JFK).
3. "Hearing before the Subcommittee on Parks and Recreation of the Committee on Interior and Insular Affairs, United States Senate, Ninetieth Congress, First Session on S. 1161, March 20, 1967" (U.S. Government Printing Office, Washington, DC: 1967).
4. "Simple ceremony marks opening of Kennedy house," *The Brookline Chronicle Citizen*, June 5, 1969, as cited in Alexander von Hoffman, *John F. Kennedy's Birthplace: A Presidential Home in History and Memory* (National Park Service: 2004), 154.
5. John Bodnar, *Remaking America: Public Memory, Commemoration, and Patriotism in the Twentieth Century* (Princeton: Princeton University Press, 1992), 13–14.
6. David M. Lubin, *Shooting Kennedy: JFK and the Culture of Images* (Berkeley: University of California Press, 2003), x–xiii.
7. Patricia West, *Domesticating History: The Political Origins of America's House Museums* (Washington, DC: Smithsonian Institution Press, 1999), 162. On collective memory, see Bodnar, *Remaking America;* Benedict Anderson, *Imagined Communities: Reflections on the Origins and Spread of Nationalism* (London: Verso, 1983), Paul Connerton, *How Societies Remember* (New York: Cambridge University Press, 1989), Eric Hobsbawm and Terence Ranger, eds., *The Invention of Tradition* (New York: Cambridge University Press, 1983), Michael Kammen, *Mystic Chords of Memory: The Transformation of Tradition in American Culture* (New York: Knopf, 1991), and David Lowenthal, *The Past Is a Foreign Country* (New York: Cambridge University Press, 1985).
8. See, for example, Michael Jackson, *Existential Anthropology: Events, Exigencies, and Effects* (New York: Berghan Books, 2005).
9. Janice Hodson, *Historic Furnishings Assessment: John F. Kennedy National Historic Site* (Boston: U.S. Department of Interior, National Park Service, Northeast Museum Services Center, 2005), 13.
10. Superintendent, Minute Man NHP to Regional Director, Northeast Region, memorandum, March 24, 1964, Resource Management Files, JFK.
11. Nancy Waters, *Collections Management Plan: John F. Kennedy NHS* (Boston: U.S. Department of Interior, National Park Service, Northeast Museum Services Center, 1999), 6–7.
12. Hodson, *Historic Furnishings Assessment,* 14.
13. See Jackson, *Existential Anthropology,* especially chapter 1.
14. Merrill Hassenfield to Robert F. Kennedy, September 14, 1966, Rose Fitzgerald Kennedy Papers, SCPF 1964–1968, John F. Kennedy Library.
15. Gary Kayakachoian, "JFK Birthplace Returns to Kin," *Boston Globe,* November 1, 1966.
16. Mrs. Joseph P. Kennedy to Secretary of the Interior Steward Udall, March 15, 1967, (emphasis added), Resource Management Files, JFK.
17. Rose Fitzgerald Kennedy, *Times to Remember* (Garden City, NY: Doubleday, 1974), 505.
18. Jacquelyn Dowd Hall, "'You Must Remember This': Autobiography as Social Critique," *Journal of American History* 85 (September 1998): 439–53, as cited in *Where These Memories Grow: History, Memory, and Southern Identity,* ed. W. Fitzhugh Brundage (Chapel Hill: University of North Carolina Press, 2000), 13.
19. Ibid.
20. Hodson, *Historic Furnishings Assessment,* 10–11.
21. Ibid., 17–19.

22. Supervisory Park Ranger to Superintendent, memorandum, September 27, 2003, Central Files, JFK; and Hodson, *Historic Furnishings Assessment*, 18.
23. Edwin Small to Regional Director, Memorandum, April 5, 1967, Resource Management Records, JFK.
24. Robert Luddington to Thomas Walsh, January 16, 1967, Joseph P. Kennedy Papers, Box 12, Folder 5 and pamphlet collection in Rose Fitzgerald Kennedy Papers, (Col. 139), Series 8 Subject Files, John F. Kennedy Library.
25. Supervisory Park Ranger to Superintendent, memorandum, September 27, 2003, Central Files, JFK.
26. Rose Fitzgerald Kennedy, interview by Nan Rickey, November 1967, Resource Management Files, JFK.
27. Kennedy, *Times to Remember*, 279.
28. Ibid., 186–87.
29. Ibid., 281.
30. Ibid.
31. Rose Fitzgerald Kennedy, interview by Harry Reasoner for *CBS News Special: "Who, What, When, Where, Why: J.F.K.—The Childhood Years, A Memoir for Television by his Mother"* (transcript), October 31, 1967, Rose Fitzgerald Kennedy Personal Papers, Box 107, John F. Kennedy Library.
32. Memorandum, Bud Dutton, Audio Production Specialist to Nan Rickey, November 24, 1967, Resource Management Files, JFK.
33. Ibid. [emphases added].
34. Rose Fitzgerald Kennedy, interview by Rickey, 14.
35. Harry Reasoner, *CBS News Special*.
36. Mrs. Carol Szazynski to Mrs. (Rose) Kennedy, October 31, 1967, Rose Fitzgerald Kennedy Personal Papers, Box 107, John F. Kennedy Library.
37. Mrs. Wallace Connor to Mrs. (Rose) Kennedy, November 3, 1967, Rose Fitzgerald Kennedy Personal Papers, Box. 107, John F. Kennedy Library.
38. Rose Fitzgerald Kennedy, interview by Rickey, 43 (emphasis added).
39. Kennedy, *Times to Remember*, 32, 81.
40. Rose Fitzgerald Kennedy, interview by Rickey, 2.
41. Ibid., 9, 37.
42. Doris Kearns Goodwin, *The Fitzgeralds and the Kennedys: An American Saga* (New York: St. Martin's Press, 1987), 142–44; James O'Toole, *Militant and Triumphant: William Henry O'Connell and the Catholic Church in Boston, 1859–1944* (Notre Dame, IN: University of Notre Dame Press, 1992), 143–72.
43. Goodwin, *The Fitzgeralds and the Kennedys*, 144.
44. Rose Fitzgerald Kennedy, audiotaped interview by National Park Service, May 22, 1969, Resource Management Records, JFK (hereafter cited as Rose Kennedy Tour).
45. Rose Fitzgerald Kennedy, interview by Rickey, 21, 23–24; Gloria Swanson, *Swanson on Swanson* (New York: Random House, 1984), 380–97.
46. Rose Kennedy Tour, n.p.
47. Craig H. Roell, "The Piano in the American Home," in *The Arts and the American Home, 1890–1930*, ed. Jessica H. Foy and Karel Ann Marling (Knoxville: University of Tennessee Press, 1994). Katherine C. Grier, "The Decline of the Memory Palace: The Parlor after 1890," in *American Home Life, 1880–1930: A Social History of Spaces and Services*, ed. Jessica H. Foy and Thomas J. Schlereth (Knoxville: University of Tennessee Press, 1992), 54, 61, 66.
48. Kennedy, *Times to Remember*, 74.
49. Bradley C. Brooks, "Clarity, Contrast, and Simplicity: Changes in American Interiors, 1880–1930," in *The Arts and the American Home, 1890–1930*, ed. Jessica H. Foy and Karel Ann Marling (Knoxville: University of Tennessee Press, 1994), 29–30.
50. Thomas A. Denenberg, "Consumed by the Past: Wallace Nutting and the Invention of Old America" (Boston University, Ph.D. diss., 2002); Janna Jones, "The Distance from Home:

The Domestication of Desire in Interior Design Manuals," *Journal of Social History* 31, no. 2 (1997): 314–15.

51. Rose Kennedy Tour, n.p.

52. Goodwin, *The Fitzgeralds and the Kennedys*, 303–8.

53. Rose Fitzgerald Kennedy, interview by Robert MacNeill for the British Broadcasting Corporation, 1974, John F. Kennedy Library.

54. Cathy Caruth, "Introduction: Recapturing the Past," in *Trauma: Explorations in Memory,* ed. Caruth (Baltimore: The Johns Hopkins University Press, 1995), 153; Jackson, *Existential Anthropology,* 20, 116–18; Besse A. van der Kolk and Onno van der Hart, "The Intrusive Past: The Flexibility of Memory and the Engraving of Trauma," in *Trauma,* ed. Caruth,163.

55. Timothy J. Meagher, *Inventing Irish America: Generation, Class, and Ethnic Identity in a New England City, 1880–1928* (Notre Dame, IN: University of Notre Dame Press, 2001), quoted in Hodson, *Historic Furnishings Assessment,* 6.

56. Goodwin, *The Fitzgeralds and the Kennedys,* 183–89.

57. Gloria Swanson described Rose as "sweet and motherly in every respect." Swanson, *Swanson on Swanson,* 386.

58. Kennedy, *Times to Remember,* 314–25; Goodwin, *The Fitzgeralds and the Kennedys,* 717–19.

59. Lubin, *Shooting Kennedy,* 82–84.

60. Jacqueline Kennedy to journalist T. H. White, December 1963, quoted in John Hellman, *The Kennedy Obsession: The American Myth of JFK* (New York: Columbia University Press, 1997), ix.

61. Rose Fitzgerald Kennedy, interview by Rickey, 43 (emphases added).

62. Rose Kennedy Tour, n.p.

63. Rose Fitzgerald Kennedy, interview by Rickey, 48.

64. Rose Kennedy Tour, n.p.

65. Rose Fitzgerald Kennedy, interview by Reasoner, 13–14.

66. Rose Fitzgerald Kennedy, interview by MacNeill., n.p.

67. Arthur Stratton, "Mother Gives JFK Birthplace to Nation," *Boston Globe,* May 29, 1969, Resource Management Records, JFK (emphasis added).

68. Hodson, *Historic Furnishings Assessment,* 26–27.

69. "JFK Birthplace National Site," *Boston Herald Traveler,* May 30, 1969, Resource Management Records, JFK.

70. "A Birthday Visit to the Home of JFK Is Moving Experience" and "Open House Tomorrow at the Kennedy Birthplace," *Providence Journal,* May 28, 1972, Resource Management Records, JFK.

71. "A Rose Still Grows at the Birthplace of JFK," *Brookline Citizen,* August 29, 1985, Resource Management Records, JFK.

72. Nan Rickey, *Interpretive Prospectus: John Fitzgerald Kennedy National Historic Site* (Washington, DC: U.S. Department of Interior, National Park Service, Office of Environ-mental Planning and Design, 1969), 13 (emphases added).

73. "Suggestions and Comments Made by Mr. Dorman," undated typed manuscript, Resource Management Records, JFK.

74. Quoted in Janice Hodson, "Report on the Status of Collections: John F. Kennedy National Historic Site" (Boston: U.S. Department of Interior, National Park Service, 2003), 13.

75. Associate Regional Director to Files, memorandum, February 19, 1976, Resource Management Records, JFK.

76. Hodson, "Report on the Status of Collections," 6.

77. Von Hoffman, *John F. Kennedy's Birthplace,* 64–66, 86–87, 94–98.

78. Kevin S. Peters to Senator Edward Kennedy, 3 March 1993, JOFI Files (Central Records).

79. Hall, as cited in Brundage, ed., *Where These Memories Grow,* 13.

80. Mircea Eliade, *The Sacred and the Profane: The Nature of Religion* (New York: Harcourt Brace Jovanovich, 1959).

Jimmy Carter Boyhood Home, Old Plains Highway (Lebanon Cemetery Road), Plains vicinity, Sumter, Georgia, photographed by Mark Harrell in 1989. Library of Congress, Prints and Photographs Division, Historic American Buildings Survey, HABS GA,131-PLAIN.V,1-4.

～3～

If remembering President Kennedy's birth flummoxed federal historians eclipsed by his mother's long shadow, imagine then the challenge of doing good history at the birthplace of a living president. This is precisely the situation that Zachary J. Lechner describes in Plains, Georgia, where former President Jimmy Carter was born and where he still lives today. From his vantage point as a historian of twentieth-century American culture, Lechner finds strengths and weaknesses in the stories told at the Carter National Historic Site. The birthplace paradigm, he contends, has enabled interpretation there to refute the "naturalness" of racism. And, at the same time, Lechner wonders why, if we are to believe that being born in Plains explains Carter's adult successes, it didn't catapult his neighbors to similar heights. A weighing here of competing memories suggests that birthplace commemoration, unless situated in the broadest historical context, risks obscuring the raw complexity of adult lives.

Commemorating Jimmy Carter and Southern Rural Life in Plains, Georgia

ZACHARY J. LECHNER

One of the defining characteristics of any historical birthplace is the connection between person and place, particularly the notion that one must know where an individual comes from in order to understand him or her. This is certainly the message in Plains, Georgia (population 776), the birthplace and current home of President Jimmy Carter and his wife Rosalynn.[1] Thanks to the efforts of local citizens, the Georgia congressional delegation, and Carter himself, President Ronald Reagan signed legislation in 1987 establishing the Jimmy Carter National Historic Site and Preservation District, which is managed by the National Park Service (NPS). Besides the buildings and property administered by the NPS, much of the town is federally protected as part of the Jimmy Carter National Preservation District. It encompasses the historic downtown area and other locations important to the lives of the Carters. With the support of the Plains community, NPS officials have created a unique commemoration of the life of Jimmy Carter and the southern rural and small-town existence from which he emerged.

The NPS has chosen an expansive approach, forgoing a narrow interpretation of the building in which Carter was born (Wise Sanitarium, a hospital). The agency and sympathetic locals have maintained the integrity of Plains's historical appearance and preserved locations integral to telling the story of Jimmy Carter's rise from a boy growing up on a farm in Archery, Georgia, just outside Plains, during the Great Depression, to the most powerful man in the world. The NPS is thus dedicated to interpreting the entire locale in which Carter came of age. As Georgia Democratic Senator Sam Nunn, a strong proponent of the site's establishment, explained in 1987, "in preserving only the homes of major historical figures, we tend to lose much of the essence of ordinary life that would illuminate those times. We may not realize what made the 'typical' places unique until they have been so changed that they have become unrecognizable."[2]

Although the NPS's interpretation is most influential in shaping visitors' experiences in Plains, the federal government is not alone in commemorating Carter and the town. The former president himself has frequently participated in, and often collaborated with, both federal and local commemorations. The Plains Historical Preservation Trust, a group in which the Carters serve in leadership roles, has been a valuable ally to the site, helping to raise money for park efforts and serving as a de facto friends group. Through its book, *History of Plains, Georgia,* and its public events, the Trust presents a relentlessly positive portrait of Jimmy Carter and Plains that focuses on white history and draws little involvement from black residents. President Carter has also played a key role in assisting the NPS with invaluable information, and he has served as a highly prominent booster of local history.

In some respects, the NPS's depiction of Jimmy Carter and southern rural and small-town life in Plains errs by glossing over controversial elements in the Georgian's pre-presidential political career. Like the Trust, the NPS fails to voice adequately the black community's historical experience. Despite these drawbacks, the NPS succeeds in overcoming many of the challenges of interpreting a living historical figure and his environment. And it does so while preserving historical complexity. The Park Service's efforts serve as a fascinating meditation on the role of race, federal-local interaction, controversial material, and objectivity in historical commemoration and elucidate both the strengths and weaknesses of the historical birthplace commemorative model.

A Living Commemoration for a Living President

The origins of the Jimmy Carter National Historic Site date to early 1981, shortly after the Georgian left office. At the former president's request, park officials met with him and Rosalynn in March at their home in Plains. The NPS reported that "President Carter asked for a conceptual study of a proposed historic site encompassing some of the homes and other structures in Plains that are significant to his life and his ascent to the Presidency."[3] The Carters actively supported the site's establishment, as did several preservation groups and entities within Sumter County, Georgia, and Plains, especially the Plains Historical Preservation Trust.[4] The Georgia House delegation introduced legislation in January 1985, followed by hearings in Plains and Washington, DC. The legislation mandated that the federal government acquire key sites related to Carter's life in Plains and Archery. These locations included Plains High School, where both Rosalynn and Jimmy were educated; a section of the Carter boyhood farm in Archery; the Plains Train Depot, which served as the Democrat's campaign headquarters during the 1976 presidential campaign; and, finally, the Carters' present home in Plains, to be administered by the NPS upon their deaths.

Key obstacles delayed the legislation's enactment. First, the site was proposed during a period of intense debate regarding further expansion of the National Park Service system. In 1981, Secretary of the Interior James Watt declared a moratorium on the creation of new sites. Watt's decision found support among other elements of the Reagan administration and the new Congress. It echoed the viewpoint of NPS director Russell E. Dickinson, who proposed that the NPS focus on stewardship of existing sites rather than growth.[5] In this context of conservative thinking, the legislation's sponsors contended that the site's buildings and lands could be acquired and operated at a bargain. Some government officials alternately worried about the appropriateness of creating a site commemorating a living president. Finally, there was the problem of Plains High School. The location had sat abandoned since the consolidation of county schools in 1979, and its restoration required heavy funding. The bill's author, Representative Richard Ray (D-GA), managed to negotiate a compromise, including a stipulation that federal funding would be limited to no more than 60 percent of the costs of the high school's restoration. The rest of the money would have to be raised locally.[6] The solution pointed toward the direction of the 1990s when the NPS turned to cost-saving public-private partnerships as a way to protect federal and non-federal lands.[7] Ray's efforts paid off. The bill won passage in the House and the Senate before President Reagan signed it into law in December 1987.

The Jimmy Carter National Historic Site has been in an almost constant state of transition since its establishment. Between February 1988 and September 1996, limited resources necessitated a stripped-down interpretation of the history of Carter and Plains. The small Plains Depot served as a visitor center and museum.[8] After a long, difficult process, the Park Service completed the restoration of the decrepit Plains High School and, on October 1, 1996, debuted it as the site's new visitor center. Staffers redesigned the depot to relate the story of the 1976 presidential campaign and dedicated it in 1997. With the opening of the Boyhood Farm three years later, the site, as laid out by Congress, was complete.

While Plains High School underwent renovations, the NPS finished the site's General Management Plan (under which it still operates) in 1993. The plan revealed the Park Service's desire to discuss the influence of Plains on Jimmy and Rosalynn Carter and vice versa. It is bolstered by seven major interpretive themes that outline the trajectory of the Carters' life from Plains to Washington, DC, and back to Plains. As well as highlighting Jimmy's early political career and the Carters' ample post-presidential activities, the plan mandates that the NPS present Plains as "a typical—and an atypical—town in southwestern Georgia" while advancing the notion that the Carters' lives "are reflected by the physical and cultural environment of Archery and Plains, Georgia."[9] These concepts are premised on the notion that Plains uniquely shaped the lives and values of the Carters and that they and the town are inextricably linked. In short, the plan outlines an interpretive strategy that seeks to answer the question: What does the relationship between the Carters—particularly Jimmy—and Plains tell us about both?

Due to its isolated location, 130 miles south of Atlanta, the Jimmy Carter National Historic Site receives a modest number of visitors per year. Visitation has ranged from a low of 22,857 in 1988 (opening year) to a high of 94,945 in 2005. In 2010, an estimated 64,849 people toured the location.[10] Most visitors come from the southeastern United States. Generally, it is the type of site that the public must make an effort to visit. It is not located near major highways, nor is it "on the way" to other major tourist attractions. Rather, much of Plains's charm lies in its remote-ness. It still feels much like the sleepy southern town of Jimmy Carter's childhood, home to one restaurant and a single chain store. The NPS encourages the public to partake of this wistful image. "Jimmy and Rosalynn Carter," reads the site's webpage, "learned the impor-tance of hard work, honesty, virtue, love and mercy in the quaint, rural town of Plains, Georgia."[11] The site's interpretation works in many ways to mitigate against nostalgia, but the allure of both real and imagined small-town America and the rural South colors visitors' encounters with Plains.

Carter and Plains: One and the Same?

The site's General Management Plan reflects the calls of NPS histo-rian William Patrick O'Brien to devise an ambitious, multidimensional interpretive approach that highlights the interrelationship between Jimmy Carter and Plains. In his *Special History Study* (1988), O'Brien presented "the social history of Plains as it applies to Jimmy Carter and his political evolution and career."[12] He offered a thoughtful analysis of the role of agriculture, race, religion, education, and family in this small southern town from prehistory to the present. While he notes the ways in which Carter's environment and rearing drove his ambition and success, O'Brien's Plains is not idyllic. Carter's experience grow-ing up around blacks helped to foster his sense of racial progressivism, but, the historian maintained, life for blacks in Sumter County in the early-to-mid-twentieth century was characterized by struggle, exclusion, danger, and intermittent violence. O'Brien urged the site to guard against nostalgia for the supposed good old days of the rural South. "Care should be taken," he wrote, "that the story of the Carters is not antisepticized, idealized or translated into a 'log cabin' mythology that distorts the actual facts surrounding a region and people remarkable and unique in their own right."[13] The NPS has, with important exceptions, largely carried out O'Brien's recommendation of a nuanced portrayal of Jimmy Carter and Plains. A closer look at Plains High School, the Boyhood Farm, and the Plains Depot makes the point.

Integrating History at Plains High School
Opened in 1996, after several years of renovation, the restored Plains High School is the centerpiece of the site's interpretative landscape and functions as its visitor center. One exhibit briefly highlights the work and philosophy of Julia Coleman, an instructor and later principal and superintendent who deeply influenced the future president. Tourists may also explore a replica of Miss Julia's classroom and a room dedicated to Rosalynn Carter's life. The main interpretive section of the visitor center is contained in three rooms, each designed to address a different period in the life of Jimmy Carter and the history of Plains: Carter's birth through his departure from Plains in 1942; his and Rosalynn's return in 1953 through his 1976 presidential campaign; and the post-presidential years, 1981 to the present. The concept of both continuity and change is critical. "Exhibits in these rooms," according to the script, "focus on the changing and enduring qualities of both Plains and Jimmy Carter."

The three rooms manage the difficult task of explaining Jimmy Carter's early life within the context of Plains's social history. The site's emphasis on the connections between person and place is particularly strong and well executed here. In the first room, visitors examine agricultural tools and learn about the progression of farming practices. Text points to the close-knit nature of the community and the centrality of religion, family, and work in both black and white lives. But it also counters nostalgia for southern rural life, as demonstrated by its inclusion of the memories of one Plains resident: "I call them the good old days, but the good old days like to kill me. You'd say that it was a happy time, when in truth we worked." Changing exhibits broaden the view further. A temporary display donated by the Carter Center in Atlanta, and on display in 2010, positions Plains in a global story by highlighting Carter's international work.

The Jimmy Carter National Historic Site's Advisory Commission deserves credit for pushing NPS staff to present visitors with a fuller portrait of the local historical experience. The site's establishing legislation mandates that the Commission "consist of a group of five nationally recognized scholars with collective expertise on the life and Presidency of Jimmy Carter, the 20th-century rural south, historic preservation, and the American Presidency."[14] "I recall," said Commission member Don Schewe, a former director of the Jimmy Carter Library and Museum in Atlanta, "that we were quite insistent on expanding the historical interpretation to include a focus on 'life in a small town in the 1st half of the 20th century', and 'farming in the South', including the relationship between blacks and whites." The high school exhibits certainly reflect these recommendations, particularly the Commission's "insisten[ce] that relations between the races needed to be included in the interpretation."[15] Explaining that "African Americans suffered many indignities," visitors are told that nonetheless "they successfully preserved a culture which enriched their daily lives." An exhibit titled "Schooling: Black and White" describes the inequities in the black and white educational systems. It notes the high-quality education at white Plains High School and contrasts it with the inferior opportunities available to black students.

Although the town's reliance on racial division as a defining social feature is smoothly articulated, the NPS's interpretative focus in this area generated local controversy. Some blacks and whites in the community questioned the appropriateness of discussing race relations at what was an all-white high school.[16] One black resident's comment to Superintendent Fred Boyles suggests that some locals felt no stake in Plains High School. "I ain't got nothin' in that school," she told him during the building's renovations.[17] In weathering this minor controversy, the NPS and its Advisory Commission managed to avoid softening the pain of Plains's racial history.

By expounding the connections between Plains, Archery, and Jimmy Carter, the high school exhibits chart Carter's growing racial consciousness from being a boy whose best friends were black, to a governor who boldly declared at his 1970 gubernatorial inauguration, "the time for racial discrimination is over," to a president and former president who fought not only for racial equality but also for human rights. The NPS reiterates Carter's own narrative that he slowly awakened to the evil of racial inequality. Text in the exhibit's second room states that "Although Carter was not an outspoken advocate of racial justice [following *Brown v. Board of Education* (1954)], he refused to join the States Rights Council and condemned the Ku Klux Klan." Visitors are also told of the Carter family's brave stand against their church's decision to bar blacks in 1965. The NPS presents Carter as an individual who essentially did what he could to challenge racism. His racial progressivism fully emerged only once he became governor, as evidenced by his concerted efforts to advance the cause of black Georgians while in office. In this instance, the site's emphasis on a birthplace narrative is highly successful in showing that many Americans are born into racial attitudes, which are further shaped by family and upbringing. Carter's relationship to race, the site suggests, was born of the pathological racism of many early-to-mid-twentieth-century white Southerners. But by highlighting the president's efforts to come to terms with local prejudices, the birthplace interpretation destroys the "naturalness" of racism. It instead demonstrates how both racist and equalitarian thinking are cultivated in a struggle between individual and environment.

This narrative is useful, yet in the NPS's hands, it succumbs to the pitfalls of progressive history. The idea that Carter gradually shook off the burden of his racist surroundings is somewhat complicated by an event that receives very little discussion in the second room: his 1970 Georgia gubernatorial bid. "Despite his conservative campaign," a short description reads, "Governor Carter was soon heralded as a 'New South' leader eager to throw off the shackles of racism." This narrowly true interpretation ignores the fact that he designed his "conservative campaign" to appeal to white segregationist voters. Describing himself during the campaign as "basically a redneck," Carter spoke in defense of private schools established after the *Brown* decision in order for white families to avoid schooling their children with blacks.[18] One of the Democrat's radio ads declared his independence from the "block" vote. As Carter biographer Betty Glad asserted, he "slurr[ed] over the crucial word so one could hear it as 'black.' "[19] Other race-baiting tactics were employed on his behalf. Historian E. Stanly Godbold, Jr., maintained that Carter's staff perpetrated these "nefarious tricks," yet regarding the candidate's own knowledge or involvement, "the truth remains unknown."[20] Visitors have the option of watching a series of short videos that touch on Carter's solicitation of conservative Georgians' votes, the accusations of racism, and the candidate's dismissal of these claims. Despite this effort to add more substance to a difficult subject, it is doubtful that most visitors will bother to view this material.

The site rightfully emphasizes Carter's call to end discrimination during his inauguration; however, downplaying the unsettling tactics of the campaign is bad history. When asked why there is not more thorough coverage of this event, Fred Boyles said that NPS planners debated the issue at length. "Whether consciously or unconsciously," he admitted, "I kind of thought, let's just leave that one alone."[21] It is easy to see why. On the surface, Carter's behavior in 1970 is antithetical to the racial narrative advanced by the visitor center exhibits. Still, contextualizing this material and presenting it more prominently would complicate, but not undermine, the overall depiction of Carter's racial views. The NPS might explain his appeals to racist voters as indicative of necessary political expediency and the difficulty of moving beyond the politics of racial division in the Deep South during the late civil rights era. One could argue that the campaign was largely a lesson in a candidate using less than admirable means to arrive at a just end. The point is that in a discussion of Carter's politics and racial views—in which the site is obviously interested—visitors deserve fuller disclosure on the 1970 race. In this respect, the site could better serve visitors, as the General Management Plan stipulates, by prompting them to "appreciate controversial and/or complicated stories—such as those dealing with human rights and politics" and "feel encouraged to make their own judgments of controversial and complicated events."[22]

The 1970 gubernatorial campaign further suggests the limits of birthplace commemoration. As in this case, the birthplace narrative leads to inevitable contradictions, for no one is a pure product of his or her youth. Indeed, adult decisions stem from more varied origins, and that is especially true for politicians like Carter. The site's decision to discuss the Georgian's racial views with a strong emphasis, like everything else, on his early development limits the type of narrative it can tell. A better discussion of the campaign—and one that does not entirely abandon the birthplace model—might contend that Carter's upbringing taught him that in the rural South race was *the* social and political issue. It was both an albatross and an easily exploitable tool. The site's current use of the birthplace model obscures the progression of white racial thinking in the twentieth-century rural South. It was not simply a matter of whites rising above racism and then never having to worry about it again. If that were so, Carter should have had no difficulty taking the high road in 1970. Apparently, even a forward thinker could not escape the sinister contours of the race issue.

Another problem besets the racial content of the high school exhibits. Despite an effort to recover the "feel" of living in Plains during the era, the experience of blacks is noticeably lacking. As we will see, the Boyhood Home location succeeds magnificently in its interpretation of the mostly black Archery settlement. Yet visitors are not given enough information about what it was like for blacks to endure Plains's racial caste system of the early-to-mid-twentieth century. Part of the reason, as the site's curator, Kate Funk, points out, is that the NPS's interpretation is limited by the types of buildings that the federal government owns.[23] Until its integration in 1969, Plains High School was the white secondary institution, and it therefore allows the Park Service an easy avenue to discuss at least educational aspects of the white experience. A bigger hindrance is the site's dearth of oral history accounts. Fred Boyles regrets that the NPS did not do more to collect the remembrances of both black and white residents during the site's early years, citing the time commitment required for various restoration efforts as an obstacle to the project.[24] Most of those memories are now lost forever.

Challenging Nostalgia at the Boyhood Farm

A few miles outside of town, tourists encounter the site's Boyhood Farm. It comprises seventeen acres of the Carter family's original 360-acre farm. Opened in November 2000, it commemorates Carter's early life, beginning with his family's move to the location when he was four. The farm features a series of wayside exhibits that enable visitors to explore the topics of pre-modern farming, family, and more deeply, race. It is restored to its pre-1938 appearance, before rural electrification, and includes seven renovated or reconstructed structures, such as the Carter family home, a blacksmith shop, general store, windmill, and barn. Carter's perspective—very much in evidence throughout the site's interpretation—is omnipresent at the farm. Several markers feature audio recordings of him reminiscing about his rural upbringing.[25] Other markers quote his writings extensively. By telling the story of the Boyhood Farm largely in Carter's own words, the NPS offers visitors a visceral encounter with history while acknowledging the former president's continued impact on the Plains area.

Life on the farm, according to the exhibit text, was difficult but not without its rewards. Quoting Carter, the Boyhood Farm brochures tells readers, "the early years of my life on the farm were full and enjoyable, isolated but not lonely. We always had enough to eat, no economic hardship, but no money to waste. We felt close to nature, close to members of our family, and close to God."[26] The NPS's interpretation at the Boyhood Farm presents a balanced portrait of southern rural life, one that undercuts nostalgia by placing the riches of this life against its significant challenges. Jimmy enjoyed the benefits of a comfortable, well-furnished home and a loving family. He had the opportunity to explore the outdoors, getting away to fish, collect arrowheads, and play with friends. At the same time, his father, Earl, made sure that he stayed productive by helping with the taxing farm work.

Just as Plains High School presents Jimmy Carter's life against the backdrop of the town's social history, the Boyhood Farm firmly contextualizes his upbringing within the predominantly black settlement of Archery. Carter's family was prosperous, though not rich. Earl Carter employed black laborers to bring in his crops, including cotton and peanuts. We learn that in Archery, as in Plains, racial inequality ruled. But the necessities of farm work required that blacks and whites worked alongside each other. This situation resulted in an intimacy between the races that eluded the strictures of Jim Crow. The site, then, presents visitors with a nuanced depiction of race relations in the early-to-mid-twentieth-century South, one that shows rural blacks and whites locked in a mutual—though grossly unequal—dependence on each other.

The Jack and Rachel Clark cabin at the Boyhood Farm serves as the central vehicle in the interpretation of black Archery. The Clarks were day laborers employed by Carter's father. Jimmy spent many hours with them and grew to view Rachel almost as a surrogate mother. A marker out-side the cabin elucidates his early feelings of kinship with blacks: "I felt at ease in the homes of the other black families in the neighborhood. My childhood world was really theirs." Rachel Clark is treated less as an indi-vidual in her own right than as an element in Jimmy Carter's elevation to greatness and his claims of insight into black culture. Here the focus on Carter's upbringing pushes the personal stories of the Clarks to the background.[27] They are notable only because they happened to touch the life of a future president. Inside the austere Clark home, tourists receive a valuable lesson in post–Civil War black southern history. Photographs and text provide substantive coverage of blacks' transition from the bondage of slavery to the serfdom of sharecropping and tenant farming, the emer-gence of the New South, and rural southern women's roles.

The interpretation at the Boyhood Farm echoes Jimmy Carter's view that his rural upbringing instilled in him strong, traditional values that allowed him to achieve great heights without ever forgetting from where he came. It is an alluring notion. One is left to wonder, though, why Carter? If the environment of his upbringing was so influential, why did more people in Plains and Archery not achieve similar greatness. These questions are unanswerable, but surely the answers involve the intan-gibles of Carter's own inner drive and ambitions as well as the consider-able economic resources at his family's disposal. Nevertheless, asking these questions suggests an inherent fallacy at the heart of any birthplace commemoration, even one as encompassing as the NPS sites in Archery and Plains. Although unique places are certainly important in creating extraordinary people, they can also limit the opportunities of others. Responsible birthplace commemoration must account for both.

The Plains Depot: Spinning Carter and the 1976 Presidential Campaign
The flawed exhibit at the Plains Depot highlights the difficulty of inter-preting the life of a living president. The site's General Management Plan mandated that, after moving the visitor center to the high school, the NPS repurpose the depot for an exhibit on the 1976 presidential race. The project sat in limbo until 1995, though, as it required a substantial investment of time and money. At that time, Jimmy Carter encouraged the Carter Political Items Collectors (CPIC), a subsidiary of the American Political Items Collectors, to collaborate with the Park Service to create

the exhibit.[28] The CPIC was founded in 1984 by A. Neil LeDock of Tucker, Georgia. "Neil thought that [the] group would be a way of returning and restoring Jimmy Carter to a place of dignity, honor and respect," one member later wrote."[29] Unfortunately, the Park Service allowed the CPIC to design the exhibits and write much of the accompanying text.[30] The portrayal of the 1976 race, despite NPS oversight, succumbs to the worst impulse of the birthplace narrative and borders on hagiography. It is a notable aberration from the site's other interpretations.

A sign at the entrance to the exhibit sets the tone: "The campaign efforts of Jimmy Carter's family, friends, and supporters displayed the democratic process at its best. Their commitment to the campaign continues to be an inspiration to this Nation. This museum is dedicated to telling their story." The interpretation at the depot definitely captures the excitement of Carter's 1976 campaign and his march through the Democratic primaries, but it lacks a substantive discussion of the stakes involved. We are told that "[Carter] campaigned on his personality and character as well as on issues," yet the exhibit offers no sense of those issues. Carter was a highly controversial candidate. His lack of national experience, his southernness, his evangelical religion, and his purported "fuzziness on the issues" provoked unease among portions of the electorate. None of these points are explored. In light of the site's efforts to connect Carter with his southern rural upbringing, the absence of the national focus on his southern origins is especially puzzling.

Controversies related to Carter, not surprisingly, are ignored or lack explanation. Visitors learn nothing of the criticisms of the "Anybody But Carter" camp of Democrats, only that they were "desperate." Fred Boyles recalled that NPS staff defended, against the opposition of some locals, the exhibit's reference to Carter's infamous *Playboy* interview (the accompanying exhibit includes a tastefully obscured facsimile of the November 1976 issue's cover).[31] While the NPS deserves credit for including this material, its description of the piece lacks substance and clarity for those not familiar with the resulting public blowback. A caption states, "Carter's honesty and total disregard for political correctness in *Playboy*'s interview caused consternation in some, while others seemed fascinated by his openness." What is lost in this brief aside is Carter's attempt in the interview to allay many Americans' lingering concerns about a Southern Baptist occupying the White House.

The NPS must expand beyond the grassroots nature of the Carter candidacy and examine his bid with a more critical eye. The General Management Plan maintains the value of a more complex interpretation: "The story of the campaign provides insight into our political process and America in the 1970s."[32] The inclusion of Carter-related controversies at the depot and the visitor's center would assist tourists in gaining a broader portrait of the former president, the South, and the United States throughout the twentieth century. Whether these absences result from Carter's close physical proximity, or are simply indicative of a historical site struggling with the rose-tinted perspective of the birthplace narrative, they result in missed interpretive opportunities.

Commemorating the President Who Lives Down the Road

It is obvious that Jimmy Carter's local presence creates a unique experience for tourists and, in the case of the farm, supplies information that is not easily recoverable. Rarely do historical figures permanently return to the birthplaces that we commemorate in their honor. Birthplace commemorations in fact often take advantage of people's absences in order to rewrite their life stories. In Plains, however, Carter has helped to shape his own history. Although he has made great efforts not to interfere with the independence of the site's interpretation, the NPS's failure to adequately address controversial issues in Carter's past raises questions about historical objectivity at a site where the person being commemorated is alive and active. The "living history" element supplied by Jimmy and Rosalynn Carter's continued residency in Plains creates both a one-of-kind situation and a potential threat to the site's interpretative autonomy.

In order to mitigate against such weaknesses and "to provide advice on achieving balanced and accurate interpretation of the historic site," independent of the Carters' or locals' pressures, the site's Advisory Commission has played a critical role.[33] As noted earlier, in its shaping of the NPS's interpretation of segregation and farming practices, the Commission served a valuable function during the Park Service's formative years in Plains. More recently, with the interpretation solidly in place, it has met less often while working closely with the NPS to combat real estate development efforts in the area that would negatively impact the site's integrity.[34]

The Commission keeps Carter well informed about its work. Member Don Schewe stated that, after conferring in private, the Commission generally meets with Jimmy and Rosalynn to discuss its recommendations. Schewe recalled no disputes with the former president over issues of interpretation. "Very often," he said, "President Carter would listen to our report and agree with it, or, if he disagreed, [he would] do so in a questioning way, and then say something like, '[W]ell, if you say so.'" Carter has occasionally grown frustrated with the NPS's inability, due to budget constraints, to push through projects quickly enough, and "on a couple [of] occasions he used his influence to get faster action."[35] The Commission does an admirable job of keeping Carter involved while maintaining its independence from him. Likewise, the former president must be credited for allowing the Commission to conduct its business without his interference. This relationship has helped to ensure a public presentation of Carter and Plains that, though not without its flaws, provides visitors with a complex understanding of the past.

Carter's involvement with the Commission and other aspects of the NPS's interpretation demonstrates the double-edged sword of commemorating a living president. On the one hand, it provides tourists with an unparalleled, fully immersive historical experience. It also gives the NPS an incredible resource, particularly in relating the history of Archery. And yet it raises an obvious, but unanswerable question, about whether Carter's presence has moved the site's planners to interpret less critically some of the challenging issues concerning the former president. What is clear is that the resulting analysis of Plains and Archery is frequently outstanding while occasionally displaying an unbalanced perspective on Carter's pre-presidential political career.

Local commemorations outside of the auspices of NPS interpretation lack balance for entirely different reasons. The major non-NPS interpreter of Carter's and Plains's history in the town is the Plains Historical Preservation Trust. It was incorporated in October 1977, during President Carter's first year in office. The organization lobbied diligently in support of the Jimmy Carter National Historic Site, and its representatives testified on its behalf before House and Senate subcommittees in 1985 and 1987, respectively. Since the site's establishment, the Trust has built a strong record of collaboration with the National Park Service, raising funds for the purchase of historic buildings and land in the area. The Trust, on behalf of the Park Service and the local community, spearheaded fundraising efforts for the Plains High School renovation. In short, the Plains Historical Preservation Trust has been a valuable asset to the NPS's operations in the community.

The Trust also acts as an auxiliary interpreter of Plains's and Carter's history outside of the dominant Park Service umbrella. It has placed various markers at historical sites in Archery and Plains. Its commemorations rely on a standard version of the birthplace narrative that presents Plains as an idealized American small town and incubator for the young Carter. In 2003, the Trust compiled a volume titled *History of Plains, Georgia,* featuring contributions from the local community, including Jimmy Carter, who is a member of the organization and sits on its Board of Directors. As a work of local history, the book tilts unsurprisingly toward nostalgia and offers a look back at the seemingly good old days. References to segregation and past racial strife, while not absent, are muted. In general, the book avoids controversial issues in the community's past. The Trust would have been wise to emulate Carter's more straightforward discussion of the area's troubled past, as featured in his 2001 book *An Hour before Daylight: Memories of a Rural Boyhood.* Carter similarly wrote wistfully of the rhythms of southern rural and small-town life without ignoring the racial tensions in Plains where as a boy he heard whites complain about "the worthless niggers."[36]

History of Plains, Georgia's entry on Carter's former house of worship, Plains Baptist Church, embodies the Trust's selective history. At the end of the 1976 presidential campaign, controversy erupted over the church's eleven-year-old whites-only policy. The resulting fallout gained substantial national coverage.[37] Eventually nearly thirty members left Plains Baptist Church and formed Maranatha Baptist Church. Euphemistically, the Plains Baptist Church piece in *History of Plains, Georgia,* describes this dispute as "a continuous disagreement about the future direction of the church."[38] It is not surprising that the Trust is less willing than the Park Service to take on unpleasant issues. It is, after all, comprised mostly of local individuals who are interested in advancing Plains's image as the quaint little town that Jimmy Carter made famous in 1976. The Trust's purpose, unlike that of the NPS, is not historical balance. Thus, the organization's less nuanced treatment of Plains is expected.

A more problematic aspect of the Plains Historical Preservation Trust's commemorations involves its nearly exclusive focus on the history of the white community. This situation is due neither to racism nor to an effort to exclude black history. Rather, it is a byproduct of the Trust's emphasis on preserving the history related to Jimmy Carter, as well as the black community's lack of participation in local history events. Blacks comprise a small portion of the Trust's membership and less than half of its Board of Directors.[39] Despite representing 42 percent of the town's population, black residents rarely attend Trust events.[40] The organization's members lack definitive explanations for this dearth of interest. Milton Raven, a black member of the Board of Directors and a lifelong friend of Jimmy Carter, suggested that it may have to do with "custom." According to Raven, the legacy of black and white social separation still lingers years after the death of Jim Crow, and some blacks do not feel comfortable in groups like the Trust.[41] Advisory Commission member Don Schewe implied that the organization's commemorations are simply not relevant to blacks. "Those events [held by the Trust] commemorate events that are predominately the actions or accomplishments of whites . . . Thus[,] I would guess the African-American community doesn't have much incentive to participate."[42] Mary Minion, another black leader in the Trust, noted that its efforts to engage the black community have not been successful.[43]

The consequences of the Trust's inability to connect with local blacks are personified in its annual folk play *If These Sidewalks Could Talk*, first produced in 1997. Written by Kim Fuller, a niece of Jimmy Carter, the play includes a dramatized series of "songs, jokes, and anecdotes" that vary each year, with townspeople playing area historical figures or relating incidents in their own lives.[44] Mary Minion has in various productions contributed recollections of her growing up in Archery and her experience of attending Carter's presidential inauguration. But Minion's participation is anomalous. She estimates that of the more than two dozen participants in the 2009 *If These Sidewalks Could Talk* program, perhaps three were black. And whites far outnumbered blacks in the audience, suggesting the latter's indifference to the Trust's commemorations of Carter and Plains.[45]

The View from Plains

The NPS's version of the birthplace narrative in Plains and Archery succeeds more than most attempts to memorialize a historical figure's upbringing using only a single restored building. The Jimmy Carter National Historic Site has woven a fuller portrait of Carter's upbringing and early life than might be expected. By placing his story within a rich social history of rural and small-town life in south Georgia, the NPS provides visitors with a nuanced view of the elements that influenced Carter's character and beliefs. Even so, despite federal efforts, the birthplace narrative cannot control for certain intangibles and convincingly explain how this southern boy rose to the presidency.

Similarly, the site's discussion of the uncomfortable topic of racial oppression in Plains's and Archery's histories is often well executed while still exhibiting notable weaknesses. The black community's underrepresentation in local commemorations is particularly unfortunate because it exacerbates the scarcity of black voices in NPS commemorations. Like the Trust's, the Park Service's attempts to engage area blacks, despite its serious coverage of race and civil rights history, have failed.[46] Perhaps if the Plains Historical Preservation Trust and the NPS made a concerted effort to more fully interpret the town's rich black history, eventually the community would enjoy a more unified—and diversified—program of historical remembrance. This effort, of course, would require that both the NPS and locals address the area's history that exists outside of Jimmy Carter's experience. In 1976, Carter frequently presented Plains as a town whose citizens had overcome the complications of race. That was not entirely the case then, and it is evidently still not the case in the early twenty-first century. As elsewhere in America, race still matters in Plains. Both whites and blacks must realize the deficit that results from anything other than an equal sharing in their intertwined histories.

As the NPS captures some of the uncomfortable truths of a racist and segregated southern past, it glides over the controversies of Carter's pre-presidential life. Carter was a more complicated figure than the site suggests. He was, in short, a politician—someone who espoused high ideals but sometimes found it difficult, if not impossible, to always put them into practice. The act of commemoration, and to some extent the act of childhood commemoration, does not necessarily lend itself to clear-eyed critiques of historical actors.

Commemorating a *living* historical figure is a still trickier endeavor, made more hazardous by the active involvement of the individual in the commemoration. Common sense dictates that establishing a site in honor of a living person should generally be avoided. As historian Joan Hoff-Wilson argued in testimony before Congress in 1985, "in most instances the final designation of a national historic site probably should be delayed until after any individual president's death in the interest of historical objectivity."[47] It can all too easily fall prey to abuse, as in the instance of Lyndon Johnson's efforts to reconstruct his Texas birthplace home. Thanks to the hard work of NPS staff and the Advisory Commission and the former president's courteous deference, the Carter site has managed to avoid many of the pitfalls of a "living" memorial. It would in fact be difficult, if not impossible, to tell the story of the inseparable relationship between Carter and Plains without the former president's input. Regardless, one wonders if the NPS might have treated the public to a more critical assessment of Carter's pre-1977 political career if Congress had chosen to establish the site after the former president's and first lady's passing.

Their deaths and those of the townspeople they know will mark the end of the "living history" component of commemorations in Plains. Although local events there will likely continue to offer a less sophisticated corollary to the Park Service's interpretation, the agency's work will definitely change. A proposed expansion of the site and the need for a new general management plan will offer Park Service officials opportunities to reassess the site's interpretation and perhaps devise a more critical perspective on Jimmy Carter's public career while maintaining its impressive social historical analysis of Plains and Archery. Even in its current incarnation, the NPS has fulfilled a great service to the public. Its exploration of rural and small-town life in the twentieth-century Deep South, one that probes that society's joys, difficulties, and inequalities, far exceeds the ambitions of an older generation of commemorative birthplaces.

NOTES

The author would like to thank Fred Boyles for his generous assistance during this project's research stage.

1. U.S. Census Bureau, 2010 Census, "Race" (via topic search for "Population" and geography search for "Plains, GA"), http://factfinder2.census.gov/faces/nav/jsf/pages/index.xhtml.

2. Sam Nunn to Dale Bumpers, November 10, 1987, in Congress, Senate, *Big Bend National Park and Jimmy Carter National Historic Site and Preservation District: Hearing before the Subcommittee on Public Lands, National Parks and Forests of the Committee on Energy and Natural Resources*, 100th Cong., 1st sess., November 12, 1987, 14.

3. Department of the Interior, National Park Service, Southeast Region, "Proposed Jimmy Carter National Historic Site: A Report Prepared for President Jimmy Carter," June 1981, 1, in Congress, House, *Jimmy Carter National Historic Site: Hearings before the Subcommittee on National Parks and Recreation of the Committee on Interior and Insular Affairs*, 99th Cong., 1st Sess., June 22, 1985, and October 29, 1985, 209.

4. See Richard Ray to Bruce F. Vento, March 4, 1985, in Congress, House, *Jimmy Carter National Historic Site: Hearings before the Subcommittee on National Parks and Recreation of the Committee on Interior and Insular Affairs*, 99th Cong., 1st sess., June 22, 1985, and October 29, 1985, 241.

5. Department of the Interior, National Park Service, *The National Park Service: Shaping the System* (Washington, DC: Department of the Interior, 2005), 86, www.nps.gov/history/history/online_books/shaping/index.htm.

6. Fred Boyles, "Jimmy Carter National Historic Site," in *History of Plains, Georgia*, comp. Plains Historical Preservation Trust (Plains, GA: Plains Historical Preservation Trust, 2003), 149.

7. Department of the Interior, National Park Service, *The National Park Service*, 87.

8. Steve Theus, interview by author, February 19, 2010.

9. Department of the Interior, National Park Service, *General Management Plan/Development Concept Plan: Jimmy Carter National Historic Site and Preservation District* (Washington, DC: U.S. Government Printing Office, 1993), 19.

10. See "Annual Park Visitation (All Years)" under "Jimmy Carter NHS Reports," www.nature.nps.gov/stats/park.cfm?parkid=125.

11. "Home Page," Jimmy Carter National Historic Site, www.nps.gov/jica/index.htm.

12. Department of the Interior, National Park Service, *Special History Study: Jimmy Carter National Historic Site and Preservation District*, by William Patrick O'Brien (Denver: Denver Service Center, 1991), 1.

13. Ibid., 126.

14. *An Act to Establish the Jimmy Carter National Historic Site and Preservation District in the State of Georgia, and for Other Purposes*, Statutes at Large 101, sec. 4, 1436 (1987).

15. Don Schewe, e-mail message to author, April 24, 2010.

16. Ibid.

17. Fred Boyles, interview by author, March 30, 2010.

18. "How Southern Is He?" *Time*, September, 27, 1976, www.time.com/time/magazine/article/0,9171,918353-3,00.html.

19. Betty Glad, *Jimmy Carter: In Search of the Great White House* (New York: W. W. Norton, 1980), 133.

20. E. Stanly Godbold, Jr., *Jimmy and Rosalynn Carter: The Georgia Years, 1924–1974* (New York: Oxford University Press, 2010), 153.

21. Fred Boyles, interview by author, March 30, 2010.

22. Department of the Interior, National Park Service, *General Management Plan*, 21.

23. Kate Funk, interview by author, January 4, 2010.
24. Fred Boyles, interview by author, March 30, 2010.
25. These audio clips are available at http://jica.libsyn.com.
26. Quoted in Department of the Interior, National Park Service, "Boyhood Farm" (undated brochure), www.nps.gov/jica/planyourvisit/upload/New%20Boyhood%20Farm%20Bro chure%20WEB.pdf.
27. It should be noted that since 2005 the site has occasionally hosted a play for schoolchildren about the life of Rachel Clark that features an actress portraying Clark. The tendency to tell Clark's story as a subset of Carter's is indicated by the play's title, *Raising a President: The Story of Rachel Clark and Jimmy Carter*. The production discusses issues like segregation and sharecropping, but the emphasis is placed on Carter's upbringing. See Carly Farrell, "Carter's Childhood Told through Clark's Eyes," *Americus (GA) Times-Recorder*, February 10, 2010, http://americustimesrecorder.com/local/x878566016 /Carter-s-childhood-told-through-Clark-s-eyes.
28. Boyles, "Jimmy Carter National Historic Site," 151.
29. Bob Linzey, "Carter Political Item[s] Collectors," in *History of Plains, Georgia,* comp. Plains Historical Preservation Trust, 159.
30. Boyles, "Jimmy Carter National Historic Site," 151. Steve Theus stated that NPS staff had editorial control over the text. Steve Theus, interview by author, February 19, 2010.
31. Robert Scheer, "Playboy Interview: Jimmy Carter," *Playboy,* November 1976, 63–64, 66, 68–71, 74, 77, 81, 84, 86.
32. Department of the Interior, National Park Service, *General Management Plan,* 20.
33. *An Act to Establish the Jimmy Carter National Historic Site and Preservation District in the State of Georgia, and for Other Purposes, Statutes at Large* 101, sec. 4, 1436 (1987).
34. Jay Hakes, interview by author, April 12, 2010.
35. Don Schewe, e-mail message to author, April 24, 2010.
36. Jimmy Carter, *An Hour before Daylight: Memories of a Rural Boyhood* (New York: Simon and Schuster, 2001), 65.
37. See, for example, Wayne King, "Carter's Church Is in Turmoil Over Rule on Blacks," *New York Times,* November 5, 1976, A15; and Kenneth L. Woodward, "Showdown in Plains," *Newsweek,* November 22, 1976, 81.
38. Marian Harris and Amy Wise, "Plains Baptist Church," in *History of Plains, Georgia,* comp. Plains Historical Preservation Trust, 76.
39. Mary Minion, interview by author, April 15, 2010.
40. U.S. Census Bureau, 2010 Census, "Race" (via topic search for "Population" and geography search for "Plains, GA"), http://factfinder2.census.gov/faces/nav/jsf/pages/index.xhtml.
41. Milton Raven, interview by author, April 6, 2010.
42. Don Schewe, e-mail message to author, April 25, 2010.
43. Mary Minion, interview by author, April 15, 2010.
44. Jimmy Carter, "1981–2002," in *History of Plains, Georgia,* comp. Plains Historical Preservation Trust, 51. See also Becky Holland, "If These Sidewalks Could Talk," *Americus (GA) Times-Recorder,* September 23, 2008, http://americustimesrecorder.com/local /x4 89060357/If-these-Sidewalks-could-Talk.
45. Mary Minion, interview by author, April 15, 2010.
46. Fred Boyles, interview by author, March 31, 2010.
47. Joan Hoff-Wilson, "Testimony on H.R. 235: A Bill to Authorize the Establishment of the Jimmy Carter National Historic Site in the State of Georgia," in Congress, House, *Jimmy Carter National Historic Site: Hearings before the Subcommittee on National Parks and Recreation of the Committee on Interior and Insular Affairs,* 99th Cong., 1st Sess., June 22, 1985 and October 29, 1985, 180.

Mark Twain's supposed birthplace cabin in Florida, Missouri, as it appeared ca. 1910, and likely the same now on display at the Mark Twain Birthplace State Historic Site. Library of Congress, Prints and Photographs Division, LC-DIG-ggbain-36277.

~ 4 ~

In the previous two chapters, we've seen how claims of authenticity—carefully crafted in one case by a president's mother and, in the other, vouchsafed by the president himself—are essential to the commemorative enterprise at birthplace monuments. What happens, then, when doubt is cast on the ties that bind a hallowed birthplace to its honoree? If that person happens to be Mark Twain, then, in Hilary Iris Lowe's assessment, the possibilities for clever interpretation only multiply. Lowe, a literary historian, appreciates how fitting it is that America's most famous raconteur left the secret of his birthplace swaddled in a confusing web of myths and mistruths. But has our fondness for Twain's fiction excused the keepers of his birth memory from coming to terms with the difficult history of more recent pasts? Lowe takes us on a fascinating journey into the heyday of early twentieth-century birthplace commemoration when a preoccupation with authenticity somehow inscribed inauthenticity as the defining feature of Twain's birthplace(s). Along the way, we discover that our search for the "real" has largely distracted us from recognizing what lessons may exist for today's heritage tourists in the failed hopes of those who would profit from Twain's birth memory.

Authenticity and Interpretation at Mark Twain's Birthplace Cabins

HILARY IRIS LOWE

Samuel Clemens's birthplace in Florida, Missouri, has changed a great deal since he was born there in 1835. In the intervening years, Clemens—or, more accurately, "Mark Twain," his nom de plume—has become a household name. He is undoubtedly one of the most recognizable Americans, and his image is an icon even to those who have never read a page of his work. Even a hundred years after his death, Twain's autobiography, published unabridged for the first time in 2010, soared to the top of the best-seller lists. The village where Clemens was born, however, is largely lost to time. Florida supported about sixty families in Clemens's day, but today none remain. Those Twain pilgrims who make the journey to Florida find his birthplace in two places. At one, they encounter an empty field with a commemorative plaque showing old photographs of Florida. A few miles down the road, at the Missouri Department of Natural Resources' Mark Twain Birthplace State Historic Site, they can visit a Clemens "birthplace cabin."

The exact spot where Clemens was born remains a bit of a mystery. Locals have claimed over the years that any of several cabins mark Clemens's birthplace. Some newspaper reports indicate that relic seekers carried away Clemens's actual birth cabin piece by piece sometime before 1905. Others say that the house was whittled down into mementos and sold at any number of World's Fairs. More recently, site administrators have argued about the birthplace cabin's authenticity and whether "visitors are entitled to know" a fuller story.[1] Clemens's birthplace is not unique in this regard. The National Park Service, for instance, has grappled with similar problems of authenticity at Abraham Lincoln's birthplace in Hodgenville, Kentucky, and George Washington's birthplace near Colonial Beach, Virginia. Since 1931, however, the state of Missouri has largely ignored all of these concerns in celebration of its Mark Twain birthplace cabin. Whether or not the site's visitors and the state taxpayers are entitled to know whether the cabin is the birthplace of Sam Clemens, it is likely that they never will.

Ultimately, however, the birthplace's tenuous claims to authenticity may not matter as much as other stories that this place can tell us about its curious history. Perhaps a pioneer site in Missouri that promotes a famous Missourian is enough to keep interested tourists coming through the doors. If the site's authenticity matters at all today, it does so in its relationship to the history of Florida in recent memory and in exploring why it has become so important to remember Clemens's birth there. What follows then is a history of the current birthplace cabin and its claims to authenticity. It may be fitting that a historical site associated with our nation's greatest teller of tall tales has been plagued by inauthenticity. Its history raises important questions about how, why, and where we remember literary birthplaces and presents interesting interpretive opportunities that speak to Missouri's recent past.

One Man, Many Births

Nearly 20,000 people visit Samuel Clemens's birthplace every year.[2] They have been coming since before his death in 1910 and at least since Clifton Johnson wrote *Highways and Byways of the Mississippi Valley* (1906), the first guidebook to "Mark Twain Country." Johnson's first-person travel narrative mimics Clemens's use of dialect as he describes the rugged road to Florida "as if it had been ploughed by Satan and his imps to plague mankind."[3] Roads notwithstanding, Johnson might have never found the birthplace without the help of a local woman. She explained that the author was born in the kitchen of a two-room framed house that the family occupied before moving into a new log home only weeks later. Both buildings, according to Johnson's account, stood as late as 1905 although the log home had been "pretty near [torn] to pieces!" Relic hunters had carried "off brick-brickbats from the chimney and pieces of glass from the windows and splinters of wood from the doors and other parts, until they'd got everything but the logs."[4]

Johnson arrived too late to gather relics from the log home where Clemens had spent his first four years. Much of the framed birth house, however, was intact, even if dilapidated.[5] What Johnson does not tell his readers is that relic seekers picked the log house apart because they believed *it* was the author's birthplace. As at other birthplaces, including Abraham Lincoln's, log cabins had become popular tourist attractions, and therefore a log cabin associated with Clemens connoted authenticity, facts notwithstanding.[6] As early as 1890, in fact, locals debated where exactly Clemens was born. Some said he was born in another small log house. Some favored the framed house that Johnson visited. Others suggested that he was born in an entirely different two-story log cabin, while still others identified another local framed house. His Uncle John A. Quarles's house was also a contender, although still others argued that Clemens was actually born one county over. The uncertainty was so significant that Twain pilgrims eventually destroyed most if not all of the buildings that might have been his actual birthplace.

The desire to remember Clemens had become so great by 1890

that what remained of one of these reported birthplaces went on a road show. The *Monroe County Appeal* reported that the Sam Clemens birthplace had been sold for $600 and was on its way to the 1893 Chicago World's Fair. Its journey anticipated the travels of Abraham Lincoln's fictitious birth cabin all across the United States.[7] In the case of Clemens's birthplace, the "new owners" were to "send wagons and cars from Chicago to move the building entire, so that [his] numerous admirers may behold the place of their hero's birth." The Monroe County reporter poked fun at this development, saying that "more old [Mark Twain] houses . . . can be bought for half the price as this one."[8] This birthplace, however, proved too difficult to move, and it remained in Florida.[9] The reporter's quip suggests that perhaps some of that difficulty was owing to the obvious credibility gap surrounding any cabin that claimed to be associated with Clemens.

Similar concerns surfaced seven years later, when the *Monroe County Appeal* editor, Sam Pollard, alerted readers that W. G. Roney had recently purchased a Clemens birth home specifically to make souvenirs of it. He guaranteed that "Mr. Roney . . . is one of the best men in the county and no one need have any fear of being humbugged."[10] And again, by the time the next American exposition was being planned, rumors surfaced of the birthplace being moved to the site of the celebration, although this time the cabin was to be "in pieces." The *Paris Mercury* recalled that "a frame house was cut up into canes, which were sold at the St. Louis World's Fair as having been made from the timber in the house where Sam Clemens was born," and added, "we are doubtful if anyone knows for certain now in what house Clemens was born."[11]

Despite reports that the birthplace had succumbed to memento seekers, one Florida resident in particular argued that the building survived. Merritt Alexander "Dad" Violette was born in Florida in 1849. It was Violette's mother, Eliza Damrell (Violette) Scott—very likely the same woman who led Johnson to the Clemens birth site—who showed Clemens's biographer, Albert Bigelow Paine, the "real" birthplace during his visit to Florida in 1907.[12] Paine was interested in the birthplace because neither Clemens, nor his older brother Orion, nor their mother could remember where exactly he was born since they had lived in a number of small cabins of roughly the same description.[13] Nonetheless, having consulted with Eliza Violette, Paine wrote:

It is still standing and occupied when these lines are written, and it should be preserved as a shrine for the American people; for it was here that the foremost American-born author—the man most characteristically American in every thought and word and action of his life—drew his first breath, caught blinkingly the light of the world that in the years to come would rise up and in its wide realm of letters hail him as king.[14]

Paine's urging may have convinced Dad Violette to preserve the cabin that his mother had identified. Violette purchased the tumbledown house in 1915 and moved it onto his property for restoration. His was one of the earliest efforts in the United States to preserve a literary birthplace, second only to John Greenleaf Whittier's birthplace, which opened to the public in 1893. The *Hannibal Courier Post* reported that Violette planned to build "a platform . . . in front of which touring parties can have their pictures taken."[15] He recognized the site's appeal, added campsites, tourist cabins, and a clubhouse, and led regular tours of the birthplace.

While camping in the area in 1922 with the Girl Reserves, a Christian girls' camping club based in Moberly, Missouri, sixteen-year-old Ruth Lamson began a conversation with Dad Violette about the future of the cabin.[16] The enterprising young woman suggested that the cabin should belong to the state of Missouri and convinced her father, Frank B. Lamson, to join her cause. During the summer of 1923, Ruth Lamson helped run tours of the birthplace on Sundays. Her father, already a Mark Twain admirer, formed the Mark Twain Park Memorial Association with H. J. Blanton and the Northeastern Missouri Pressmen's Association to raise endorsements, money, and support for a state park in Florida to memorialize Sam Clemens's birth. The Missouri Pressmen were particularly proud that Clemens had begun his career as a typesetter and editor in northeastern Missouri.[17]

Frank Lamson wrote in the association's promotional literature that "if the plans of the Mark Twain Park Association . . . are realized, little Florida will become a literary shrine as famed as Stratford on Avon, England's Memorial to the immortal Shakespeare."[18] The association raised money to purchase the land needed to establish a state park, and Frank and Ruth Lamson convinced Violette to donate his cabin. "Florida has but one claim to greatness," wrote Frank Lamson, and "the old Scotch Presbyterians of that section declare that [it] was foreordained to become his birthplace . . . only one place can lay claim to his birth and that is the little hamlet of Florida."[19] With the support of local businessmen, broad public interest, successful fundraising, and Dad Violette's generous donation of the birthplace cabin all seemed certain to make the birthplace Missouri's first state park. The association chose and purchased the original one hundred acres for the park because of their remarkable view of the Salt River Valley. Although Sam Clemens may have roamed this area when he visited his uncle and aunt on their farm near Florida, however, there was no concrete connection between the park site and Clemens. Nevertheless, in late 1924, the state accepted the land and opened Mark Twain State Park to the public, and, though the view from the bluff at the new state park was lovely, visitors did not find the birthplace cabin there.

Visitors could not visit the cabin at Mark Twain State Park because questions about the cabin's authenticity reemerged. As we have seen, not everyone accepted, as had Albert Bigelow Paine, the Violette family's identification of the Clemens house. When it came time for the birthplace to be officially sanctioned by the state, rumors surfaced that the house was not *the* birthplace. These rumors had evidently caused enough concern that, although the state agreed to accept the gift of land for its new park, plans did not proceed for making the birthplace cabin its centerpiece. Rather, the cabin stayed in Dad Violette's yard, where he tended to it every day, waiting for the state to relocate it to the new state park. Centerpiece or not, the house garnered plenty of attention. In 1927, Violette explained to Frank Lamson that the guest register already contained "about 50,000 names of people from everywhere." He continued to believe that "[they] are going to build a house to enclose [the] Mark Twain birth house," and that he would "turn the house over to the State when they make the proper arrangements to enclose it."[20] And yet, no one was certain that the house was really the place where Clemens was born.

The disparity prompted local newspapers to investigate the "unfortunate question as to the authenticity of the old house." In 1929, Violette and the editor of the *Monroe County Appeal* claimed that Clemens's father, John Marshall Clemens, had "built the present house" after settling in Florida, but soon thereafter built a second home for his growing family. Although the second house had been torn down, M. A. Violette purchased the "first" house and "with rare vision for the future, preserved it for posterity."[21] Violette added, in an accompanying letter to the editor, that his grandmother was "no doubt present when Mark Twain was born," and that "Bigelow Payne [sic] was here and decided that this was the Mark Twain birth house and the State Commissioner that erected the marker investigated the place where he was born and erected their marker accordingly."[22] He pleaded, "I hope that you'll have the house moved to the Park . . . I am eighty years old now and would like to see the house removed while I live."[23]

A year later, in June 1930, Violette got his wish. Because the state of Missouri had officially accepted the land and the cabin as gifts from the Association when it had authorized Mark Twain State Park, it had to take responsibility for the cabin on Violette's property, whether it was really Sam Clemens's birthplace or not. Using one horse and an outfit ordinarily employed to pull tree stumps, workers jacked up the cabin, set it on wheels, and transported it to a bluff overlooking the Salt River. Two boys rode atop the house, one dressed as Tom Sawyer and the other as Huck Finn. Later that year, the park erected a temporary protective building around the birthplace cabin to guard it from the elements and from curio seekers. The structure, little more than a shed with a lock on it, provided visitors with a view of the cabin through wire-screened windows. Violette walked to the state park on Sundays to open the birthplace for tourists until he died on January 30, 1931.[24] The birthplace cabin remained largely unaltered in its shed for the next thirty years.

The Shrine Today

Missouri, like the rest of the nation, saw historical tourism grow after World War II, and intensify in anticipation of the nation's bicentennial. In Missouri, this meant that historic sites gained separate status from other parks that celebrated Missouri's natural resources within the state park system. As the park surrounding the birthplace grew in size and a plan for a lake there became a reality, the "shrine" site became a separately managed entity. Throughout the 1950s, local Mark Twain enthusiasts lobbied state representatives for a proper birthplace museum.

Their efforts paid off in 1960 when the state dedicated considerable energy and resources to providing a proper memorial and a "shrine" building to replace the old shed.[25]

This new home is what visitors encounter when they visit the state park today. A sign over the entrance reads, "Mark Twain Memorial Shrine." The birthplace "shrine" building is modern in the extreme. A "hyperbolic parabaloid . . . forms the roof," which swoops up like a stealth bomber made of limestone, glass, and concrete.[26] But visitors must go inside or read a nearby plaque in order to determine what kind of Mark Twain shrine they have happened upon. Nothing here tells visitors that it is a birthplace, a historic site, and a museum. Once inside, visitors discover one wing of the museum devoted to the "birth cabin" and another to a small Twain collection. In the cabin wing, visitors look through the windows and doorways into an 1830s two-room home. One room is set up as a multipurpose kitchen with a fireplace filled with cast iron cookware, a kitchen table, a bed and trundle made up with the requisite log cabin quilt, child-sized chairs, and marbles scattered across the pine floor as though a child still lives and plays here. The other room is recognizable as a bedroom with a large ornately carved bed with pineapple bedposts, elaborate coverlet, wardrobe, trunk, chamber pot, and, of course, a cradle. If this was the house where Sam Clemens was born, he would only have lived here as an infant for a few months. How the Clemens family and their slave, a woman named Jennie—ten people in all—lived in the tiny cluttered cabin is unclear.

The house has three doors and three windows through which visitors admire the arrangement of historic objects. The staff has neatly whitewashed the inside, and the house is cozy with hand-woven rugs and period decorations in both rooms. Setting the scene outside the cabin is a wood-chopping block and woodpile, a hand-hewn bench made from a log, and a discarded rattlesnake skin. The tableau is classic pioneer Missouri, typical of other Missouri history sites that commemorate western expansion before the Civil War. Nothing stands out here except for a few very nice pieces including the carved bed, its coverlet, and several stuffed cats that conspicuously recall the author's fondness for felines.

The shrine's museum wing exhibits items that belonged to Sam and Olivia Langdon Clemens alongside cases full of Mark Twain memorabilia. Highlights include a comb used by Olivia Clemens, a carriage, a desk, a divan, and many other items that probably belonged to the family when they lived in Hartford, Connecticut, from 1873 to 1891. These items appear in no particular order and have little to do with Clemens's time in Missouri. What visitors find here does not tell them very much about Sam Clemens or about his connection to Florida. In fact, despite the 1960s building and ongoing efforts to revise the site's interpretive master plan, interpretation at the museum remains much the same as it was in 1960.[27] This shortcoming certainly owes something to ongoing state budget concerns. Even high-ranking officials in the Department of Natural Resources have failed to effect the most basic of improvements, such as dealing with the site's chronic lack of effective signs.[28]

More likely, however, the site's interpretive stasis results from persistent questions about its authenticity. The Twain site has never received the kind of state funding needed to develop it into a major tourist destination. This problem has not been lost on the site's staff. As recently as 1983, site administrator and architectural historian Stan Fast set about studying the cabin itself for evidence of its age and history. Fast knew that, "as for the authenticity of the cabin . . . this museum holds no incontrovertible documents." "A few longtime local residents have an oral tradition that the real birthplace either burned down or fell down before the state got possession," but, "in the absence of proof to the contrary such traditions die hard."[29] Fast's resulting study did not "vindicate" the cabin.

Fast found, through an extensive analysis of nail types, tool marks, and other structural clues, that Dad Violette's claim that the cabin was 80 percent "original" to the time of Clemens's birth was unfounded. Most of the nails, boards, shingles, siding planks, and even the door and window frames were newer than the period in which the Clemens family would have lived there. Fast discovered evidence that the cabin was cobbled together from a number of sources. Although this would not have been uncommon among poor settlers, much of the cobbling looked to Fast as though it had happened long after the time of the Clemens family's residence. Even so, Fast concluded that "the question of authenticity remains unanswered." "Much additional research must be done," he argued, because "the site's visitors are entitled to know, is this the cabin faithfully though amateurly [sic] restored or is it Violette's replica . . . ?"³⁰

Fast's report has had no impact on the way that the state and the staff at the site continue to present the cabin, and no other research has been done to further establish the cabin's origin. The reluctance to do further research may be owing to a larger unwillingness to cast doubt on the only resource for which this site is significant. Even Fast, despite his research, is still "pretty convinced that that cabin had a direct association with Mark Twain." Although no physical evidence supports his conviction, Fast doubts that Dad Violette would "perpetrate a hoax on people just simply for the few dimes and nickels that he might be getting by just showing that cabin."³¹ All of the claims of authenticity at the site come down to whether you can believe Violette's account above all evidence to the contrary. The state has never officially acknowledged the rift between its presentation of the house as authentic and the physical evidence that the house provides.

Old Problems, New Opportunities

This is not to say that the state of Missouri should or must officially recognize this rift, but the site's questionable status as the building in which Sam Clemens was born might make it a place where other interpretive discussions could thrive. At least three major interpretative opportunities exist within the history of the park itself that illuminate aspects of Missouri and United States history more vibrantly than the relatively limited story of Clemens's first three months can. One opportunity is to interpret local history—specifically the history of race in Missouri—through the story of the Civilian Conservation Corps's (CCC) importance to Missouri State Parks and the resistance that black enrollees met in Florida. A second concerns the story of the long-deferred and controversial creation of Mark Twain Lake by the Army Corps of Engineers and the various attempts to commercialize the lake area as a Mark Twain–themed attraction. The last and perhaps most compelling opportunity for interpretation at the museum involves Clemens's own celebration of literary and historic birthplaces. Clemens was decidedly skeptical about the relationship between place and genius, but he worked to commemorate two birthplaces during his lifetime. His interest in literary and historic commemoration provides a unique window through which to view Florida's history as well as the broader history of commemoration in the United States.

Florida, Missouri, and the Civilian Conservation Corps

Interpreting the story of the Civilian Conservation Corps at Mark Twain State Park would connect the park to the history of racism in the United States, the Great Depression, and the New Deal. During the Great Depression, many state parks across the country found support in the relief programs of the New Deal, and particularly in the widespread efforts of the CCC. But when news came to Florida that it was to receive CCC Company 1743, a "colored Junior Company," many residents, including Dad Violette, resisted and argued that "a camp composed of white boys will fit into our economical and social life much better than colored boys."[32]

Florida was an all-white village when, in early October 1939, Florida residents Charles Hamilton and John Massey delivered a petition to the State Park Department in Jefferson City with twenty-eight signatures that indicated residents would not welcome a "colored" CCC camp. Florida was "surrounded by thirteen (13) towns that have a negro population" and signers of the petitions believed "that it would be just a matter of time until this town and county would also have an excess population of negroes." Additionally, "the women folks of Florida" feared that the camp "would be a menace to their safety and welfare."[33] I. T. Bode, Missouri representative for the CCC, came to nearby Paris to speak with local residents about their opposition to Company 1743. Bode explained that the issue "might resolve itself into a choice between getting a big job done by well-behaved Negro workers or not getting it done at all."[34]

Residents eventually rescinded their petition and stipulated that Company 1743 was to "go right ahead with its plans" for developing the state park, but without "enter[ing] the village of Florida at any time for any purpose."[35] One enrollee recounted his experience with the CCC in Florida, saying that "when we came to Mark Twain, things were a little hard at first." "We couldn't go into Florida or Stoutsville," he continued, "the people didn't want us, but things turned out all right. They thought a group of Colored boys was gonna be unruly but we were like everyone else, we came to do a job."[36] Eventually, when residents realized that

Florida businesses were missing an opportunity to cash in on enrollee paycheck dollars, they allowed the black workers to enter the village.

The park was still in an early stage of development, and it needed the infrastructure that the CCC could offer. The Missouri State Park Board and the National Park Service had devised a plan for Company 1743 at the Mark Twain Memorial State Park to span six years, constructing a man-made lake and building a lodge, cabins, new campgrounds, a marina, boat ramps, fishing facilities, roads, and trails. Most important to the history of the birthplace cabin, this plan included "a museum dedicated to Mark Twain and removal of the author's birth cabin back to its original location in the village of Florida."[37] Such a museum would have given the residents the literary shrine that they had dreamed of since Ruth Lamson and her father first envisioned a state park along the lines of an American Stratford.

World War II cut the efforts of the men in Company 1743 short. In July 1942, Company 1743 disbanded, and many of the enrollees transferred into active military duty. They had only just begun their work at the park but had been able to develop trails, campgrounds, a park office building, and a working water system. The museum would wait another twenty years.[38] Between 1993 and 1994 the Mark Twain Birthplace State Historic Site's staff celebrated the efforts of Company 1743 with a short-lived poster board display developed for Black History Month as part of a larger effort of the Missouri state park system to document the work of the CCC. The exhibit was carefully edited to mitigate the depiction of the community's racism and opposition to the CCC enrollees, and was removed when the staff decided to develop an exhibit to celebrate Ruth Lamson.[39]

Celebrating Twain's Birth with "Flat-Water Recreation"

Ironically, fulfillment during the 1980s of the CCC's plans for a lake at Mark Twain State Park may be what will keep visitors coming back to the Mark Twain Birthplace and Historic Site. In 1984, the Army Corps of Engineers flooded the Salt River Valley after constructing the Clarence Cannon Dam.[40] The development of the lake led to the destruction of a number of small towns, individual farms, and properties that lay in the lake's footprint. Though these controversies were largely settled in the 1980s, the lake itself destroyed much of the landscape that would have been important to understanding historic Florida, Missouri. Today, the birthplace museum gleams in the sunlight reflected off the water.

In direct ways, the lake hinders the site's ability to make the usual claims about the importance of the surrounding landscape to Clemens's early life. At other birthplaces, landscape is incorporated into the essential story of who an individual becomes in later life. At Florida, however, this story cannot be told with the existing countryside.[41] The site cannot claim Clemens's literary genius, for instance, because tourists literally cannot visit any place there that retains a sentimental connection to Sam Clemens. Although the original impetus for Mark Twain State Park was the celebration of the author, currently the park caters to people interested in boating, fishing, and other forms of outdoor recreation. According to former Site Administrator Stan Fast, more than half of the people who come into the museum today come in to ask directions to somewhere else. Upon finding that they are at the Mark Twain Birthplace State Historic Site, they exclaim, "Oh, my goodness, this is one of America's, if not the most famous, author[s] we've ever produced; we'd better spend a little time here."[42]

Not long after the creation of the lake, out-of-state developers sought to cash in on the growing number of tourists by creating a Mark Twain theme park.[43] A number of area residents invested in the plan only to see their money used to draw up plans for a theme park that would never materialize. More recently, the Army Corps of Engineers has invited proposals for a more modest conference center and resort.[44] There seems to be abundant interest in ways to make money from Clemens's legacy in the area, but little effort to coordinate planning for these enterprises with preserving the historic environment and exploring the Missouri history that contributed to who he was and what he wrote.

Clemens and Birthplaces

Clemens's own interest in relics and historical preservation is a crucial place from which to think about the site's most fertile possibilities for interpretive programming linked to critical self-reflection. The writer believed that birthplaces were *sometimes* essential to understanding important figures. In a 1907 *New York Times* editorial, for example, he argued that the Abraham Lincoln Farm was a "birthplace worth saving." Clemens wrote, "The association [between Lincoln and his birthplace] had substance to it. Lincoln belonged just where he was put. If the Union was to be saved, it had to be a man of such an origin that should save it."[45] Clemens saw Lincoln's connection to his Kentucky birthplace as central to who Lincoln would become.[46]

In the case of Lincoln, the narrative was deterministic, and his birthplace was preordained like that of no other American figure, save for George Washington. In the face of growing national interest in the commemoration of "historically significant" great men and the belief that American history was the result of these great men's actions, Clemens still understood that such places become shrines akin to religious relics for the people who visit them. He even understood that a great number of people made pilgrimages to shrines where their reverence might be misplaced.[47] He cautioned that "some people make pilgrimages to the town whose streets were once trodden by Shakespeare . . . Shakespeare might have lived in any town as well as in Stratford."[48] Shakespeare might have been born anywhere, but Lincoln's birthplace mattered. It is paradoxical that historians then suspected and now recognize that the log cabin that the Lincoln Farm Association secured as Lincoln's birthplace was counterfeit. The cabin had been cobbled together long after Lincoln's birth.[49]

In 1902, during his last trip to Missouri, Clemens set aside time in a busy schedule, which included receiving an honorary doctorate and piloting a steamboat on the Mississippi, to dedicate a plaque that commemorated the birthplace of his fellow Missourian the poet Eugene Field. Field is largely forgotten today, though he wrote popular children's poems including "Little Boy Blue" and "Wynken, Blynken, and Nod." Clemens unveiled the plaque saying, "We are here with reverence and respect to commemorate and enshrine in memory the house where was born a man who, by his life, made bright the lives of all who knew him, and by his literary efforts cheered the thoughts of thousands who never knew him."[50] But this birthplace was short-lived. Less than a week after its dedication, the poet's brother revealed that the historical commission had enshrined the wrong building. Although a number of newspapers covered the mishap, at least one acknowledged that it was an easy mistake to make because the family, like Clemens's own, had lived in two houses during the writer's early childhood.[51]

When Albert Bigelow Paine, Clemens's biographer, made him aware of the Field mishap, Clemens merely replied, "Never mind. It is of no real consequence whether it is his birthplace or not. A rose in any other garden will bloom as sweet."[52] Perhaps Clemens would laugh off the troubled history of his own birthplace with the same nonchalance. One way or the other, his conflicting thoughts on the value of birthplace commemoration provide a perfect starting point to discuss the problem of authenticity in Florida and how even "inauthentic" places can be meaningful. After all, Lincoln and Clemens were important enough—to the people who decided to commemorate them and to those who made pilgrimages to their birthplaces—to construct anew.

For scholars of Sam Clemens, historians, and others invested in the idea that state-funded historic sites should do their best to educate the public and present local history accurately, the Mark Twain Birthplace and Historic Site leaves much undeveloped. Its refusal to embrace the cabin's inauthenticity has prevented the site from engaging Clemens's literary origins and his very real connection to the state of Missouri. If anything, its struggle should remind us that at historic sites, like Twain's birthplace, inauthenticity does not have to be antithetical to good history. In some cases it can be an asset. Twain's spurious birth cabin creates wonderful opportunities to explore the history of Florida and its demise as well as the part that the development of Mark Twain State Park played in it. The story of the development of the park—Ruth Lamson, the community's resistance to African American CCC workers, the long dispute about the legitimacy of the cabin, and the largely unmined history of the building of the lake—are more interesting than the story told at the "birthplace" today and might say a good deal more about Missouri history in the meantime. Replicas do not keep tourists away from "historic" sites. In fact, while tourists value "authenticity," authenticity can reside in the discovery that things are not always what they seem. If nothing else, the story of Mark Twain's birthplace cabins reminds us that birthplaces and origins matter and that they may matter most when we cannot find them.

NOTES

Many thanks to John Huffman for his hospitality at the Mark Twain Birthplace State Historic Site, Ralph Gregory, Stan Fast, Alan Gribben, and John Cunning, who all gave interviews about their time at the birthplace, and Heather Rudy at the Missouri Department of Natural

Resources Archive, who helped me wade through the state's records for the birthplace. For reading this chapter in various forms, many thanks are due to the generous Susan K. Harris, Cheryl Lester, Marilyn Watley, Jennifer Heller, and Seth C. Bruggeman.

1. Stan Fast to Samuel J. Wegner, memorandum, March 4, 1983, Mark Twain Birthplace State Historic Site, Florida, MO (herafter cited as MTB).
2. According to park attendance figures for January 1–December 31, 2008, Missouri Department of Natural Resources Archives, Jefferson City, MO (herafter cited as MDNR).
3. Clifton Johnson, *Highways and Byways of the Mississippi Valley* (New York: Macmillan, 1906), 170.
4. Ibid., 178–80.
5. Ibid.
6. See Edward Pessen, *The Log Cabin Myth: The Social Backgrounds of the Presidents* (New Haven: Yale University Press, 1984); and Dwight Pitcaithley, "Abraham Lincoln's Birthplace Cabin: The Making of an American Icon," in *Myth, Memory, and the Making of the American Landscape*, ed. Paul A. Shackel (Gainesville: University Press of Florida, 2001), 240–54.
7. Pitcaithley uncovers the questionable trajectory of Lincoln's birthplace from the time it was "identified" in 1895 to when it was stored and, consequently, its logs intermingled with the Jefferson Davis birthplace cabin in the Bowery section of New York City in 1897, in "Abraham Lincoln's Birthplace Cabin," 242–44.
8. Johnson, *Highways and Byways of the Mississippi Valley*, 178–80.
9. Joe Burnett, *The Paris Mercury*, Paris, MO, October 17, 1890.
10. Sam Pollard, *Monroe County Appeal*, Paris, MO, June 18, 1897.
11. Recollections of the 1904 exposition appear in *The Paris Mercury*, Paris, MO, June 22, 1934.
12. Ralph Gregory, *M. A. "Dad" Violette: A Life Sketch* (Florida, MO, 1969).
13. Ralph Gregory, "Orion Clemens on Mark Twain's Birthplace," *Mark Twain Journal* 20, no. 2 (1980): 16–18.
14. Albert Bigelow Paine, *Mark Twain: A Biography, the Personal and Literary Life of Samuel Langhorne Clemens*, 3 vols., vol. 1 (New York: Harper and Brothers, 1912), 12.
15. As cited in Gregory, *A Life Sketch*, 3.
16. "Park Originator," *Kansas City Post*, March 22, 1924.
17. Duis Bolinger, "Letter to the Editor," *Missouri Life*, August 1986. Ruth Lamson Armstrong, "Fulfilling a Vision: A Letter to the Missouri Department of Natural Resources," *Hannibal Courier Post*, June 5, 1995. "Historical Notes and Comments: Mark Twain Memorial Park Association," *Missouri Historical Review* 18, no. 2 (1924).
18. Frank Lamson, "Statement by F. B. Lamson, Secretary Mark Twain Park Association," 1924, MTB, 2.
19. "Historical Notes and Comments," 290. Missouri State Parks, "Evolution of the System," 1991, MDNR. Frank Lamson, "Statement by F. B. Lamson," 1.
20. M. A. "Dad" Violette to Frank B. Lamson, 1927, Ruth Lamson File, MTB.
21. See coverage of Violette's response in "Settles Controversy About Twain Home," *Enterprise*, Perry, MO, October 24, 1929. For more on competing claims, see Ralph Gregory, "Orion Clemens on Mark Twain's Birthplace."
22. "Settles Controversy About Twain Home."
23. Ibid.
24. Gregory, *A Life Sketch*.
25. On Victor and Edith Turner's arguments about the nature of contemporary religious pilgrimage and its connection to literary tourism, see Lawrence Buell, "The Thoreauvian Pilgrimage: The Structure of an American Cult," *American Literature* 61, no. 2 (1989): 179.
26. Charles Hammer, "A Home at Last for the Old Twain House," *Kansas City Star*, November 22, 1959.

27. New interpretative master plans were drawn up in 1961, 1979, and 1985, but never implemented. See Missouri State Park Board, "Museum Prospectus for Mark Twain Birthplace Memorial Shrine, Mark Twain State Park," 1961; Nancy Honerkamp, "Notes on Interpretation: Mark Twain Shrine State Historic Site," 1979; and Daniel Holt, "Museum Assessment Program Grant—Mark Twain Birthplace," 1985, MDNR.

28. For an account of the various internal complaints about signage over the years, see William C. Holmes to Jack Hilton, memorandum, 1980; and Ann Nickell to Frank Wesley, 1995, MDNR.

29. Fast to Wegner, March 4, 1983.

30. Ibid.

31. Stan Fast, telephone interview with author, November 20, 2007.

32. R. H. Hamilton, R. E. Rouse, et al. "Statement: Florida, Missouri August 30, 1939," MDNR.

33. Ibid.

34. "The Park Problem," *Monroe County Appeal,* October 12, 1939.

35. "Will Not Let Them Go into Park Town," *Monroe County Appeal,* October 26, 1939.

36. "Interview with Unnamed Company 1743c Enrollee," 1997, MTB.

37. John Cunning, "CCC Company 1743: The Thunderbirds," *Preservation Issues* 6, no. 1 (1996).

38. Ibid.

39. John Huffman, interview with author, January 7, 2008.

40. See U.S. Army Corps of Engineers, "Mark Twain Lake," www.mvs.usace.army.mil/mark twain/.

41. For a discussion of birthplaces and this typical literary birthplace narrative, see Aaron Santesso's "The Birth of the Birthplace: Bread Street and Literary Tourism before Stratford," *English Literary History* 71 (2004): 377–403. See also Nicola Watson, *The Literary Tourist: Readers and Places in Romantic and Victorian Britain* (New York: Palgrave Macmillan, 2007), chapter 2.

42. Fast, telephone interview with author.

43. Ron Powers, *White Town Drowsing* (Boston: Atlantic Monthly Press, 1986), 128–30.

44. See U.S. Corps of Engineers, "Mark Twain Lake Resort Development," www.mvs.usace .army.mil/marktwain/.

45. Mark Twain, "A Lincoln Memorial: A Plea by Mark Twain for the Setting Apart of His Birthplace," *New York Times,* January 13, 1907, 8.

46. For a longer discussion of the role that Lincoln's birthplace played in his election and presidency, see Pessen, *The Log Cabin Myth.*

47. Clemens's skepticism about pilgrimages and relics is most evident in this passage from *Innocents Abroad:* "We find a piece of the true cross in every old church we go into, and some of the nails that held it together . . . I think we have seen as much as a keg of these nails . . . And as for bones of St. Denis, I feel certain we have seen enough of them to duplicate him if necessary." Mark Twain, *The Innocents Abroad; or, the New Pilgrim's Progress* (Hartford: American Publishing Company, 1870), 165.

48. Mark Twain, "A Lincoln Memorial."

49. Pitcaithley, "Abraham Lincoln's Birthplace Cabin."

50. "Eugene Field Tablet, Birthplace Memorial Unveiled by Mark Twain," *St. Louis Globe Democrat,* June 7, 1902.

51. About the mishap see "Note and Comment," *Springfield Daily Republican,* June 14, 1902.

52. Albert Bigelow Paine, *Mark Twain: A Biography, the Personal and Literary Life of Samuel Langhorne Clemens,* 3 vols., vol. 3 (New York: Harper and Brothers, 1912), 1175.

Stratford Hall, birthplace of Robert E. Lee, State Route 214, Stratford, Westmoreland County, Virginia, photographed by Jack E. Boucher in 1969. Library of Congress, Prints and Photographs Division, Historic American Buildings Survey, HABS VA,97-____,4-4.

~ 5 ~

Perhaps it's a tribute to the exuberance of early twentieth-century monument mak-
ers that so many commemorative birthplaces celebrate the memories of people who
didn't remain where they were born for very long. Whether or not a matter of hap-
penstance, this peculiarity has freed the guardians of birth memory to populate
these places with a remarkable variety of meanings. Paul Reber and Laura Lawfer
Orr, both experienced birthplace stewards, offer a case in point, like Lowe's, from
the golden age of American birthplace commemoration. They explain how the
preservation of confederate General Robert E. Lee's Virginia birthplace—which
Lee left at age three—resulted from the efforts of displaced southern women more
concerned after the Civil War to promulgate Lost Cause ideology than to confront
the complexities of Lee's life and legacy. With little more than the first years of a
newborn to make their point, these progenitors of Lee's memory moored his legacy
in Stratford Hall's colonial past. The result, as Reber and Orr show us, is less a
memorial to Lee than a fascinating glimpse into how twentieth-century Americans
enlisted the eighteenth century in what is still a volatile struggle to shape how we
understand the nineteenth's most defining moment.

Stratford Hall

A Memorial to Robert E. Lee?
PAUL REBER AND LAURA LAWFER ORR

Stratford Hall is a historic home set on 1,900 acres in Westmoreland County on Virginia's Northern Neck Peninsula. Constructed circa 1738 by Thomas and Hannah Lee, it was home to four generations of the Lee family. These four generations included many well-known figures who shaped American history. Two of Thomas and Hannah's sons, Richard

Henry and Francis Lightfoot, signed the Declaration of Independence, and three other sons—Thomas Ludwell, William, and Arthur—played key roles in the struggle for independence. Their sister Hannah became an early proponent of women's rights. Stratford Hall is best known as the birthplace of Robert E. Lee. While he lived there for less than four years, Robert E. Lee is the personality that most often attracts visitors to the site.

Today, Stratford Hall is a private nonprofit historic site administered by the Robert E. Lee Memorial Association. In addition to the historic house, Stratford Hall's extensive land holdings and location on the Potomac River provide many opportunities for its 30,000 annual visitors to learn about both history and the environment. Stratford Hall's mission is to preserve the legacy of the Lee family and its plantation community; to inspire an appreciation of America's past; and to encourage commitment to the ideals of leadership, honor, independent thought, and civic responsibility. Although Stratford Hall now focuses on the importance of the entire Lee family, including its enslaved population and indentured servants, that has not always been the case.

The history of Stratford Hall's preservation and transformation into a nationally significant historic site can be illustrated by the contrasting views of two women: May Field Lanier and Ethel Armes. They cooperated in their efforts but looked at Stratford Hall from different perspectives. One celebrated its role as the birthplace of Robert E. Lee while the other celebrated its architecture and the legacy of its eighteenth-century occupants. Looking closely at these two perspectives provides useful insight into the struggle over public memory as manifested in two social movements prevalent in early twentieth-century America. The first was the principally southern effort to redefine the origins and legacy of the Civil War, a notion widely characterized as the "Lost Cause." The second involved the aesthetic movement referred to as the Colonial Revival. Considering Stratford Hall's history in light of these two movements allows us to explore how the professionalization of museums and a female-dominated preservation movement shaped politics and gendered notions of the past.[1]

The Northern Roots of a Southern Memory

In spring 1928, Ethel Armes, a writer from Washington, DC, conducted research in Virginia about George Washington's adult home at Mount Vernon and his birthplace at Wakefield in Westmoreland County. She came across Stratford Hall only by chance. Its appearance struck her as "bleak and gaunt in the center of a bare grass-grown quadrangle . . . scrawny blinds of the eighteen eighties, hanging on broken hinges, and dingy window casings made ugly patches of green and white against the red walls." Armes believed it was too "solitary, so forgotten by the world," and should be preserved and made accessible to the public. When she arrived home, she immediately wrote a letter to her friend May Field Lanier in Greenwich, Connecticut, suggesting that the United Daughters of the Confederacy purchase and maintain it, "precisely as Mount Vernon is cared for and given to our country for all time?"[2]

At almost the same time that Armes was writing her letter, Lanier, daughter-in-law of Georgia poet laureate Sidney Lanier, found an unpublished speech delivered by her father-in-law following the death of Robert E. Lee in 1870. It resolved that a monument be built in Lee's honor and that "such a monument should assume its best propriety in the form of a great hall of fame to be built by . . . voluntary contributions." A few days after receiving Armes's letter, Lanier read a few phrases from her father-in-law's address at a meeting of the William Alexander, Jr., chapter of the United Daughters of the Confederacy (UDC) in Greenwich. She hinted at the possibility of Stratford Hall serving as the memorial he envisioned. With the support of the William Alexander, Jr., Chapter, Lanier planned to take the proposal to the November 1928 National UDC Convention in Houston, Texas, hoping that the UDC would agree to support the effort by taxing each member $5.00 for the acquisition of Stratford as a memorial to Lee.[3]

The Connecticut origin of the movement to create a Lee memorial appears unusual, but it was not. Louis C. Cramton, a congressman from Michigan, for instance, spearheaded legislation to create the Lee Mansion National Memorial to preserve Lee's adult home at Arlington in 1925. Stratford Hall's story, however, was tied more directly to the northward migration of Southerners eager to escape the dismal economic conditions that prevailed in the postwar South. These immigrants concentrated in certain areas of the North—Connecticut, Pennsylvania, Washington, DC, and Massachusetts—and their descendants formed new chapters of the UDC. Members of northern UDC chapters, like May Field Lanier, descended from prominent south-ern families. According to historian Karen Cox, by the end of World War I, "members of the first generation of the UDC, women who had experienced the Civil War firsthand or had grown up in its aftermath, were being replaced by a new generation of Lost Cause women." This new generation included the members of the William Alexander, Jr., Chapter of the UDC established by May Field Lanier in 1926 in honor of her uncle who died at the Battle of Shiloh.[4]

On her journey to Houston in November 1928, Lanier made two stops. She met with a fundraising firm in New York City, and in Washington, DC, she met with Armes's real estate agent to negotiate a preliminary purchase agreement for Stratford with its owner, Charles Stuart. After some hard bargaining, Stuart agreed to a sixty-day pur-chase option on Stratford for $200,000. Lanier set off for Houston with the option in hand, but her high hopes were not realized. The politics of a large organization like the UDC made consensus on such a momentous undertaking impossible. Instead, the UDC delegates voted to study the matter and report back in March 1929. Lanier was despon-dent until a friend told her that the William Alexander, Jr., Chapter could take up the option independent of the national organization. Elated at this revelation, Lanier sent a telegram to the real estate agent accepting the option's terms.[5]

Lanier next turned her attention to the $200,000 she needed to acquire the property. Hilton Railey, representing the New York fundrais-ing firm, had given the impression that these funds could be secured from New York businessmen. When Lanier pressed the matter upon her return, however, Railey requested a payment of $15,000 before he would begin work. This impossible request made Lanier conclude that "we will simply have to do the best we can within our own ranks and raise what funds we can." In the meantime, Lanier also retained an attorney who renegotiated the purchase agreement with Stuart to increase the acreage from 300 to 1,100 and the purchase price to $240,000.[6]

Recognizing that this represented an audacious challenge for a UDC chapter with only 25 members and very little money, Lanier decided she would need to create a national organization. There were several organiza-tional models to choose from. Both men and women participated on the board of the Wakefield National Memorial Association, actively restoring

George Washington's birthplace a short distance west of Stratford Hall. Perhaps inspired by her friend and close associate Mary Van Deventer, who served on Mount Vernon's board, Lanier selected the nation's oldest and most prominent preservation organization for her model: the Mount Vernon Ladies Association of the Union. The Association was formed in 1856 to acquire and preserve George Washington's Mount Vernon. In February 1929, Lanier and her fellow preservationists established the Robert E. Lee Memorial Foundation with all-female board members representing their various states. The role of women in historic preservation, either as leaders or in all-female associations, was not unusual in the first decades of the twentieth century. The presence of women in the preservation movement served, as some historians have argued, to emphasize the domestic role of women in creating and establishing the character of great men like George Washington and Robert E. Lee. It also provided a place where women might exercise political influence free from interference from men.[7]

Throughout its initial organizing efforts, the Foundation's mission was to establish Stratford Hall as a memorial to Robert E. Lee. While Ethel Armes had a broader understanding of the complex history of the site and its other Lee family occupants, the women did not acknowledge or define how any of this would factor into the Foundation's mission in these first years.

Stratford Hall and Sectional Reconciliation

The Association chose a propitious time to create a memorial to Lee. Sixty years after the conclusion of the Civil War, Robert E. Lee's role as a mythic, unifying national figure had been firmly established by the efforts of Lost Cause advocates in the South and North. The narrative of Lee as an exemplar of all that was good and noble received further validation with the publication of Douglas Southall Freeman's Pulitzer Prize–winning biography of Lee in 1934, which presented a unidimensional image of a man raised to near godlike status. Franklin D. Roosevelt also validated Lee's importance when he sent a letter of support to the Foundation in 1932.[8]

When selecting members for the new Foundation board, Lanier chose wisely, locating "the wealthiest and most energetic group to be found in the United States in the 1930's." Its illustrious and affluent board ensured that the Foundation could make the first payment on its loan in July 1929. Even so, Lanier realized that she would need significantly more money to purchase and restore Stratford Hall. She also knew that, to get it, she needed a communications plan to highlight Lee's significance and draw national attention to the Foundation's cause. The plan that Lanier and her committee devised, which encompassed special events and outreach to the national media, provides a useful perspective on the Foundation's agenda and into national attitudes about the Civil War during the early twentieth century.[9]

"Stratford Day" served as the centerpiece of their plan. Robert E. Lee was born on January 19, 1807, an inconvenient time of year for an outdoor celebration. So, rather than celebrate Lee's birth, the Foundation decided to stage its first "Stratford Day" on October 13, 1929, one day after the fifty-ninth anniversary of Lee's death. The board, led by publicity chair Irene Gibson of New York, planned the event and made certain to include dignitaries of national significance. A number of unnamed Missouri congressmen and Virginia Lieutenant Governor Junius West attended, as well as various officials from West Virginia, Kentucky, Alabama, and Virginia. One local newspaper referred to Stratford Day as "one of the most notable gatherings near Fredericksburg since the laying of the cornerstone of the Mary Washington monument, more than thirty years ago." It added, "Already every train is bringing in guests of national distinction" and that all of the inns and hotels in the immediate area were fully booked for the weekend.[10]

The program included a variety of speakers with messages intended to appeal to Americans in both North and South. Senator Alben W. Barkley of Kentucky noted that "Robert E. Lee was the perfection of the genius and character and high ideals that grew in this old house. He was an example of what breeding means in men as in animals. In him was the fruition of all that was best and noblest in the Lees, who lived in this house." Similar words came from Missouri Senator Harry B. Hawes: "The Lee I like to think of . . . is not the general leading armies, but 'Marse Robert,' the kindly man, the man who won the love of the country." These expressions were all common elements of Lost Cause rhetoric, which emphasized the dignified leadership of the South's prominent families and their devotion to duty and country.[11]

Of all the esteemed attendants, one person more than any other captivated the audience: Giles Cooke, the last living member of Robert E. Lee's Civil War staff. The ninety-one-year-old veteran showed his support for the Foundation by attending the entire day's festivities. Also significant among the speakers was Albert Bushnell Hart, professor emeritus at Harvard and son of a Union prisoner of war. Even Hart, an opponent of the Lost Cause model, praised Lee's character. Hart's address, titled "What I think of Robert E. Lee," claimed Lee as a "brother American and one of a small group of superlative Americans."[12]

Press coverage of the event focused on the theme of sectional reconciliation. One northern newspaper, the *Cincinnati Enquirer*, reported: "Lee came of a noble line . . . Is it not time to symbolize a united country by the creation of a worthy memorial to the greatest among the Confederate leaders? Lee is deserving of this honor. It would be . . . evidence of a proper appreciation of the virtues of a truly great American, one whose name illuminates the pages of our history."[13]

Southern newspapers used the same theme and vigorously applauded the efforts to preserve Stratford Hall. The *Richmond Times-Dispatch* was especially effusive in its praise, writing that "among the people of this country bitterness engendered during the War Between the States now is scarcely more than an unpleasant memory" and that "the average citizen is thoroughly convinced that differences which separated North and South in the history-making sixties were settled long ago." The *Nashville Banner* advertised "National Stratford Day" with an illustration that depicted Robert E. Lee looming in the clouds above Stratford Hall. The front of the illustration depicted a rolled-up document that read, "Plans for converting Stratford-on-the-Potomac into a National Shrine." A small piece of paper floated behind it, reading, "Stratford Hall: The birthplace of two signers of the Declaration of Independence and the best loved of Southern heroes—General Robert E. Lee." Interestingly, while this paper mentioned the signers of the Declaration of Independence who lived in the house prior to (and longer than) Robert E. Lee—which most Stratford Day speakers failed to note—the main focus, consistent with the general thrust of the Foundation's communication efforts, was the unifying message and image of Robert E. Lee.[14]

Employing the same theme of national reconciliation, but from a different perspective, other newspapers chose to focus attention on the fact that a northern chapter of the UDC had purchased Stratford Hall. The *Louisville Courier-Journal* reported that "it is not altogether strange, or inappropriate, that a New England chapter of the Daughters of the Confederacy has purchased Stratford Hall. It is a graceful gesture [that the] adopted daughters of the North should set on foot the movement to preserve the old home of the best loved of Southern heroes."[15]

Northern newspapers praised the preservation efforts with equal vigor. *The Press,* a newspaper from Escanaba, Michigan, reported the peculiarity of a Connecticut organization's purchase of Stratford for the American people, but it agreed with the southern newspapers regarding the overall merits of the move. One reporter stated that "a couple of decades ago there undoubtedly would have been a good deal of unthinking hostility to such a plan. In many parts of the North there would have been protests against honoring 'a rebel.'" But now, the paper continued, "North as well as South, it is now universally realized that Lee, for all that he fought against the Union, was a great man and a splendid American . . . It is perfectly safe to predict that the movement to turn his birthplace into a national memorial will not meet a dissenting vote."[16]

The message of sectional reconciliation was not universal. *The State,* a paper from Columbia, South Carolina, recognized that the Foundation carried "a silent loyalty and love of the old 'cause,' which, like all great causes can never wholly die. But they are now residents—citizens—of a New England state, in a region in which has burned most steadily and most hotly the fires of resentment toward the South." This, however, was the only negative voice surrounding an event that celebrated the reunification of the nation. Both the North and South placed Robert E. Lee at the center of the narrative as Lee became a symbol for the dominance of the Lost Cause rhetoric. As historian Douglas Southall Freeman noted, "If there is an ideal in the Old South, it is Lee, he stands for all that was best and brightest there." Placing Lee at the center of Civil War remembrance ensured that people ignored the role of slavery in bringing about the conflict. The marginal role of African Americans in Stratford Day celebrations was consistent with the effort to obscure their role in the history of the conflict.[17]

The Ambiguity of a Birthplace

Despite the _rhetoric of reconciliation_ and some positive press, the Foundation confronted an awkward reality when making Stratford the memorial it envisioned and that people, in both the North and South, seemed to expect. While it is true that Lee was born at Stratford in 1807, he, his mother, and his siblings left there three years later for Alexandria, Virginia, where he spent all of his youth save for occasional visits to Stratford Hall as an adolescent. Hoping to link Lee more firmly to his birthplace, the Foundation made special note of references to Stratford Hall found in Lee's Civil War letters. Lee's letter to his daughters in 1863 described his birthplace affectionately, stating that it had been "a great desire of my life to be able to purchase it." Lee expressed similar sentiments to his wife, Mary Custis Lee, two weeks later: "In the absence of a home I wish I could purchase Stratford."[18] Despite his expressed desire, there is no record that he ever saw his birthplace after the war, even when visiting the homes of friends nearby. None of these sentiments made Stratford Hall exceptional. George Washington had an almost equally tangential relationship to his birthplace located just down the road from Stratford Hall.

The Foundation's brochures, primarily the work of Ethel Armes, grappled with the ambiguity of Lee's relationship to the site by presenting a more nuanced history of Stratford Hall. May Field Lanier distributed the first publication, _Stratford-on-the-Potomac,_ at the UDC meeting in Houston. It included Sidney Lanier's address, a chapter containing Lee's reflections on his life at Stratford, and two other chapters on the significance of Stratford's eighteenth-century occupants. In another early publication, "Twelve Reasons Why Stratford Should Become a National Shrine," Armes noted that Stratford Hall was "a rare and surprising example in America of Seventeenth century English architecture, noble and impressive . . . the only American home built in part with funds given by a British sovereign." In actuality, the house does not invoke seventeenth-century English architecture, nor did a British sovereign give funds to build it, but these statements appealed to Americans who revered the colonial period and its connections with England. Armes touted Stratford Hall's eighteenth-century history as well. She noted that "it was the home of the first native born President of the Colony of

Virginia, Thomas Lee, it was the birthplace of Richard Henry Lee, Francis Lightfoot Lee, Signers of the Declaration of Independence, and their patriot brothers and sisters," and that "it exemplified the highest pinnacle of cultural, social and plantation life of the Colonial and Revolutionary Periods of Virginia."[19] All of these facts, save for Stratford Hall being the birthplace of Richard Henry Lee and Francis Lightfoot Lee, were true. Armes and the Foundation did not discuss how all of this was compatible with Stratford Hall as a memorial to Robert E. Lee, however.

In a March 1930 letter to Giles Cooke, Armes agreed that "the movement [to preserve Stratford Hall] is no way sectarian and that is one of the reasons why we wish to stress the colonial and revolutionary periods."[20] In this context, "sectarian" referred to regional sectionalism. This suggests that Armes believed that the cause of national reconciliation was so much a part of the Foundation's message that it was best served by emphasizing the eighteenth-century aspects of Stratford's history.

Fiske Kimball and the Politics of Memory

Rumors in circulation by 1930 that the reconstructed George Washington birthplace house had been built in the wrong place surely explain, in part, the Robert E. Lee Memorial Foundation board's determination that its restoration plans be supervised by experts. These experts played a significant role in shaping the restoration. Mary Van Deventer, chair of the restoration committee, was especially committed to this course of action. The experts she contacted included furniture scholar Herbert Putnam, preservation advocate Leicester Holland, and historian Charles Andrews. Van Deventer also contacted Fiske Kimball. In 1930, Kimball was the Director of the Philadelphia Museum of Art and had made his reputation as the foremost scholar of Thomas Jefferson's architecture. He served on the board of Monticello's Thomas Jefferson Memorial Foundation and Colonial Williamsburg's architectural advisory board. As one reviewer noted, "the amount and quality of Kimball's scholarship is a challenge to all architectural historians."[21]

Van Deventer's first letter to Kimball in July 1930 sought advice on the restoration and on what parts of the house could be considered "original." Kimball responded that the dominant thought should not be restoration, but preservation—that the greatest care should be exercised on changing anything "back to the way it was supposed to formerly have been," and the house should be kept as it currently stood. He added that "more harm has been done to historic buildings by ill-judged restoration than by neglect," and "any changes made down to the time of the Confederate war, should be undisturbed." Van Deventer evidently liked what she heard, and in August 1930 asked Kimball if he would serve as the Foundation's architect. Kimball said he would be pleased to have the commission and suggested that the process begin with a study to recommend priorities.[22]

Although the deepening Depression prevented the Foundation from contracting with Kimball in 1930, Ethel Armes's research project continued. As Armes described it, the research effort would inform "every phase and aspect of Stratford Hall's history and restoration plans." Aleen Bingham, chair of the house furnishings committee, agreed that Armes's effort would proceed with the utmost care and attention to authenticity. Contrary to Kimball's advice, however, Bingham remarked that the mission was to restore an eighteenth-century Virginia mansion. Bingham's remark is an indication of a shift in the objectives of the restoration. It is also clear this shift was encouraged by Armes and the "experts" enlisted to support the research effort.[23]

The Foundation also engaged Luke Vincent Lockwood and Francis P. Garvan, both noted collectors of American decorative art, as consultants. In April 1930, Lockwood recommended refurnishing the house with "nothing later than the year 1800 and emphasize the pre-Revolutionary styles." He approved of the Foundation's first acquisition—an eighteenth-century French toile bed set—and described it as "perfect for Stratford." Lockwood's wife explained her interest in Stratford Hall's restoration in terms of its "uniqueness and importance" from an eighteenth-century perspective.[24]

At the same time, Garvan—who with his wife had recently created the Mabel Brady Garvan Institute of American Arts and Crafts at Yale University—offered "to assist the board in its restoration of Stratford." Respected Yale architect Everett V. Meeks directed the research project, and Yale faculty joined Ethel Armes, who continued to play an important role. After visiting Stratford Hall on August 14, 1930, Meeks expressed his admiration for the place, stating that "when the records are complete and restoration is carried out accordingly, we are going to be able to see an extraordinary house and grounds of the early eighteenth century." Meeks was not alone. Cazenove Lee, an eminent member of the family and author of several books on the Virginia Lees, agreed that the "determination to restore the house and grounds to their condition in 1750—the golden age of the plantation—is quite proper." The Daughters of the American Revolution even resolved to support the restoration of Stratford "in recognition of the illustrious services of Richard Henry Lee and Light Horse Harry Lee."[25]

By 1932, the Foundation had raised sufficient funds to pay off the Stuart loan and finalize its agreement with Kimball. Kimball's first task was to complete a survey of the house as he had outlined to Van Deventer two years before. Prior to delivering the survey, however, Kimball outlined urgent repair work, adding that some "artistic restorations" might be undertaken to the roof, outside stairs, and interior millwork. The significance of this statement became apparent when Kimball delivered his survey report, "Stratford: Yesterday, Today and Tomorrow," in fall 1932. In it, Kimball justified his "artistic" restoration by arguing that the Northern Neck had become a "backwater devoid of good craftsmen" by the late eighteenth century. Although its rooms "were as they were when Robert E. Lee was born" and "as he saw them in his childhood," Kimball believed that the "quality of design and workmanship" of the renovations undertaken by Robert E. Lee's father "are not comparable to that of the time of Thomas Lee." By suggesting that the restoration should value aesthetics and workmanship above historic fabric, Kimball opened the door to the approach he warned against in 1930.[26]

He argued, for example, that Stratford Hall's south stairway had replaced an aesthetically superior original. To the modern-day visitor, the staircases on the north and south elevations of the main house rank among its most imposing features. The exterior stairs remain Kimball's most controversial additions to Stratford Hall. Current research indicates the brick and sandstone stairs present at the time of the restoration were likely built by "Light Horse Harry" Lee. Robert E. Lee probably knew those stairs in his youth. Kimball submitted plans for the restoration of the south stairs in 1935 based on stone fragments found around the house that he believed formed part of an earlier stone stair and balustrade. Colonial Williamsburg's landscape architect, Arthur

Shurcliff, responsible for most of the archaeological excavations around the house, protested. He pointed out that his excavations did not substantiate Kimball's design for the new stairs. Stratford Hall's Resident Superintendent, Benjamin Cheatham, and restoration contractor Herbert Claiborne both expressed their skepticism. Kimball dismissed all of their objections by arguing that the archaeological evidence was from inferior, early nineteenth-century additions. The evidence also did not fit his preconceived notion that Stratford Hall's design should follow English Baroque precedents.[27]

Initially, Kimball had been given a free hand to manage the restoration process. But after the controversy over the exterior stair restoration, interior restoration became a contentious negotiation between the architect and various members of the Foundation Board. Kimball and the Board acknowledged that most of the interior dated from the renovation completed by Robert E. Lee's father in the late eighteenth and early nineteenth centuries. However, as Kimball's research gradually revealed more of the original mid-eighteenth-century construction, the board members' interest in seeing it restored grew. Of particular interest were the decisions that ultimately led to the restoration of the dining room, in the northeast corner of the house, back to its conjectural appearance during the time of Thomas Lee. It was Kimball's original recommendation to leave this room with its Federal period woodwork intact; however, many board members came to believe there was greater value in restoring the original Thomas Lee interiors. In an attempt to avoid the removal of the Federal period elements, Kimball offered compromises and suggestions. The Board rejected them all and directed Kimball to restore the room to its colonial period appearance.[28]

Another debate ensued over the restoration of the parlor in the northwest corner of the house. Like the northeast room, this room also retained much of its original Federal period woodwork. This time, Kimball was less inclined to compromise, describing his preferred preservation course as "antique and real." Ethel Armes complicated final resolution of this issue by writing a lengthy report arguing that the woodwork had been installed by Stratford Hall's first non-Lee owner, William Somerville, because Henry Lee could not have afforded the expense. Based on this argument, Armes concluded that all the rooms except the southeast room where Robert E. Lee was allegedly born should be restored to the earlier period "as faithfully as the genius and great ability of Mr. Kimball can render it." Kimball successfully rebutted Armes's arguments. He prevailed primarily because of his alliance with restoration committee chair Mary Van Deventer. On the bottom of a letter from Kimball to Van Deventer noting that evidence of the original Thomas Lee woodwork had been found, Kimball wrote: "This is merely reported for information, as nothing is to be done unless there is some further action taken by council." The minutes are silent on whether or not Van Deventer ever conveyed this information to the Board. With memories of the recent struggle over the dining room in mind, she may have taken Kimball's subtle suggestion to heart and kept this revelation to herself. In fall 1938, the Board voted to accept Kimball's recommendation to leave the Federal period woodwork undisturbed.[29]

Fiske Kimball is frequently criticized for his treatment of the exterior of Stratford Hall. As much as these decisions seem misguided to us today, it is equally clear that he stood in the way of a near gutting of the interior of the house. Nonetheless, the final result of the restoration is a confusing mix of restored and original finishes without a lot of integrity to any one particular period. Kimball left only one section of the house basically undisturbed: the rooms in the southeast corner where Robert E. Lee was supposedly born and the adjacent nursery where he spent most of his first three years. It is interesting to note that the Board restored and refurnished these two rooms with the only funds received directly from the UDC. One is tempted to speculate whether things would have been different if the UDC had agreed to take on the entire project, as May Lanier initially proposed.

Stratford Hall as the Birthplace of a Family

If the final result of the restoration was not a memorial to Robert E. Lee, it was something perhaps more creative—a memorial to four generations of the Lee family. In this sense, the Robert E. Lee Memorial Foundation was a pioneer, resisting the prevalent trend to restore to a single time period and instead creating an experience that allowed it to interpret the many important national figures who called Stratford Hall home. It is not clear whether this was a conscious decision from the start, or possibly more an accident of Board politics, the twists and turns of the restoration, and the very ambiguity evident from the Foundation's origins in 1929. Inside the house, Kimball counseled against the acquisition of objects based solely on their aesthetic appearance or uncertain claims of originality. Research for his furnishing plans followed the procedures used by modern museum curators, which include using architectural and documentary evidence such as probate inventories, and selecting furnishings of the appropriate period and style. Kimball's interpretation of the interior told the story of the four generations of the Lee family though, as was typical at the time, without any serious mention of the enslaved Africans and African Americans who represented the majority of Stratford's eighteenth- and nineteenth-century residents.[30]

But where did this fifty-year transition leave the original concept of Stratford Hall as a memorial to Robert E. Lee? By the 1970s, Lee's stature as a national hero and symbol of sectional reconciliation had been significantly diminished. What is more, the donation of a prestigious collection of American furniture and the looming celebration of America's Bicentennial encouraged the implementation of an interpretive and furnishing plan reminiscent of a decorative arts museum. Board members considered the Colonial Revival—with its emphasis on a more gendered and genteel presentation of the past—more compelling than the early nineteenth-century world of Robert E. Lee's birth. It was a successful strategy: attendance hit 45,291 by 1975 and reached over 60,000 in 1976. If we define "memorial" in the usual sense—as a place to keep the memory of someone alive—by the 1970s, Stratford Hall became a memorial to the eighteenth-century Lees and the sanitized vision of their world that was at the heart of the Colonial Revival.[31]

Robert E. Lee still remains part of Stratford Hall's story, though only his birth is enshrined in one of the Great House's rooms. In this sense, Robert E. Lee's Lost Cause role as a unifying national figure has been preserved, symbolically linked with his father and Lee cousins who were instrumental in creating the nation he fought against.[32] Currently, Stratford Hall is undergoing a third major transformation since its acquisition in 1929 by the Robert E. Lee Memorial Foundation. It will reverse some of the restoration decisions made in the 1930s and restore the Federal period appearance of some of the rooms. Many objects acquired since 1929 have been de-accessioned, and the house will be refurnished with pieces more appropriate to the period of Lee occupancy. While

Stratford Hall's current mission is to tell the story of four generations of the Lee family and its free and enslaved servants, Robert E. Lee remains a central figure in this tale—and so he will always be.

NOTES

1. See Richard Guy Wilson, "What Is the Colonial Revival?" in Richard Guy Wilson et al., *Re-creating the American Past, Essays on the Colonial Revival* (Charlottesville: University of Virginia Press, 2006), 1–10. The role of women is best described by Patricia West, *Domesticating History* (Washington: Smithsonian Institution Press, 1999).

2. Ethel Armes, *Stratford Hall* (Richmond: Garrett and Massie, 1936), 443; Ethel Armes to Mrs. Charles Lanier, May 24, 1928, Robert E. Lee Memorial Association Archives, Stratford, VA (hereafter cited as RELMA).

3. Walter B. Jones, "General Lee's Home," *The Montgomery Advertiser,* no date. A thorough account of the creation of the Robert E. Lee Memorial Foundation can be found in Charles B. Hosmer, Jr., *Preservation Comes of Age,* vol.1 (Charlottesville: University Press of Virginia, 1993), 190–201.

4. There is no evidence to suggest whether Cramton's efforts or the existence of other Lee memorials influenced Lanier's plans. Karen L. Cox, *Dixie's Daughters: The United Daughters of the Confederacy and the Preservation of Confederate Culture* (Gainesville: University Press of Florida, 2007), 7; United Daughters of the Confederacy (UDC), chapter application, UDC Business Office, Richmond, VA; Murray H. Nelligan, *Old Arlington: The Story of Arlington House, the Robert E. Lee Memorial* (Burke, VA: Chatelaine Press, 2001), 447.

5. Lanier to Armes, November 15, 1928, and Lewis to Armes, November 19, 1928, A2-29, RELMA; "Report of Mrs. Charles D. Lanier," November 28, 1928, A2-2a, RELMA, 1–2.

6. May Field Lanier to Hilton Railey, December 7, 1928, Folder A2-2a/Appendix, RELMA; Hosmer, *Preservation Comes of Age,* 196.

7. Seth C. Bruggeman, *Here, George Washington Was Born* (Athens: University of Georgia Press, 2008), 81; West, *Domesticating History,* 159–61; James M. Lindgren, *Preserving the Old Dominion* (Charlottesville: University Press of Virginia, 1993), 28–29.

8. David W. Blight, *Race and Reunion* (Cambridge: The Belknap Press of Harvard University Press, 2001), 258, 267; Elizabeth Brown Pryor, *Reading the Man* (New York: Viking, 2007), 467–70; Gary W. Gallagher, "Shaping Public Memory of the Civil War," in *The Memory of the Civil War in American Culture,* ed. Alice Fahs and Joan Waugh (Chapel Hill: University of North Carolina Press, 2004), 39–63; Franklin D. Roosevelt to May Field Lanier, August 5,1932, 1932 minute book, RELMA.

9. Hosmer, *Preservation Comes of Age,* 190–201.

10. "Services to Mark Lee Anniversary," unknown newspaper, October 2, 1929; "Big Crowd Here for Stratford," unknown newspaper, October 12, 1929.

11. "National Stratford Day Opens Drive for Funds," unknown newspaper, October 14, 1929; "Many Honor Lee on Stratford Day," unknown newspaper, October 14, 1929.

12. "Many Honor Lee on Stratford Day," unknown newspaper, October 14, 1929; Albert Bushnell Hart, "A Tribute to General Lee," (Greenwich, CT: Robert E. Lee Memorial Foundation, n.d.).

13. "The Lee Memorial," *Cincinnati Enquirer,* date unknown.

14. "Lee's Birthplace," *Richmond Times-Dispatch,* date unknown; "Honor to Honor's True Son: A Shrine to Lee," *Nashville Banner,* October 11, 1929.

15. "'Marse Robert's' Home," *Louisville Courier-Journal,* no date.

16. "A Shrine to General Lee," *The Press*, Escanaba, MI, February 10, 1929.

17. "Connecticut Honors General Lee," *The State*, Columbia, SC, January 22, 1929; Blight, *Race and Reunion*, 267–71; Mary Tyler Freeman Cheek, *A High Calling: Douglas Southall Freeman: Reflections by His Daughter, His Research Associate and a Historian*, ed. Robert A. Armour (Richmond: Friends of the Richmond Public Library, 1986), 8. The memory of the Civil War has been explored in a number of publications. See, for example, Blight, *Race and Reunion;* Fahs and Waugh, *The Memory of the Civil War in American Culture;* Elizabeth Brown Pryor, *Reading the Man: A Portrait of Robert E. Lee Through His Private Letters* (New York: Penguin Group, 2007), 467–70.

18. Ethel Armes, *Stratford-on-the-Potomac* (Greenwich, CT: William Alexander Chapter, United Daughters of the Confederacy, 1928), 9–10.

19. Ibid.; Ethel Armes, *Twelve Reasons Why Stratford Should Become a National Shrine* (Greenwich, CT: National Headquarters, The Robert E. Lee Memorial Foundation, 1929).

20. Ethel Armes to Giles Cooke, June 13, 1930, RELMA.

21. Mary Kane, *A Bibliography of the Works of Fiske Kimball* (Charlottesville: University of Virginia Press, 1959), i.

22. Emerson Newell, Memorandum to Emergency Committee, March 10, 1930; and Report of the Restoration Committee, Minutes of the 2nd Council, October 1930, 1930 minute book, RELMA. Fiske Kimball to Van Deventer, July 15, 1930, RELMA.

23. Report of the Committee on Historical and Architectural Research and Report of the House Furnishings Committee, Minutes of the 2nd Council, 1930 minute book, RELMA.

24. Luke Vincent Lockwood to May Field Lanier, April 29, 1930; Report of House Furnishings Committee, October 1930 Meeting, 1930 minute book; and Report of Grounds Committee, October 1933 Meeting, 1933 minute book, RELMA.

25. "A copy of Mr. Garvan's Statement," Folder B2-3/45; Everett Meeks to Mrs. Emerson Newell, September 3, 1930, Folder B2-3/45; Cazenove Lee to May Field Lanier, August 24, 1931; President's Report, October 13, 1931, 1931 minute book; and Minutes of Emergency Committee, May 14, 1932, 1932 minute book, RELMA.

26. Minutes of Emergency Committee, May 14, 1932, 1932 minute book; Kimball to Restoration Committee, May 13, 1933, 1933 minute book; Fiske Kimball, "Stratford: Yesterday, Today and Tomorrow," October 1932 Meeting Minutes, 1932 minute book, RELMA.

27. Claiborne to Fiske Kimball, November 25, 1935, Folder B2-6a/70; and Kimball to Van Deventer, May 18, 1935, Folder B2-6A/70, RELMA; Mark Wenger, *Historic Structures Report for Stratford Hall* (Albany, NY: Mesick, Cohen, Baker Architects, 2011), 59.

28. Joint Meeting of the Emergency and Finance Committees, May 8, 1933, 1933 minute book; Kimball to House Restoration Committee, August 14, 1933, Folder B3-2a; Lanier to Kimball, November 20, 1933, Folder B3-2a; Minutes of the Emergency Committee Meeting, May 8, 1934, 1934 minute book; Lanier to Kimball, May 16, 1934, Folder B2-6a; Minutes of the Emergency Committee, April 2, 1935, 1935 minute book; Kimball to Lanier, April 15, 1935, Folder B2-6a; Minutes of the 8th Council, October 1936, 1936 minute book; and Minutes of the 9th Council, October 1937, 1937 minute book, RELMA.

29. Armes to Newell, January 6, 1938, Folder B2-6a/81; Kimball to Van Deventer, March 2, 1938, Folder B2-6a/74; and Minutes of the 9th Council, October 1937, 1937 minute book, RELMA.

30. Cummin to Lanier, September 26, 1941; Kimball to Bingham, September 14, 1945; Bingham to Kimball, June 1, 1945; Bingham to Kimball, May 9, 1947; Bingham to Kimball, no date; and Joseph Downs to Kimball, March 14, 1946, RELMA.

31. Cheek to Hollister, July 22, 1974; Mary Tyler Cheek, "Minutes of the Special Committee to Consider the Foulke Gift," June 18 and 19, 1974, Folder A2-2l/301; Mary Tyler Cheek, notes on conversation with John Sweeney, June 18, 1974; "John Sweeney's List for use in Places Other than the Great House," Folder A2-2l/301; and "The Foulke Collection at Stratford Hall," no date, RELMA.

32. Robert E. Lee Memorial Association Minutes, April 25–29, 1976, RELMA, 6.

The Joseph Smith birthplace monument, 357 LDS Lane, South Royalton, Vermont, as it appeared ca. 1905. Photo courtesy of the Royalton Historical Society.

~ 6 ~

Historian Keith Erekson rounds out our encounter with the early days of American birth commemoration by challenging us to rethink how we've come to understand "sacred" pasts. Americans have grown accustomed to thinking of war monuments, for example, in terms of civic religion and sacred space. Similarly, birthplace monuments, by their very nature, suggest a messianic impulse. But as Erekson demonstrates in his consideration of Joseph Smith's birthplace monument, generalizing too broadly about the sacred qualities of secular memory may prevent us from appreciating the mnemonic significance of real sacred places. Such is the case of Smith's towering monument in central Vermont. By interrogating the motivations of its builders and the anxieties of its neighbors, Erekson provides a new perspective on the debates about origins and citizenship that explain, in part, the proliferation of birthplace monuments during the early twentieth century. At the same time, he shows us how secular commemorative strategies played an important role in modernizing the Mormon Church and expanding its reach. Considered in light of Mormonism's prominent role in recent presidential politics, the story of Smith's birthplace reminds us too of the remarkable power of America's log cabin mythology to cut across all lines of cultural difference.

Memories, Monuments, and Mormonism

The Birthplace of Joseph Smith in Vermont

KEITH A. EREKSON

A large stone on the side of a hill near South Royalton, Vermont, bears a plaque with these words: "Around this hearthstone and its glowing fireplace, two days before Christmas 1805, the Smith family washed,

dressed and cuddled the future organizer of 'God's Kingdom Restored.'"
The baby referenced in the inscription grew to be Joseph Smith who, in
his thirty-eight-year life, published the *Book of Mormon*, established The
Church of Jesus Christ of Latter-day Saints, founded the city of Nauvoo
on the Mississippi River in northern Illinois, commanded the Nauvoo
militia, and aspired to the presidency of the United States. He was a
memorable man—tall, handsome, and charismatic—and his life story
as a prophet of God drew thousands of converts to the fold before his
assassination in 1844 seared his place in American history and in the
memory of the faithful.[1]

The memorial stone and its plaque, placed in 1963, sit about eight
feet below the actual location of the original hearthstone. Left behind
by the Smiths just three years after Joseph's birth, the hearthstone survived pillaging neighbors who repurposed the walls of the wood-frame
house to build their own homes and barns. By 1905 the hearthstone,
along with the crumbling cellar wall, was all that remained of the
Smiths' frontier home, but it was enough to provide a foundation for
more than a century of commemoration. On the centennial of Smith's
birth, the Church he organized dedicated a fifty-foot granite monument
and a new "Memorial Cottage" that incorporated the old hearthstone
into its new decorative fireplace. Half a century later, when the cottage
had become too small for the growing number of tourists, the hearthstone again survived the "extensive terracing" by dynamite intended to
emphasize the granite monument. As a result, the original hearthstone
was moved approximately thirty yards down an engineered hill from
the memorial stone where it remained for many years in a museum,
preserved in front of an elaborate faux mantle and flanked by velvet seat
cushions.[2]

Dynamite and velvet underscore the fact that memories of the past
can be both obliterated and romanticized with the passage of time.
Even those artifacts that remain—a two-hundred-year-old hearthstone,
for example—can be dramatically re-imagined within new interpretive contexts. Over the course of a century, Joseph Smith's birthplace
became a site of religious expression as memories of prophecy and
preaching coalesced into monumental reality. Ironically, at this site
that celebrates the birth of a child on the frontier in the early Republic,
the plaque on the rock makes the only reference to the experience of

motherhood and childbirth. Furthermore, the site became an impetus to additional monument-building and an administrative opportunity for managerial experimentation that cast the site variously as a resort for missionaries, a proselytizing center, a profit-producing dairy farm, a center for congregation-building, and a tourist destination.

The history of Smith's birthplace is also significant for its mingling of historic and religious interpretation. Scholarship on historic sites focuses extensively on so-called secular places related to nation-building or local history. When it is invoked by historians, religion tends to be employed either as a descriptor for Native American sites or as a metaphor—as "civil religion"—for illustrating how old-fashioned religious sentiment has been repurposed in a secular modern world.[3] From the perspective of religious studies, sacred sites are most commonly viewed from an anthropological standpoint that examines the division of sacred space from the profane or the role of pilgrimage in personal devotion or community formation. Occasionally writers have reached across the disciplinary divide to cherry-pick from the work of Maurice Halbwachs, though often without systematically examining the entwined relationship of history, religion, and memory.[4] At the birthplace of Joseph Smith, however, a century of commemoration efforts reveals new forms of sacralization distinct from the sacred history celebrated at the site. And, in an interesting inversion, the commemoration of a sacred site became part of an effort to emphasize the Americanness of Mormonism, a project that has grown increasingly visible in recent years owing to the presidential aspirations of prominent Mormons. And instead of simply demarcating the sacred from the profane, the site has invariably fallen into "profane" contests over religious and regional politics, prompting experimentation with a variety of commemorative and religious practices. Joseph Smith's birthplace mingles religion, history, and memory in a space designed for public visitation.

Memories into Monuments

Joseph Smith loomed large in the memory of nineteenth-century Mormons both as a prophet and as a Vermont schoolboy. Over the course of his lifetime, thousands had met him, listened to him speak, and believed him to be a prophet like the Old Testament figures Moses or Elijah. John M. Chidester remembered that "my impression on behold-ing the Prophet and shaking hands with him was that I stood face to face with the greatest man on earth." Angus M. Cannon recounted how "I never heard [Joseph Smith] speak when it did not electrify my whole soul." Luke S. Johnson recalled that Smith healed his mother. Newell Knight, Levi Hancock, and Zebedee Coltrin all bore witness that Smith cast "devils" and "evil spirits" out of them.[5] Mormons also remembered Smith as a poor boy raised in Vermont. Smith customarily began his life sketches with emphasis on the "indigent circumstances" of his childhood that "deprived [him] of the bennifit [sic] of an education."[6] After his death, Smith's lack of scholarly credentials served as circum-stantial evidence for the truthfulness of his message in general and the Book of Mormon in particular—"No Vermont schoolboy wrote this," summarized a century of Mormon testimony.[7]

As the nineteenth century drew to a close, Mormons—by now num-bering in the thousands—found themselves with greater opportunities to commemorate the past. Having been expelled by neighbors in both Missouri and Illinois in the 1830s and 1840s, invaded by the U.S. Army in the 1850s, and targeted by federal anti-polygamy laws throughout the 1870s and 1880s, Mormons were relieved that the admission of Utah to statehood in 1896 brought a period of relative peace.[8] But peace in the intermountain West coincided with the deaths of persons who had known Smith in life. In 1894, on the 89th anniversary of Smith's birth, a gathering in Salt Lake City produced fewer than two dozen people who had known or seen the Prophet. At the gathering, Smith's nephew Joseph F. Smith who, like most living Mormons, had grown up in the West, called for wider celebration of his uncle's birth, and the next few years saw community fasts and musical programs. In 1901, Joseph F. Smith became president of the Church and directed local congrega-tions to hold commemorative services on the Sunday nearest Joseph Smith's birth each December. In 1903, the Church purchased the site of Joseph Smith's 1844 assassination—a jail in Carthage, Illinois— and the following year began work on a statue of Smith that would be erected in Salt Lake City in 1911.[9]

Within this context of increased commemorative interest, the pro-posal to commemorate Smith at his birthplace in Vermont came to

Church leaders from outside ecclesiastical lines. In 1894, Utah-born Mormon Junius F. Wells visited the site of Smith's birth while on a business trip to New England. A dabbler in mining, politics, and publishing, Wells founded an organization for young men and edited a youth magazine in which he described the abandoned condition of the site and hoped for a day when something might be done to improve it. After another trip to Boston in the spring of 1905, Wells offered his proposal to Joseph F. Smith and was authorized to identify the site and purchase it. Wells returned to Vermont where he traced land titles to identify the present location of the tract owned by the Smith family and then solicited oral testimony from longtime residents who pointed to a crumbling cellar hole as the only remains of the home in which Smith had been born. Wells returned to Salt Lake City in May with the title to the property and submitted a design proposal to erect a monument and memorial in time to celebrate the centennial of Joseph Smith's birth in December.[10] Possibly because of the opportunity, probably because of the novelty, and certainly because of the expense, leaders of the still debt-stricken Church deliberated over Wells's proposal for three weeks. The details of their discussion are not available, but in the end of June they gave Wells the green light and carte blanche to carry out his proposal.

Wells envisioned a towering monument and a modern visitor's cottage to mark the site of Joseph Smith's birth. The three-story cottage was built on the site of the old cellar hole and incorporated the Smith family's hearthstone and doorstep into its larger footprint, complete with furnace and running water upstairs. The monument was set about thirty yards from the cottage on a slight rise in the landscape. Unfortunately, Wells left no written description of his design process, though analysis of the design and inscriptions on the monument indicates that he created a composite of nineteenth-century memories of Joseph Smith. The dominant element of the polished Vermont granite monument is a thirty-eight-and-one-half-foot-tall obelisk—one foot for each year of Smith's life. In the world of turn-of-the-century monument making, obelisks had become passé because Civil War commemorators preferred equestrian generals, standing soldiers, or kneeling slaves. In the American national context, however, obelisks were linked strongly with the Revolutionary War, the Bunker Hill monument in Boston and the Washington Monument in the nation's capital being the most renowned examples.[11] Confederate veterans and their daughters erected a massive obelisk near the Jefferson Davis birthplace in Fairview, Kentucky, for instance, to draw explicit parallels between the president of the Confederacy and the first president of the United States.

Whether or not Wells intended his obelisk to convey similar meanings, it appears that he at least appreciated the obelisk's simplicity. It rests on a series of rectangular bases that give the entire monument its approximately fifty-foot height. Two sides of the base bear inscriptions penned by Wells; one cites the dates of Smith's birth and death and the other, titled "Testimony of Joseph Smith," lists Smith's religious accomplishments, including visions, angelic visitations, translation of sacred scripture, and organization of the Church. This latter inscription concludes by mentioning that "over a million converts to this testimony have been made throughout the world" who "love and revere him as a Prophet of God." The inscriptions emphasize Smith's prophetic role, while the memory of the Vermont schoolboy is emphasized by the monument's placement at his birthplace and by its Vermont granite.

Since historic sites of all kinds are so commonly referred to as "sacred," it's worth pointing out that Smith's monument really is. Historians have shown how words like "sacred" account metaphorically for devotions paid to secular activities. Battlefields are made "sacred," for example, by the deaths of soldiers. In contrast, the birthplace of Joseph Smith actually commemorates the life of a religious leader whose teachings were accepted as sacred by his followers.[12] There is an important difference, however, between Smith's birthplace and any number of holy sites throughout the world where pilgrims travel in search of miracles and to commune with the divine.[13] The Church of Jesus Christ of Latter-day Saints has never promoted the birthplace as a place of healing or miracle work. Nor does making a pilgrimage there hold the same theological significance for Mormons as does, say, making a pilgrimage to Mecca for Muslims. Indeed, Mormons don't go to Smith's birthplace to encounter the divine; they go to demonstrate that they have already found it. Though the Church certainly values the birthplace's sacred associations with its faith's founder, the monument also bears witness to the *miracle* of Smith's followers having overcome persecution to secure an enduring place in the community, which is evidenced in their ability to be tourists and to visit the site. In the end, both the details of Smith's life and the testimony of his followers sanctify the birthplace.[14]

In hindsight, it appears that Wells's mingling of Smith's memory with the visual iconography of early century secular commemoration made the sacred past more readily available to modern Americans. Its inscribed "Testimony" universalized Smith's legacy by grounding it in the expressions of the faithful who would come, even in the future, to demonstrate their faith. Even those visitors who might not believe Smith was a prophet would be viewed by Wells as the fulfillment of a promise Smith received from an angel that his "name should be had for good and evil among all nations." To the unbeliever, Wells reasoned, "you of the world, unbelievers in 'Mormonism,' have been speaking the name of Joseph Smith for evil; we Latter-day Saints have built this monument and this memorial to show our love, our admiration and our testimony . . . So, between you and us we have fulfilled the words of the angel of God, and proved Joseph Smith . . . a prophet of God."[15]

In July, Wells returned to Vermont to oversee the monument's six-month construction process, an amazing engineering feat carried out against all odds by quarrying granite blocks, transporting them by rail and horse power, shoring up sagging bridges, crossing frozen mud holes, and beating winter storms.[16] The formal dedication occurred on December 23, and was presided over by LDS Church president Joseph F. Smith. In his dedicatory prayer, the nephew of Joseph Smith referenced the ground as a symbol of the church's foundation of prophets and apostles, the base as the rock of revelation that made Joseph Smith a prophet, the obelisk "as a token of the inspired man of God whom Thou didst make indeed a polished shaft in Thine hand, reflecting the light of heaven, even Thy glorious light, unto the children of men," and the entire monument as "signifying the finished work of human redemption." Speakers on the occasion emphasized the kindness of local Vermonters, the Church's connection to the Green Mountain State, and Mormon American patriotism. Musical selections included "The Star-Spangled Banner" and "We Thank Thee, o God, for a Prophet."[17]

Thus, influential mist-like memories of Joseph Smith were symbolically translated into the Joseph Smith Birthplace Memorial Monument in December 1905. Memories that had circulated for decades were emphasized by specific individuals in the context of early twentieth-century concerns. Joseph Smith the uneducated schoolboy was not forgotten, but his ties to the Green Mountain State and its virtues were emphasized. A monument to a religious leader found a home within New England's regional heritage. The commemoration did not directly point toward national icons but instead used the language of patriotism to connect a prophet's birth with the figurative birthplace of Yankee America, a sentiment that some years later would help create an image of Joseph Smith as an "American Prophet." Though not the first monument proposed to Joseph Smith, the Joseph Smith Memorial Monument in Vermont became the first monument completed, making it the first monument erected by the LDS Church in what would become a century of commemoration and celebration of Mormon heritage. But individuals also found their own meaning in the monument. Wells saw it as an expression of testimony of contemporary Latter-day Saints. Joseph F. Smith dedicated it as a witness of the work of human redemption. And Vermonters of all stripes debated its meaning for another two decades.

More Memories, More Monuments, and the "Mormon Affair"

Sacred though Smith's birthplace may have been, the Joseph Smith Memorial Monument ended up in its share of "profane" contests over religious and local politics. Ed Linenthal and David Chidester have emphasized the crucial role of contestation in defining and defending American sacred sites. They root these contests in the question of ownership, both of physical space and of the meanings attached to it. At the birthplace of Joseph Smith, the latter category drew the most attention as various believers in Joseph Smith debated the particularities of his legacy and as Vermonters debated among themselves how best to integrate the site into their own community and history.[18]

As Latter-day Saints translated their memories of Joseph Smith into monumental form, they also provoked questions of polygamy and patriotism from religious competitors, anxious Americans, and neighboring Vermonters. The range of public reactions to the monument reminds us that memories, though intangible and mist-like, are real and highly influential. In late June 1905, after an unsigned Associated

Press article falsely claimed that the proposed monument had outraged local Vermonters, the leaders of the Reorganized Church of Jesus Christ of Latter Day Saints (RLDS, now Community of Christ) publicly announced their opposition to LDS commemoration.[19] For the over half century since Joseph Smith's death, the LDS and RLDS Churches had vied for ownership of the institutional legacy of Smith's Church, contesting each other's claims in the courts and while proselytizing. The RLDS "Open Letter to All People" essentially restated differences between the two Churches: the Mormons of Utah, they argued, followed Brigham Young and thereby had rejected Joseph Smith; Joseph Smith never practiced polygamy; and the LDS were un-American, a charge then under congressional investigation after Utah had elected the first Mormon to the U.S. Senate. The letter closed with a "protest against the further stigmatization of Joseph Smith's name by the present Mormon authorities through their malfeasance and the erection of mocking monuments."[20] RLDS leaders continued their protest by sending lecturers to Salt Lake City and a representative to the monument's dedication who was largely ignored.

The letter and the debate among rival Mormon groups over the legacy of Joseph Smith both captured national attention. Articles in *The Nation,* the *New York Times,* and the *Burlington* (Vermont) *Free Press* entered the fray, while a piece in New England's *Interstate Journal* characterized Mormonism as "a species of deep-sea octopus, with ever-reaching tentacles, seeking whom it may devour." In Vermont, Congregational circuit speakers found increasing success in their anti-Mormon lectures, especially those speakers who could share firsthand accounts of purportedly abject conditions in Utah.[21]

For their part, Vermonters split three ways on the propriety of the monument. On one hand, a large number stood to benefit, at least a little, from the $15,000 construction project. On the other hand, many Vermonters expressed shame that their state had produced Smith and several of the Church's prominent leaders, a shame that prompted Vermont congressmen of the nineteenth century to sponsor tough anti-polygamy legislation. Both reactions found expression in Royalton Township, the political jurisdiction that contained the Mormon property and all of the transportation routes to it. During the first week of December, Congregationalist Reverend Levi Wild of Royalton village wrote to the editor of the local paper on behalf of those "who regard with deep concern the present Mormon invasion of our community." He introduced a letter prepared by the Woman's Home Missionary Union of Vermont that argued that Smith was deplorable, the LDS hierarchy sought power, and the monument would provide a foothold in Vermont for missionary work. "This imposing monument marks the grave of the virtue of women and the sanctity of monogamy," they wrote, contrasting the geographical site of Smith's birth with the death of their definition of virtue and familial structure. Two days later, a lawyer from South Royalton village challenged the protest by arguing that "Mormons have the same right to worship God that we claim for ourselves." His letter was seconded by the forty-three other local citizens who signed a petition welcoming Mormons to the community for the monument's dedication.[22]

A third reaction to the monument called attention to Vermont's neglected past. Residents of Royalton township needed little persuasion to celebrate their township's heritage—they had hosted celebrations throughout the nineteenth century—but the arrival of the Mormon monument and the claims it made on their past changed the contours of their endeavor. The Mormon monument arrived at what was described by a local historian as "a critical time in [the township's] history."[23] Settled before the Revolutionary War, Royalton had been an important village in the early 1800s and featured the renowned Royalton Academy for teachers. The opening of the Vermont Central Railroad in 1848 prompted settlement in South Royalton, and in March 1905 township residents elected a South Royalton majority of public office holders for the first time in the township's history. In the midst of this fractious and wavering village rivalry, the monument foregrounded history in the township's cultural contest, and galvanized residents along village lines in what became a decade-long race to celebrate Royalton's past. While other Progressive Era towns debated dance halls, theater performances, public zoos, or science exhibits, the Mormon monument turned Royalton's past into present politics, giving the upstart "village of trade" new grounds on which to challenge the fading "village of culture."[24]

The result was a public contest of monuments with a gendered subtext. Levi Wild's uncle fired the first volley by giving the Royalton Woman's Club $1,000 toward the creation of a monument in Royalton

village. Club members quickly decided to commemorate the white survivors of a 1780 Indian Raid that antedated the Smith family's presence in the community and made Royalton unique among Vermont
towns and worthy of a tributary visit by Lafayette in 1825. The decision
combined the veneration of hardy pioneer ancestors with Vermont's
tradition of individualism and frontier democracy, all part of what made
Royalton inheritor of "New England's true heritage."[25] On October 16,
1905, on the one hundred twenty-fifth anniversary of the raid (and while
Wells was still only transporting the pieces of the Mormon monument
to the site), Royalton's selectmen officially granted the right to erect a
monument. That afternoon the Woman's Club hosted a groundbreak-
ing ceremony that included a recitation of the raid story to the children.[26] The women also obtained a $500 gift from the township to com-
mission a local history and invited former Royalton resident Evelyn M.
Lovejoy back from teaching in the Midwest to research and write it.

Lovejoy had lived in Royalton village in the 1880s, but after her husband died she went west where she eventually taught school, graduated
from the University of Chicago, and wrote a novel. When she returned
to the township, she settled in South Royalton, taught at the new public
school, and worked on the town history over the next five summers
before producing her *History of Royalton, Vermont,* a one thousand-page
volume with over one hundred illustrations, maps, genealogical records,
and a comprehensive index. Her research made Lovejoy one of the foremost experts on Vermont's early history, the leading expert on the township's past, and a vital asset in the new village's push for cultural promi-
nence. The year after she arrived in the village, South Royalton women
organized their own woman's club and they elected Lovejoy president as
her book rolled off the press.

Donating the proceeds from her book, Lovejoy initiated a subscrip-
tion drive to erect a monument in South Royalton village. Rather than
celebrating the raid survivors generally, South Royalton's monument
emphasized two people: Hannah Handy, a mother who pleaded for the
freedom of herself and nine children, and Phineas Parkhurst, "Vermont's
Paul Revere," who rode off on horseback to Sharon to sound the alarm.[27]
Though both monuments drew their inspiration from the same event,
the celebrated messages could not have been more divergent: Royalton
idealized an innocent community savagely attacked by the outside world,

while South Royalton recognized individuals who reached out to others in a time of distress. Whereas the LDS Church had been silent on the role of Smith's mother, Lucy Mack Smith, in giving birth to their prophet, the women of the township's two villages articulated two distinct visions of New England motherhood: in one, virtuous mothers were attacked in their domestic sphere; in the other, a mother sacrificed her life to save the community's children. Clearly, "motherhood" is not a static category or a singular construction, but is adaptable to the needs of commemorators. The South Royalton monument was dedicated not on the raid's anniversary in October, but in August 1915 at what would become an annual "Old Home Week" celebration.

As South Royalton's cultural status surged, the final confrontation came over plans for a new memorial library. Royalton's public library had begun in 1896 and, though overseen by elected trustees and funded with township money, it had yet to find a permanent home. In 1912 Lovejoy became the first woman elected to public office in the township, and she stepped into her position as a library trustee with vigor. In 1917, Reverend Levi Wild resigned from the board and was replaced by Charles Tarbell, the same lawyer who had responded to Wild's letter protesting the Mormon monument over a decade before. At the same time, a bequest to the library that had been held up in court for sixteen years became available, and so the South Royalton–dominated board purchased property in South Royalton for a new "memorial" library that would be funded by subscriptions from donors who could memorialize their ancestors on a special tablet.[28] As work progressed on the library, Lovejoy canvassed the countryside and obtained a contribution of $200 from Heber C. Smith, the adopted son of LDS Church president Joseph F. Smith and caretaker of the Joseph Smith birthplace monument. Unsurprisingly, Heber Smith asked that Joseph Smith be listed on the library's tablet.

Reverend Wild penned a note to Lovejoy on July 22, 1922. "I am told that it is proposed to memorialize the name of Joseph Smith in connection with our Library building," he began formally. "If this is the case I hereby enter my earnest protest against doing so. If it is done the name of my father, John Wild, must be left out." Soon others in Royalton threatened to withdraw past donations and more promised never to donate. The details of this explosive response were not recorded, though

Lovejoy hashed out the major issues a few months later in correspondence with Royalton resident Gertrude Laird, wife of the person Lovejoy replaced on the Library board and member of Royalton Woman's Club and Congregational Church. The letters indicate that the debate covered a range of doctrinal, historical, and contemporary concerns, including polygamy and the *Book of Mormon,* the character of the Smith family, and the presence of Mormons in their contemporary community. Laird couched her criticisms in generalized hearsay. According to her, Mormons out west had hundreds of wives and the Smith family was disreputable. Lovejoy responded from personal experience. The Mormons in town, she argued, were respectable people and she had seen "all the early records of Sharon, Tunbridge, and Royalton, and never found anything derogatory to this family."[29] Her back against the wall, Lovejoy asked Heber Smith to withdraw his contribution, and he graciously concurred. The next month, Royalton resident Clara Denison McClellan offered $200 only on condition of receiving a written statement from Lovejoy that neither she nor the library would ever accept Mormon money again. As Royalton residents saw that their mounting pressures only hurt Lovejoy's feelings, they backed down from their demands. The library was dedicated in 1923 and the memorial tablet—still hanging in the library today—never memorialized Joseph Smith. In time, however, the names of Clara Denison McClellan and Evelyn Lovejoy were added.

By paring away the personal and religious issues of the "Mormon Affair," as Lovejoy called it, she identified the motivating concern of Royalton residents: their fears about commemoration and the Mormon presence were intertwined with their anxiety over South Royalton's increasing influence. The Mormon monument served to root the LDS Church's community narrative in Royalton soil in the very moment in which the township's internal balance of economic, political, and cultural power was in flux. The commemoration of Joseph Smith's birth by outsiders forced local residents to craft their own origin story, but they had to agree on one first. Lovejoy conceded the battle of the Memorial Library to Royalton in an act that marked the older village's last effectual stand. In short order, the Royalton Woman's Club disbanded, Royalton Academy closed its doors, Gertrude Laird and Levi Wild passed away, and the Denison house was sold at auction. The

Flood of 1927 that devastated so many Vermont communities swept through the older village, taking an entire street with it and leaving Royalton "just a string of houses" along the roadside—a physical loss paralleling the symbolic loss of influence in township life.[30] Royalton's vision of an isolated community lost out to South Royalton's narrative of contact and connection with modernizing America's wider society. Not unlike Hannah Handy, South Royalton residents offered up the older village to ensure the peaceful perpetuation of the younger.

Experiments in Historic Site Management

While Vermonters struggled to fit Joseph Smith's birthplace into their local history, Mormons experimented with the uses of historic property in an ecclesiastical setting. In the first public announcement of the monument and centennial commemoration, Junius Wells announced that the property would be "converted into a beautiful summer resort" that would "afford a pleasant resting place for a day or two to missionaries enroute to and from their foreign mission fields."[31] References to the site's natural resources, local interest, and proximity to travel routes all mark this as an announcement for a turn-of-the-century railroad resort. During the second half of the nineteenth century, iron rails linked America's coasts, spawned cities, and standardized time. Anxious to encourage Americans to ride the rails, industry leaders promoted and developed resort destinations. The Northern Pacific carried people to Yellowstone, the Santa Fe to the Grand Canyon, and the Lackawanna and New York Central to Niagara Falls. In Vermont, local politicians and civic boosters initiated an effective promotional campaign that emphasized the virtues of the Green Mountain State and its maple-producing trees. In 1893, LDS Church leaders had invested in the Saltair Resort on the shores of the Great Salt Lake, spending over half a million dollars to acquire lakeside property, construct a large entertainment pavilion, and subsidize a sixteen-mile railroad spur that carried visitors to the resort where they could float in nature's salt bath.[32] In Vermont the project seemed much simpler. The Vermont Central line passed within sight of the property, and missionaries already caught ships to Europe out of Boston and New York City.

If LDS Church leaders initially cast the Joseph Smith Birthplace as a missionary resort, the two-and-a-half dozen of them who attended the monument's December 1905 dedication saw the potential of developing the site for all Church members as well. Of course, it would require over six decades—and the assistance of postwar industrial expansion, the democratization of automobile ownership, the Highway Act, and the invention of middle-class leisure time—before large numbers of Latter-day pilgrims could visit the site. Nevertheless, Wells began to develop the entire site, but particularly the Memorial Cottage, as a "historical repository for the entertainment of representative men of the Church."[33] Over the next two years, the Church made three additional property purchases that increased the size of the resort to 283 acres that were cultivated with hundreds of flowers, a lily pond, and fountains.[34] Inside the Cottage, Wells stocked a small library with doctrinal and historical books, and on the walls he hung paintings, engravings, and photographs of Joseph Smith's family, prominent Mormons, U.S. Presidents, and the monument's construction. The Cottage was built with the Smith family's hearthstone—left in its original position—as its focal point. Wells believed that "Joseph Smith was only three years old when his parents moved; so if he had any association with that hearthstone, it was as a child . . . perhaps it was where he was washed and dressed as a babe." Wells encouraged visitors (including President Smith on dedication day) to sit on the hearthstone and gaze reflectively out the window.[35]

To those looking back from the twenty-first century, the destruction of the ruins of the Smith family home in order to construct a hotel mocks our modern historical sensibilities. Our reactions are largely shaped by the fact that American preservation in the twentieth century followed a path of professionalization from the restoration of Colonial Williamsburg to the National Historic Preservation Act of 1966 that has emphasized authenticity, originality, and architectural aesthetics—unlike, for example, the Englishman John Ruskin's desire to allow buildings to decay naturally or the Frenchman Viollet-le-Duc's efforts to create out of ruins "a completed state which may never have existed at any particular time."[36]

Wells's decision struck a chord with contemporaries who were not yet influenced by the modern authenticity ethos. Susa Young Gates concluded that "sentiment is the source of all the beauty and harmony in the world. And the most delicate, artistic, and vibrating of life's unities prompted Junius F. Wells to choose [the hearthstone as] the one thing of all others most fit to form the keynote of the whole harmonic structure." Other features of the resort-repository connected visitors not with ossified relics but with the "vibrating unities of life." Weary travelers could dip their bucket in the same well that served the Smith family, or imbibe "cider, made from Grandfather Mack's own apple trees." Beginning in 1906, visitors blended the ecclesiastical with the ecological by planting trees in "Apostle's Grove" or on "Missionary Hill." One row on this hill was designated for "faithful missionaries who were true in life & death & have gone to labor with Joseph Smith & his associates in the Spirit World."[37] Thus, for Wells's generation, the past was not a "foreign country," incomprehensible to the present; rather the present flowed out of the past as smoothly and naturally as cider from ancestral apples. In contrast to "authentic" living history sites at which a costumed pioneer must "interpret" an obscure farm implement for a sunscreen-slathered audience, this type of "living history"—water, cider, and trees—needed less instruction than experience as it united member and missionary, past and present, living and dead through symbolic and literal integration in the ecological and temporal flow of time at the site.

Between 1911 and 1919, while the monument, cottage, lily pond, and groves remained, the outlying property at the birthplace changed dramatically. Church leaders appointed Frank L. Brown to manage the site *and* to experiment with a profit-producing dairy farm—with workers not to dress up as historical farmers, but to generate income as modern ones. Soon barns, a granary, two silos, and livestock appeared, and by 1918 the site had covered its expenses and the Prophet's birthplace had generated a small profit.[38] Missionaries still stopped en route to foreign lands, but they now began to perform farm work—which was often more relaxing than passing out tracts all day. Brown and his wife and child also made a subtle, but perhaps the most significant, change in administrative policy by taking up year-round residence in New England. In 1911, they held the first commemorative ceremony on Joseph Smith's birthday since the monument had been dedicated in 1905. When Brown died of influenza, former Utah state dairy and food commissioner Heber C. Smith was assigned to bring "modern business methods" to the farm. He alternated four- or five-year managerial stints with Angus J. Cannon, who raised a herd of cattle that always claimed ribbons at the local fair. The site remained a memorial and dairy farm until it fell into disrepair by the mid-1950s.[39]

The generation of LDS administrators tasked with fixing up the old farm and monument found themselves in an entirely different context from 1905 when the site was created. Widespread opposition to the Church and its message had largely subsided, the local rivalry in Royalton had been settled in favor of welcoming outsiders who minded their own business, and the prosperity of the postwar years prompted tourism and family vacations. Though the preservation movement was gaining steam on the successes of Colonial Williamsburg in Virginia and Greenfield Village in Michigan, the LDS embrace of that vision of authenticity in places like Nauvoo and upstate New York was still a couple of decades off. So Church leaders approved a $300,000 renovation that made the monument the new "focal point of the grounds" by razing the Cottage, removing surrounding terrain with dynamite to elevate the monument, adding a reflective pool, and separating the museum from the caretaker's resident into two colonial-style buildings of Vermont slatestone.[40]

The terracing obliterated all of the ground that could have been walked on by the Smith family and the new buildings broadened the Vermont site into a New England landscape. The changes also formalized the site's religious functions. As early as 1909, the lily pond had doubled as a baptismal font. The congregation of Mormon converts established in South Royalton in the 1940s outgrew its rented hall within a decade, so local Church leaders built a chapel on the property where crops had once been sown. In the 1990s, a large tract of old cattle pasture became a recreational camp space known as "Camp Joseph." The trees first planted in the early twentieth century are now decorated with lights at Christmastime in a combined celebration of Joseph Smith's birth and the birth of Jesus Christ, though the live Nativity Scene has never been paired with a live reenactment of Smith's birth on the cold Vermont frontier. Visitors to this new memorial are now greeted by full-time missionaries who explain Church history and doctrine using paintings, photographs, dioramas, and video kiosks.[41] The tour's script continues to present Joseph Smith as an American Prophet, while also emphasizing his ties to Vermont and New England.

In the 1970s South Royalton placed its monuments and memorial library on the National Register of Historic Places but the absence of physical remains precluded that option for Smith's birthplace. By the 1980s, the overwhelming majority of the estimated 40,000 annual visitors to the Joseph Smith Birthplace Memorial were faithful followers of their founding prophet. On the bicentennial of Smith's birth in 2005, the president of the LDS Church spoke live via satellite from Smith's birthplace and emphasized both Smith's role as a prophet and his place in American history—a message similar in spirit to the documentary produced by Vermont's public television station that same year, *American Prophet: The Story of Joseph Smith,* and narrated by Gregory Peck.

The Sacred, Beyond Metaphor

The story of the century-long commemorative activities of a church at the birthplace of its founder opens new avenues for considering the development of historic preservation and site interpretation in the American context. At Joseph Smith's birthplace, the concepts of sacred space and pilgrimage serve as more than just useful metaphors for understanding secularized experience. Their orientation away from the good deeds of the past toward the faithfulness of modern visitors stands in contrast to both common historical and anthropological models. The long-term histories of contestation over meanings and experimentation with practice illustrate the way that history and memory shape religious expression and that religion shapes memories and historical narratives about religious rivalry, community history, and Americanness.[42] The site's early emphasis on the "vibrating unities of life" demonstrates that the development of historic preservation in the United States has not been entirely dominated by mimetic authenticity.

Over the course of a century, memories of Joseph Smith held by faithful Mormons, wary Vermonters, and interested Americans coalesced into monumental form, prompted debate and competition, and served as the building blocks for commemorative experimentation with granite and cattle, dynamite and velvet. Just as a crumbled cellar wall was replaced subsequently by a monument, cottage, farm, and tourist destination, so too did the meanings associated with the site change over time. Members of the LDS Church interpreted the site of their founder's birth as the symbolic birthplace of their religion, and only a single brief reference now connects the site with a mother's work of childbirth in the early republic. Yet, in the early twentieth-century debate between residents of Royalton township, the place of birth became a vehicle for expressing norms about virtuous womanhood and motherhood as well as for articulating the community's position toward outsiders. An old hearthstone—saved, emphasized, moved, and reimagined—provided the foundation for a century of commemoration and consternation, community reinvention and church expansion.

NOTES

1. Richard Lyman Bushman, *Joseph Smith: Rough Stone Rolling* (New York: Alfred A. Knopf, 2005).

2. In 2005, the velvet cushions were removed and the hearthstone was placed in a setting more representative of architecture of the period.

3. Klara B. Kelley and Harris Francis, *Navajo Sacred Places* (Bloomington: Indiana University Press, 1994); Andrew Gulliford, *Sacred Objects and Sacred Places: Preserving Tribal Traditions* (Boulder: University Press of Colorado, 2000); Robert N. Bellah, "Civil Religion in America," *Dædalus, Journal of the American Academy of Arts and Sciences* 96, no. 1 (Winter 1967): 1–21; Edward T. Linenthal, *Sacred Ground: Americans and Their Battlefields* (Urbana: University of Illinois Press, 1993); Kenneth Stanley Inglis, *Sacred Places: War Memorials in the Australian Landscape* (Carlton, Vic.: Melbourne University Press, 2005).

4. Maurice Halbwachs, *On Collective Memory* (Chicago: University of Chicago Press, 1992); for a review of this literature and a critique of its reliance on Halbwachs, see Oren Baruch Stier and J. Shawn Landres, eds., *Religion, Violence, Memory, and Place* (Bloomington: Indiana University Press, 2006), 1–15.

5. Hyrum L. Andrus, *They Knew the Prophet* (Salt Lake City: Deseret Book Company, 1999), 12–13, 19–24, 30, 33; Angus M. Cannon in "Recollections of the Prophet," December 23, 1894, *Collected Discourses*, ed. Brian H. Stuy, 5 vols. (Burbank, CA, and Woodland Hills, UT: B. H. S. Publishing, 1987–1992) 5:33.

6. Dean C. Jessee, *The Papers of Joseph Smith*, 2 vols. (Salt Lake City: Deseret Book Company, 1989–1992), 1: 3–5, 13, 268–69, 429.

7. Franklin S. Harris Jr., *The Book of Mormon: Messages and Evidences* (Salt Lake City: Deseret News Press, 1953), 200.

8. Thomas G. Alexander, *Mormonism in Transition: A History of the Latter-day Saints, 1890–1930* (Urbana: University of Illinois Press, 1996), chapter 1.

9. Joseph F. Smith, *Collected Discourses*, 5:26–27; "Joseph Smith's Birthday," *The Juvenile Instructor* 33 (1898): 76; "Joseph Smith, the Prophet," *Improvement Era* 5 (January 1902): 232–33; *Improvement Era* 7 (December 1903): 138–39; *Improvement Era* 7 (August 1904): 810; "The Prophet and Patriarch," *Improvement Era* 14 (July 1911): 855–57.

10. Junius F. Wells, "Birthplace of the Prophet Joseph Smith," *The Contributor* 16 (February 1895): 202–11; Junius F. Wells in [Joseph Fielding Smith, comp.], *Proceedings at the Dedication of the Joseph Smith Memorial Monument* (Salt Lake City, [1906]), 10; (hereafter *Proceedings*); Junius F. Wells, "Report on Joseph Smith's Birthplace," June 10, 1905, 23–25,

Junius F. Wells Collection, Church History Library and Archives of The Church of Jesus Christ of Latter-day Saints, Salt Lake City, Utah (hereafter Wells Collection). Kathleen Flake mistakenly assumes an origination among the church leadership in *The Politics of American Religious Identity: The Seating of Senator Reed Smoot, Mormon Apostle* (Chapel Hill: University of North Carolina Press, 2003)

11. G. Kurt Piehler, *Remembering War the American Way* (Washington, DC: Smithsonian Institution Press, 1995), 47–91; Kirk Savage, *Standing Soldiers, Kneeling Slaves: Race, War, and Monument in Nineteenth-Century America* (Princeton: Princeton University Press, 1997); Brian Lamb, *Who's Buried in Grant's Tomb?: A Tour of Presidential Gravesites* (Baltimore: Johns Hopkins University Press, 2000).

12. John Sears, *Sacred Places: American Tourist Attractions in the Nineteenth Century* (Amherst: University of Massachusetts Press, 1999); Mike Wallace, *Mickey Mouse History and Other Essays on American Memory* (Philadelphia: Temple University Press, 1996), 168–69.

13. Victor and Edith Turner, *Image and Pilgrimage in Christian Culture, Anthropological Perspectives* (New York: Columbia University Press, 1978); John Eade and Michael J. Sallnow, eds., *Contesting the Sacred: The Anthropology of Christian Pilgrimage* (London: Routledge, 1991); Gwen Kennedy Neville, *Kinship and Pilgrimage: Rituals of Reunion in American Protestant Culture* (New York: Oxford University Press, 1987).

14. Wells, *Proceedings*, 9–10.

15. Wells, *Conference Report*, October 1926, 70.

16. Stanley F. Blomfield, "James M. Boutwell—Man and Mayor," *The Vermonter* 22 (April 1917): 57–67; Ken Bush, "Joseph Smith: Memorial Vermont Ingenuity," *Barre Life*, Winter 1997, 4–5; Darel P. Bartschi, "The Joseph Smith Memorial: A 1905 Tribute to the Prophet and His Work," *Ensign*, February 1988, 7–10.

17. Susa Young Gates, "Memorial Monument Dedication," *Improvement Era* 9 (1905–1906): 310–16; *Proceedings*, 22–24.

18. David Chidester and Edward T. Linenthal, eds., *American Sacred Space* (Bloomington: Indiana University Press, 1995), 1–42.

19. *Salt Lake Tribune*, June 26, 1905, 1

20. Frederick M. Smith, "Open Letter to All People," *Salt Lake Tribune*, July 1, 1905.

21. P. L. Allen, "The Public View of Mormonism," *The Nation* 81 (1905): 113–14; "Mormon Fight on Mormons," *New York Times*, July 2, 1905; *Burlington Free Press*, July 10, 1905; "Mormon Shrine in Vermont," *Interstate Journal* 10 (June 1905): n.p.; *Randolph* [Vermont] *Herald*, November 16, 1905, December 21, 1905.

22. Levi Wild to the editor and "A Protest from the Woman's Home Missionary Union of Vermont," *Randolph Herald*, December 7, 1905; Charles P. Tarbell to the editor, *Randolph Herald*, December 14, 1905; the original petition is in the Wells Collection.

23. Evelyn M. Wood Lovejoy, *History of Royalton, Vermont, with Family Genealogies, 1769–1911* (Burlington, VT: Burlington Free Press Printing Company, 1911), vii

24. Hope Nash, *Royalton Vermont* (Lunenburg, VT: Stinehour Press, 1975), 40.

25. Dona Brown, *Inventing New England: Regional Tourism in the Nineteenth Century* (Washington, DC: Smithsonian Institution Press, 1995), 135–67.

26. Ivah Dunklee, *Burning of Royalton, Vermont, by Indians* (Boston: Geo. H. Ellis Co., 1906), 51–52.

27. Lovejoy, *History*, 97–182.

28. Royalton Town Records, 1916–1937, 39.

29. Levi Wild to Evelyn Lovejoy, July 22, 1922; Evelyn M. Lovejoy to Gertrude Laird, October 6, 1922; Laird to Lovejoy, October 17, 1922, Evelyn M. Lovejoy Library Correspondence (Royalton Memorial Library, South Royalton, VT).

30. Hope Nash, *Royalton Vermont*, 69; Mary E. Whitney, "Royalton's Flood," *The Vermonter* 34 (July 1929): 110–11.

31. Wells, "Birthplace of Joseph Smith the Prophet," 14.

32. George H. Douglas, *All Aboard: The Railroad in American Life* (New York: Paragon House, 1992), 232–33; Jill Mudgett, "The Hills of Home: Environmental Identity in the Rural North, 1815–1860" (Ph.D. diss., University of Massachusetts Amherst, 2008); Leonard J. Arrington, *Great Basin Kingdom: An Economic History of the Latter-day Saints, 1830–1900* (Cambridge: Harvard University Press, 1958), 392–93; Nancy D. McCormick and John S. McCormick, *Saltair* (Salt Lake City: University of Utah Press, 1985); Wallace Stegner, "Xanadu by the Salt Flats: Memories of a Pleasure Dome," *American Heritage* 32 (June/July 1981): 81–89.

33. Junius F. Wells to Joseph F. Smith, November 25, 1908, Wells Collection.

34. Dana F. Dow, "Planting Plan for the Grounds of the Joseph Smith Memorial, Feb 1907," Wells Collection.

35. Wells, *Proceedings*, 15; Gates, "Memorial Monument Dedication," 315; *Montpelier* (Vermont) *Journal*, August 29, 1905; *Randolph Herald and Times*, August 31, 1905. Additionally, the doorstep of the Smith home became the back doorstep of the Cottage.

36. William J. Murtagh, *Keeping Time: The History and Theory of Preservation in America*, rev. ed. (New York: Preservation Press, 1997), 16.

37. Gates, "Memorial Monument Dedication," 310, 317; "Tree Record," Wells Collection. See also Marla R. Miller and Ann Digan Lanning, "'Common Parlors': Women and the Recreation of Community Identity in Deerfield, Massachusetts, 1870–1902," *Gender and History* 6, no. 3 (November 1994): 435–55.

38. "Tells of Improvements on Joseph Smith Farm," *Deseret Evening News*, October 11, 1915; Inventory, December 31, 1910; Inventory, [1919], "Earnings Statement," 1918, Wells Collection.

39. "Widow Honorably Released from Smith Memorial Farm," *Deseret Evening News*, April 24, 1919; "Heber C. Smith is Sent to Vermont," *Salt Lake Telegram*, April 23, 1919 ; "Angus J. Cannon to Succeed Heber C. Smith at South Royalton," *Deseret Evening News*, May 16, 1924; "Made Custodian of Joseph Smith Farm," *Deseret Evening News*, March 21, 1929.

40. *White River Herald*, August 6, 1959, October 12, 1961; Carter E. Grant, "Epochal Events at the Prophet's Birthplace," *Improvement Era* 64 (May 1961): 326; *Church News*, October 7, 1961, 4, October 14, 1961, 10.

41. Henry A. Smith, "A New Way to Tell Story of Mormonism," *Church News*, April 29, 1967, 3, 5.

42. Oren Baruch Stier and J. Shawn Landres come to the same conclusion on the relationship between memory and religion at sites of violence in *Religion, Violence, Memory, and Place*, 1–5.

The Bill Monroe birthplace at Jerusalem Ridge, 6210 US Highway 62 E, Rosine vicinity, Beaver Dam, Kentucky. Photo by author.

～ 7 ～

Although some birthplaces, as Erekson points out, may be more miraculous than others, miracles were precisely what the residents of Rosine, Kentucky, had in mind when they restored the birthplace of bluegrass virtuoso Bill Monroe during the 1990s. Rosine's coal and lumber jobs succumbed to deindustrialization during the late twentieth century, leaving residents desperate for purchase in a new economy. They found it in Rosine's only remaining renewable resource: memory. Cultural anthropologist Cynthia Miller details here how Rosine effectively reinvented itself as a shrine to Monroe's memory. At his birthplace and throughout town, residents literally make their living by recalling Monroe for visitors. Miller portrays a deeply spiritual community whose tribute to Monroe is wholly celebratory and imbued with religiosity. Rather than dwell on the intertwined histories of race, class, and popular culture that frame Monroe's legacy, Rosine simply encourages its musical pilgrims to honor the place where bluegrass was born. So far, it seems, the investment in heritage tourism has paid off. Rosine's claim to Monroe's memory, however, is not singular. In fact, Monroe built his own bluegrass museum in Tennessee. How Rosine distinguishes itself among the various claimants to Monroe's legacy suggests that the mnemonic strategies of an earlier generation linger in our nation's ongoing preoccupation with origins.

Rosine, Kentucky

Birthplace of Bill Monroe and American Bluegrass Music

CYNTHIA MILLER

The commemoration of Bill Monroe's birthplace in Rosine, Kentucky (population 41), began with a single nail that, once driven, reshaped the life of an entire town. The May 26, 2001, nail-driving ceremony marked the beginning of a restoration project, but it also drew together the people, places, and memories of the town in a singular focus on one of the leading figures in traditional American music.[1] The commemoration attests to the centrality of Monroe and his music in Rosine. It also stakes a claim for Rosine's contribution to his life by suggesting that the sights, sounds, and smells of the place created the substance of the man. The character and essence of Monroe's birthplace become *his* character and essence. And that essence became the music known as Bluegrass, the official State Music of Kentucky.

That music, along with the life and legend of the man with whom it originated, can be traced, touched, and heard throughout the town of Rosine, from the farm and historic house on Jerusalem Ridge that was the Monroe family's homestead, to the cemetery that serves as Bill Monroe's final resting place, and points in between. Monroe's life is inscribed onto the small town's landscape through memorials, markers, images, and architecture that have been reproduced and repurposed in a range of material culture that has, in turn, been marketed across the globe: maps, books, magazines, graphic art, record and compact disk covers and liner notes, and of course, sheet music and instruments. Over time, Monroe's fame has drawn attention to other exceptional, but often overlooked, local musicians: his brother Charlie; uncle Pendleton ("Uncle Pen") Vandiver; thumb-picking guitarist Arnold Schultz; and fiddler Tex Atecheson, among others, creating a culture of recognition for those who have contributed to the region's vernacular musical heritage.

As we consider Monroe's life and legacy, that picture of the relationship between the man, the place, and the music becomes not only more robust, but more complex. On one hand, the powerful influences of his birthplace are undeniable; on the other, those ties to place became more symbolically powerful as they became less binding in reality. Monroe was not the first gifted musician, or the last, to call Rosine home, and he suggested years later that the seeds sown in him, as in so many others, by life in the small town, would not have flourished without room to grow: "I guess if I hadn't left Rosine and gone up North, I'd probably be just like the other folks who live here now, farming and raising a family."[2]

The Father of Bluegrass Music

Bill Monroe was born on September 13, 1911, atop Jerusalem Ridge, just south of Owensboro, Kentucky in a small town called Rosine. He was the youngest of eight children born to James Buchanan "Buck" Monroe (1857–1928) and Malissa Vandiver Monroe (1870–1921). Buck Monroe owned a 655-acre farm that produced timber and coal, vital elements in the town's economy at the time. Proud and law-abiding, the Monroes were hearty Scots-Irish frontier stock who adhered to a life of hard work and discipline. Buck's family was wealthy by local standards, and his children well educated for the times. At a time when a fifth-grade education was considered ample, Monroe's father completed the eighth grade, and was skilled with numbers.[3] Tenant farming earned him enough to purchase land. Over the next decade, he purchased hundreds of acres of woodlands and coal reserves, leaving the family economically well positioned, but reliant on hard labor to harvest these raw materials.[4] By the time Buck married, the Monroes were considered a reserved "old" affluent family compared to the laboring, illiterate, and gregarious immigrants from whom Malissa came. Buck Monroe, many said, married beneath him, but his marriage brought music into the Monroe family, and into the lives of Buck and Malissa's children.

By the time Monroe was born, his parents were well into middle age and his siblings too old to remedy the isolation that would mark his early years, when music became his constant companion. At age ten, he began playing his signature instrument, the mandolin, because his older siblings had already laid claim to the more prestigious fiddle and guitar. The mandolin was more popular in Kentucky than in other southern states, thanks to long tradition and performers like Roy "Shorty" Hobbs and Larry Hensley. But for Monroe, the choice was made from necessity. The family farmhand, Hubert "Stringbean" Stringfield, an accomplished player in his own right, gave the boy pointers, as did African American guitar master Arnold Schultz.[5] In addition, his "Uncle Pen" gave him fiddle tunes to copy. Soon Monroe was playing for local dances and parlor parties, either in trio with his brothers, Birch and Charlie, or as back-up for Schultz or Uncle Pen. Schultz's mentorship of the young Monroe is significant because it demonstrates the influence of black music, which persists in the bluegrass sound. It also affords a glimpse into the world of a lonely young white boy in rural Kentucky in the 1920s. Monroe's marginalization from his peers created space for an abiding friendship and sense of respect for an African American man, at a time when race and class divided communities. Monroe would not acknowledge this influence until late in his career, but carried with him a long-standing admiration and interest in black music and its players.[6]

Birch and Charlie left Rosine to find work, and in 1929, after his father's death, Bill joined them, forming The Monroe Brothers band. The siblings played together for nine years, touring part-time and playing on radio shows until personal and artistic differences caused them to go their separate ways. Once the act broke up in 1938, Bill moved to Atlanta and formed the group that would launch his career and take the Grand Ole Opry by storm: the Blue Grass Boys. Over the course of Monroe's career there would be over 200 Blue Grass Boys. The band is often referred to as the "Blue Grass School of Music."[7] Monroe named his Blue Grass boys in honor of his home state, later saying, "I'd already decided on using the name 'bluegrass,' because that's what they call Kentucky, the Blue Grass State. So, I just used 'Bill Monroe and the Blue Grass Boys' and that let people throughout the country know I was from Kentucky, saved a lot of people from having to ask me where I was from."[8] Referred to by one folklorist as "folk music with overdrive," bluegrass has been lauded as a truly American art form, and studied extensively for its connections to string band music, country, jazz, gospel, blues, and the ballads of immigrants from places like Scotland, England, and Wales.[9] Monroe, however, took a somewhat different view of the music's roots. During an interview, a musicologist, eager to convey the global roots of the genre, told Monroe about the contributions of music from faraway places like Egypt, Ireland, and the Andes Mountains. He then asked Rosine's famous son where *he* thought bluegrass came from. Monroe's answer was simple: "Down home."[10]

Exactly when the genre developed is a point of contention as well. Monroe's own bluegrass style dates back to his early days at the Grand Ole Opry, but while some cite the formation of the Blue Grass Boys in 1939 as the genre's birth year, others trace the style's departure from other forms of string music to 1945, when banjo-picker Earl Scruggs joined the band. Either way, the bluegrass style is an unmistakable combination of mandolin, banjo, fiddle, guitar, and bass, with strong vocal harmonies and hard-driving rhythms. Bluegrass emphasizes instrumental virtuosity—with fierce breakdown arpeggios that often highlight individual players in solo breaks—and syncopation inspired by black dance music, in combination with "songs of faith, family, love, loss, pain, and redemption . . . anchored in a distant rural past."[11]

Much has been written about Monroe's seventy years in the music industry.[12] He performed for four presidents, received a National Medal of Arts in 1995, was awarded the first ever Grammy Award for a bluegrass recording (1989), as well as in recognition of his lifetime achievement (1993), and is the only performer to have been inducted into the Country Music Hall of Fame, Rock and Roll Hall of Fame, and the International Bluegrass Music Association (IBMA) Hall of Fame. Over the course of his career, he played with countless celebrated performers, developing what has been described as a "cult-like following," and his musical influences have been felt across genres.[13] But as a child growing up in Rosine, Monroe suffered from estropia—an inwardly crossed eye—which affected not only his sight but his confidence as well.[14] He was acutely shy and quiet, and the deep loneliness of his social world later gave shape to the plaintive tenor singing and virtuoso musical style that would characterize bluegrass music: the "high lonesome" sound that is generally credited to Monroe. Although he moved from Rosine at the age of eighteen, it was these early experiences in the town of his birth that many, like Jerusalem Ridge Foundation executive Campbell Mercer, believe shaped Monroe's identity, his music, and his career: "Bill Monroe was a genius, and he just happened to be born here. If he'd been born somewhere else, he might have been a nuclear physicist."[15]

From Pigeon Roost to Rosine

"Stereotypes about the roots of bluegrass might lead some to assume that Rosine is a little mountain hollow filled with barefoot, anti-social hillbillies who rouse themselves only to check on their whiskey stills."[16] A hundred and twenty miles west of Louisville, in western Kentucky's Ohio County, Rosine was originally called Pigeon Roost after the large flock of passenger pigeons that roosted on the hill east of town. The settlement provided the backdrop for Washington Irving's "The Early

Experiences of Ralph Ringwood" (1819–20), which tells the story of a ne'er-do-well lad who grew to be a "Kentuckian by residence and choice," although a Virginian by birth.[17] Pigeon Roost became Rosine at the hand of a banker and Kentucky state legislator, Henry D. McHenry, who named the new town after the pet name of his wife, poet Jenny Taylor McHenry. McHenry used his political influence to secure a rail line in the area with the hope of creating an urban transportation center.[18] The town was chartered in 1873 and, several months later, the name of the Pigeon Roost post office officially changed to "Rosine." Thanks to the railway, the town thrived. Hotels, bars, and poolrooms competed for cash from visitors and townspeople who worked in local industries, which encompassed a gristmill, creamery, tobacco drying houses, stave and hoop mills, and a shingle mill. Until the 1970s, Herbert Woosley's Bat Mill supplied the milled ash timber "blanks" that became the world-famous "Louisville Slugger" bats.[19]

By 1918, when a young Bill Monroe rode into town to sell farm produce and catch up on local news, Rosine was home to nearly fifty families and had a population of almost 200. Notions of progress—tied to entrepreneurship, industry, and the exploitation of natural resources—poised the town at the boundary of prosperity and persistent poverty, subject to the whim of political and economic forces far removed from the community's day-to-day realities. Most townspeople worked for the railroad.[20] This was the dominant social environment in which Bill Monroe was raised, and which worked its way into the lyrics and sentiments of his songs. The young Monroe—and his music—articulated with Rosine's social and economic environment in ways that significantly altered the trajectory of his life. His poor eyesight excluded him from many childhood pastimes, and, as he grew, from most normal occupations as well. Music became his refuge and companion, the connective tissue between a boy, the natural world, and the community that surrounded him.

Like other small communities in Kentucky and elsewhere, Rosine had a strong heritage in folk and church music, dating back to at least the early nineteenth century.[21] Homecomings, get-togethers, square dances, and jamborees all brought community members together to play and sing. It was within this environment of "family music" that Bill Monroe learned to play and sing. However, a tradition of formal music training also existed, in the form of "singing schools." Traveling teachers offered classes to children and adults, teaching the fundamentals of music and "shape notes," a system in which notes on the staff were given shapes as aids to recognition. Students learned the notes—Do, Re, Mi, Fa, So, La, Ti, Do—and only then united them with words. In Rosine, this tradition was carried on by Granville Morris, a music instructor from nearby Renfrow.[22] Morris taught church hymns and gospel songs, such as "A Beautiful Life" and "What Would You Give (in Exchange for Your Soul)," as a music ministry. These classes culminated in a "singing convention" that brought together all the area classes for a day of singing, food, and community. Monroe and his brother Charlie were among Morris's students in Rosine, and although Monroe's poor eyesight interfered with this, and other, formal education, Rosine's traveling hymn teacher added dimension to the boy's understanding of vocal harmonies and the voice as an instrument.

In communities such as Rosine, music was the language of pastimes: children's games, hearthside and front porch relaxation, and Saturday night dances. But as Robert Cantwell points out, when it became the focal point of a life, it also became a marker of difference.[23] Apart from those who traveled as music teachers for children, imparting the skills to learn spirituals, music was decidedly not an occupational choice. It was a hobby which, failing to contribute to the economic life of the community, was looked on with skepticism or disdain when it stretched beyond its traditional recreational and spiritual roles. The circumstances that combined to create the young Monroe's affinity for music marked him not only as having a gift, but also as destined for a life different from those typically found in Rosine in the early decades of the twentieth century.

Coming of age in the year that marked the beginning of the Great Depression, Monroe left a town that seemed to offer few economic alternatives for success and was increasingly reliant upon capital. He observed that "I reckon my people figured I would never make anything there, and that they should try and get me out of there to where I could make a decent living."[24] And, ultimately, they were right. Rosine's economic realities failed to live up to McHenry's early ambitions. The town continued to be a commercial center through the postwar years, largely due to the abundance of coal and timber. "Coal falls out of the ground in Rosine" according to Aaron Hutchings, founder of the Rosine Association.[25] But because of the low demand for high-sulfur coal, the town's coal industry has diminished. While the county's timber industry remains strong, jobs are scarce. Weekly wages in the county fall significantly below the state average, while unemployment ranks significantly higher.[26] Since the 1970s, Rosine has suffered from an economic and demographic trend common among rural towns in Kentucky and elsewhere. A dramatic decline in markets for coal and other resources; the demise of the family farm; employment-driven out-migration to urban centers; and the decline in traditional local patterns of socialization all contribute.

As Tom Ewing notes, however, the factors that have distinguished Rosine from other rural towns in decline are its strong musical tradition, embodied in the life and legacy of Bill Monroe, and the town's willingness to create an industry of musical heritage based on that legacy.[27] The town faded into relative obscurity until Monroe's musical heyday in the mid-1940s, but the social and cultural heritage of the community has persisted, and has been revitalized in the service of a robust program of tourism focused on Monroe and his music. Most of Rosine's current citizens are direct descendants of the town's founders, and narratives of the town's history continue to be passed down through generations, creating a body of oral history that is deeply embedded in the story of the homeplace.[28] As travelers enter present-day Rosine, the sign says simply "Hi There. Welcome to Rosine—Home of Bluegrass Music."

Pilgrimage and Hallowed Ground

"This is holy ground," according to one reporter, "the epicenter."[29] The homeplace of the Father of Bluegrass is the symbolic center for the genre and its followers. For bluegrass fans, the journey to Rosine is often framed as a pilgrimage—an experience that replaces the notion of "tourism" with one of devoted followers connecting with the source of the genre and paying homage to its patriarch—a conceptualization that finds support in the Ohio County Tourism Commission's website invitation to "Plan a Pilgrimage to the Homeplace." And plan they do, by the thousands each year. In an era of digital communication, Monroe's bluegrass fans are found worldwide, and many individuals, families, and groups from across the United States, Europe, Asia, and elsewhere, come to visit Monroe's birthplace each year, with a range of reasons and interpretations, supporting Juan Eduardo Campo's suggestion that, rather than displacing pilgrimages, globalization increases them, diversifying the reasons why those journeys are made.[30] Drawing together those diverse reasons, however, is the notion of proximity to greatness—to walk the ground of Jerusalem Ridge, to stand in the rooms that echoed with Monroe's early music—and leave feeling connected, inspired, and, perhaps, changed.

This notion of pilgrimage, of identifying with, approaching, and perhaps touching artifacts associated with the divine, has deep roots in religious tradition, and yet offers a framework of interest for thinking about the journey to Rosine. Historically, pilgrimages were made to the final resting places of spiritual patrons, in order to celebrate and commemorate their lives and works.[31] In this tradition, the pilgrim's sights are fixed on the individual, as a locus of power, and so the focus of the journey becomes that spiritual figure's physical remains. In Rosine, Monroe's life comes full circle, as both birthplace and resting place; and while "pilgrims" visit both the homestead and the cemetery, it is the historic house—the site of birth and life—that serves as the focal point and locus of power. The patriarch of bluegrass is felt more deeply *in place,* in the context of the landscape, built environment, and relationships that fostered and animated his music, than in his physical resting place, which, although highly revered, holds his remains separate from his spirit. Once again, we're reminded of Mercer's words, "if he'd been born somewhere else . . ."

And while visitors to the Monroe homestead in no way confuse the historic house on Jerusalem Ridge with the "Little Community Church" (1948) up the road, there is an element of reverence here. The Monroe farm may not be sacred space, but it is, perhaps, hallowed ground. As Duncan Cameron observes, the museum, or in this case, the historic house or homestead, is much closer in function to the church than it is to the school. It provides opportunity for reaffirmation of the faith, it is a place for private and intimate experience, although it is shared with many others; it is, in concept, the temple of the muses.[32]

For many who come to Rosine, Cameron's imagery is particularly meaningful. The claim to music that permeates the historic house and the landscape that surrounds it suggests that there are, indeed, muses at work—or that, as a writer for the *New York Times* attested, "the dirt has music in it."[33] The interpretative framework that surrounds Monroe's birthplace invokes a deep sense of place as it joins the essences of landscape, vernacular architecture, and local culture with the early life of a man and his music. If Monroe's gifts were a blending of man and place, then it is a blending that many who come to the homestead long to share, casting it as a kind of *locus sanctorum.*[34] Prior to the homestead's restoration, one "pilgrim" removed a door from the historic house, and crafted a mandolin from its wood, a relic residing in the space between the cultural and the sacred. Pilgrimage has been described as "a journey to the source and heartland of the faith."[35] To visit the homeplace then, to hear (or play) bluegrass at its source, is for many, an experience of a lifetime, but at the same time, these journeys to Rosine and the homeplace become part of the fabric of the history of the homestead, the town, and bluegrass itself.

The House That Built Bluegrass

A historic house, as Thomas Schlereth observes, has "at least two histories: its existence as an actual residence, and its past and present life as a house museum."[36] The ways in which these complexities intersect with "place" become particularly interesting as we think about birthplaces. The Monroe homeplace, cited on the National Register of Historic Places, follows a long-standing tradition of popular interest in local history, and grassroots historical advocacy. The movement to preserve and restore historic houses traces its roots to efforts in the 1850s to preserve sites associated with George Washington, and has since captured, as historian John Herbst notes, the interest, imagination, and energies of countless Americans.[37] As artifacts of local public history, however, these sites also present the challenge of integration with the local community, as they create bridges between local history and the public. The Monroe homestead, which was bought and sold several times before settling into its status as a homeplace museum, draws on local knowledge—the collective memories of Rosine's inhabitants—as well as the community's everyday life, to weave the fabric of living history throughout the town. A number of longtime local residents serve as volunteer tour guides, often blending their own memories of the Monroe family with the tour script, adding an impromptu oral history component to the experience.

Their story is one that emphasizes hard work in the face of adversity, greatness that grows from simplicity, the grace in imperfection, and the wholeness that comes from the land. The entry to the wooden farmhouse opens into a parlor, home to the fireplace where "Uncle Pen" sat and filled the house with fiddle tunes, and where the two Monroe girls slept. The house's three bedrooms, on either side of the massive fireplace, were occupied by Monroe's parents and the boys, and a kitchen holds memories of roasted chestnuts, wild game, and homemade jam. Artifacts in the homeplace include many of the family's original belongings: a trunk belonging to Monroe's parents, his mother's ironing board, and his father's walnut tool chest. A Kentucky bluegrass plate with a horse painted on it is identified as "Bill's favorite," while other household objects, original and representative, introduce visitors to the everyday lives of the Monroe family. Photographs throughout the house narrate the lives and relationships of family members. Authenticity is typically a critical issue for historical homes and similar venues, and is highly valued at the homestead as well. But in instances where "representative" objects have been used—the stove, donated by the family of a musician; "a Monroe table, maybe not *the* Monroe table;" or the mandolin, placed lovingly on the bed, which "represents the kind Bill played as a boy"—all are treated with a plainspoken honesty that reveals the homestead's *true* concern for authenticity—the preservation of an authentic down-home spirit.

Historian Stuart Hobbs has commented on the challenges of presenting history through historical houses, where interpretation often largely focuses on material culture, rather than on social history, with visitors learning "more about antiques and good taste than about history."[38] Tours of Bill Monroe's boyhood home suffer from no such lack, as tour narratives link the places and times of Monroe's early life, not only with family and community dynamics, but with the development of bluegrass music itself. "When you look at the home, unlike other famous homes, you are not only seeing where a famous person, or in this case, three famous persons, were raised, but you are seeing where an art form flourished and a new one was formed."[39] Monroe's music, visitors are told, was fueled by home, family, and place—this place—in a way impossible elsewhere. At the opening ceremonies of the International Bluegrass Music Museum, located about forty miles north in Owensboro, Steve Brechter, chairman of the museum's Board of Trustees, observed that "other art forms represent other character-istics of the human experience, but bluegrass goes down deep and is really about the journey of the soul and its quest for 'home.'"[40]

Yet, while "place"—a house, a community, a region—and the yearn-ing for an identity firmly grounded in those, are seen as the birthing ground for Monroe's music, the two are, in fact, mutually constitutive. The Monroe family homeplace is a house that music *built,* as well, and narratives of instruments learned, melodies played, and lyrics written animate the tour. Far more than restored architecture and recreated home culture, the Monroe homeplace is inextricably linked to the fam-ily's music. As Monroe scholar Richard D. Smith observes, "music was the most cherished pastime on the Monroe farm."[41] Monroe's mother was a multi-talented musician who sang and played fiddle, accordion, and harmonica, among other instruments, and encouraged each of her children to play. Not only Bill, but his brothers, Charlie and Birch, gained recognition as professionals, and they, along with Malissa's brother "Uncle Pen," played not only at home, but at local dances. Tour guides instruct visitors that "this has got to be America's most musical home," its walls embedded with, and shaped by, the notes and chords that filled it, giving it a voice of its own. From the tour guide's rendition of "I'm on My Way Back to the Old Home," to the 78-rpm record from the original 1946 pressing of the state song, "Blue Moon of Kentucky," to the mandolin carefully laid across Monroe's childhood bed, music animates the tour narrative, room by room, and memory by memory.

This intertwining of music and place is reinforced by Monroe's own insistence that "I never wrote any songs. The music was all around me in the air and I was just the first to reach up and pull it down."[42] Monroe's keen sensitivity to place—both his social environment and natural surroundings—can be heard and felt in his music. "There is that authentic wail in his high-pitched voice that one hears in the coun-try when Mother Nature sighs and retires for the night," Judge Hay, founder of Nashville's Grand Ole Opry, wrote of Monroe's music for one of the Opry's souvenir publications.[43] Monroe credits this "high lonesome" sound for combining emotions evoked by the harsher side of his young life with sounds in the natural world that surrounded him: "There was a time there when my brothers, they'd all left, you know, and my father and mother had passed away, and I lived on the farm a long time, and all that I heard was the foxhound or the birds or something like that. And I would sing kindly the way I felt."[44] Departing from what Edward Alexander has noted as the "anecdotal great man, great events approach to history," which fails to consider "economic, social, and cultural factors," the homeplace tour draws much of its strength from being firmly situated in the social and economic contexts of the Rosine community in the early twentieth century.[45]

Rosine's preservationists "want to say we have restored Bill Monroe's boyhood home, but we also want to say we've restored his birthplace."[46] The current 1,000-square-foot home was built in 1917, on the site of the Monroes' original cabin, by Monroe's parents, along with the help of family and friends. Crafted from hand-hewn logs and virgin timber, the home also contains a hand-hewn limestone chimney and fireplace built in the mid-1800s, and thought to date back to the first Monroes in Ohio County, making the house a tangible link, not only to the history of Rosine, but to that of the county as well. Monroe remained at the homeplace until 1929, when he left to join his brothers in northern Indiana. In later years, the homestead was sold, and after several failed attempts to purchase the family farm, Monroe occasionally visited his boyhood home, from 1965 until his death in 1996. Curiously, he returned to perform in Rosine only five times after becoming known professionally, appearing twice at the Rosine Barn Jamboree the year before his death.[47]

Rosine residents look on the complexities of their town's relationship with Monroe with a wide range of sentiments. As noted in an Ohio County *Times-News* story reporting Monroe's death, many expressed deep, abiding affection for the musician and native son. "Bill was a good person and never really changed much after he got famous. He's been in this place several times and I talked to him when he visited his sister just down the road. His name and the name of this little town will forever go together. Bill didn't spend a lot of time around Rosine in later years, but he did give a free concert at the old barn not too many years ago and everybody really appreciated that."[48] Herbert Napier, a native of the town, expressed great respect for the Monroe family name, and for

Monroe's pioneering vision in bluegrass music, but cautioned about looking at that relationship through rose-colored glasses: "If he had done for Rosine what some of the people of this community had done for him, Rosine could have really been some kind of a place."[49] Rosine's then-fire chief, Stoy Geary, however, argued his disagreement, noting that "if that's the case, then it's everybody's fault . . . If for no other reason, you have to appreciate that when people mention the name Monroe, they also mention the name Rosine in the same breath. That's meant a lot to this town."[50] And Monroe's niece, Rosetta Kiper, who remained in Rosine, affirmed that "he loved his hometown of Rosine enough that he requested to be buried here."[51]

The Rosine Project

Despite Monroe's fame, his homeplace had receded from the public consciousness and was nearly destroyed by vandals and souvenir-seekers by the late 1990s. After visiting the house, Nicholas Dawidoff observed:

> The glass in all the windows was gone and trees were bending in through the gaps. Plaster hung from the ceilings like old lace, a bees' nest filled a portion of one room, and the floor in another was covered with a soft dirt . . . Bill Monroe, a notoriously taciturn man who sings notoriously wistful music, grew up in one of the loneliest places I have ever seen.[52]

When Campbell Mercer, a veterinarian and bluegrass performer, sought out the farm, even Monroe's son, James, was uncertain about its location. Former Blue Grass Boy Frank Buchanan brought Mercer out to the site that had given rise to songs like "Jerusalem Ridge," "Little Cabin Home on the Hill," and "Rose of Old Kentucky," and Mercer found a structure that was being reclaimed by the land on which it stood. The foundation was sinking into the ground, the porch had disintegrated, and the roof verged on collapse. Mercer left his veterinary practice and farm to pursue his dream of restoring the Monroe homestead. He moved his family to Rosine in 2001 and began the Jerusalem Ridge Foundation. He secured an $800,000 grant from the Commonwealth of Kentucky with a vision of restoring the historic farmhouse and creating a kind of "sacred space"—a focal point for historical memory and reverence—on the outskirts of Rosine, which would draw on the power of place to tell the story of the Father of Bluegrass.[53]

Restoration work, formalized as The Rosine Project, began in May 2001. Historical building contractors restored everything from the sandstone foundation, which archaeologists suggest had been reused from Monroe's original birth cabin, to the windows that stretched nearly from floor to ceiling, letting in what Monroe's lyrics invoked as "that light I long to see." The $250,000 restoration of the 1,000-square-foot farmhouse created a focal point for the community's expanding identity as the home of bluegrass music.[54] Even so, funding challenges have thrust The Rosine Project, which is not affiliated with the Monroe family, into the spotlight on several occasions. The organization must compete with other museums and associations for Monroe artifacts, state funding, and use of the Monroe name. Mercer's band, the Cumberland Highlanders, attracts support with a televised bluegrass program, "Crossing the Cumberlands," taped weekly at the homeplace. With two former Blue Grass Boys among its members, the band creates living history, in a sense, by carrying on Monroe's legacy in a complex exchange of social and symbolic power. It draws on the heritage of the historic homestead as object and place and, in turn, renews the site's vitality and currency by infusing music back into the hallowed ground. Similarly, the annual Jerusalem Ridge Bluegrass Celebration, intended to "celebrate Bill Monroe's birth and to pay respect to his passing," is held some 400 feet from the homestead. Spanning four days and featuring over forty bands, the festival invites fans and musicians alike to become part of the history of bluegrass that is written at Jerusalem Ridge.

While the commemoration of Monroe's birthplace begins at the homestead and Jerusalem Ridge, it does not end there. The fabric of Rosine is tightly knit with Monroe's legacy. As Aaron Hutchings, former producer for the Kentucky Network (KET) and restoration volunteer, observed, "this entire hamlet is Bill Monroe's monument."[55] As visitors leave the homestead, they are encouraged to drive two miles up the road into town to the cemetery, where Monroe, "Uncle Pen," and other family members are buried. Vandiver's headstone, which bears the lyrics to Monroe's 1950 tribute "Uncle Pen," serves as an unintentionally powerful symbol joining an individual life, cultural history, and a new genre of music he helped foster in the young Monroe:

> Uncle Pen played the fiddle, Lord
> How it would ring
> You could hear it talk
> You could hear it sing

Similarly, lyrics to one of Monroe's best-known "real life" songs, "Memories of Mother and Dad," are drawn from inscriptions on his parents' headstones: "Gone But Not Forgotten," and "We Will Meet Again." Monroe's own passing, on September 9, 1996, is marked by an obelisk of white granite, twenty feet high, bearing his image (along with that of his dog, Stormy), and an engraved history, written by his son James, on a horizontal stone slab. The monument echoes with meaning, as it affirms that "Bill Monroe is Bluegrass Music!" and outlines a life of hardship, determination, and renown, inextricably linked with family, music, and place: WALK SOFTLY AROUND THE GRAVE, FOR MY FATHER, BILL MONROE, RESTS HERE, AS THE BLUE MOON OF KENTUCKY SHINES ON.

Back on the main road, the "Little Community Church" of Monroe's song, along with the General Store, and the town barn, where the Friday night Jamboree is held, continue the inscription of Monroe's life in the Rosine landscape. While the Rosine Barn Jamboree is, indeed, a performance of down-home entertainment that draws the attention of countless tourists, it is also a way of life for local residents, and one that many have attended each Friday night, for years. Victor Turner writes that "by their performances shall ye know them." As part of a common culture, the Jamboree serves a function far greater than an evening's entertainment, or even as a continued thread that binds Rosine to the Monroe legacy. It is, as Turner notes, "declarative of [a] shared humanity," while at the same time, "uttering the uniqueness" of local culture.[56] Unlike performances at the Monroe homestead, these performances, while staged as part of the Monroe tradition, are carried out in community space, in ways that valorize and reinforce community culture, and create shared memory. Although many Blue Grass Boys, like Tom Ewing, Hartford, Kentucky resident and author of *The Bill Monroe Reader*, have participated in the Friday night Jamboree, Monroe himself performed at the barn only twice after leaving Rosine back in 1939—in May and September of 1995—the year before his death.[57] The Jamboree, then, embodies a uniqueness all its own, celebrating the town's association with the Monroe legacy, while at the same time using it to independently express a shared identity and incorporate bluegrass more broadly into public history.

From Claiming Place to Placing Claim

The Rosine Project crystallized efforts not only to celebrate Monroe but also to claim him on local, regional, and institutional levels. Challenges to Jerusalem Ridge's status as the focal point of the Monroe bluegrass heritage have been present in many forms, from as nearby as Rosine to farther afield in Bean Blossom, Indiana, and country music's "capital," Nashville, Tennessee, suggesting the complexity of the politics of representation inherent in Monroe's larger-than-life status as the Father of Bluegrass. Because he was a leading figure in the town's public history, questions were raised locally about the centrality and accessibility of the homeplace in relation to the social geography of the town, with some community leaders advocating for its relocation to downtown Rosine. Citing the ties to place that so closely inform Monroe's music, Campbell Mercer successfully argued that "that ridge, that farm, that view had more to do with forging this style of music than any structure could." Referring to songs like "On My Way Back to the Old Home," in which Monroe sings "The road winds up the hill," Mercer affirmed these already acknowledged ties between place and identity, urging community leaders not to move the home, but to preserve the home*place,* road, hill, and all, insisting that "you can't just go into a museum and have photographs or paintings depict this . . . You've got to let people get out there and walk around those ridges and see how hard life was for the Kentucky hill farmer."[58]

Just as Monroe's musical fame extended outward from Rosine throughout the country, so too does his commemoration. Promotional materials for Ohio County, in which the tiny unincorporated town is located, support and showcase Rosine, beckoning tourists to "Come Home to Bluegrass," "Catch the Bluegrass Spirit in Ohio County," and "Find the REAL Home of Bluegrass" above colorful down-home images of a bluegrass jam session on the porch and lawn of the Monroe homestead, with a sepia-toned portrait of Monroe himself, looking on from an inset in the corner. Rosine takes pride of place in both the county's "Music Adventures" and "Cultural Adventures" itineraries, and the Commission's website dedicates a page to the Monroe homeplace and the family's heritage. And as both town and county prepare for Monroe's centennial, public art, public history, and public memory are drawn together for a year-long birthday party, featuring a mandolin trail, public storyboard, songwriting contest, and numerous concerts at the homestead and beyond. Collaboration for the event has been slow to crystallize among various claimants to Monroe's legacy, each seeming to prefer to celebrate their relationship with Monroe in their own way.

Similarly, Western Kentucky, known for its "Bluegrass, Blues, and Barbeque" region, celebrates Rosine and the Monroe homeplace as a significant contribution to the region. While the area is home to countless musicians, including the Everly Brothers, W. C. Handy, Mose Rager, and Merle Travis, no other birthplace is as well elaborated or well commemorated as that of Monroe. Monroe's regional influence extends northward to the International Bluegrass Music Museum and Hall of Fame, located in Owensboro. The museum, established in 1991, is an outgrowth of the International Bluegrass Music Association, dedicated to serve as the "world center for the presentation of the history, culture, and future of bluegrass music." Mandolin player Doyle Lawson, whose instrumental piece "Rosine" pays tribute to Monroe's birthplace, cites the museum as part of a grassroots effort by musicians. "I was part of a core group," according to Lawson, "that was looking to establish a home for bluegrass music. We had no home, no representation, no office, and no Hall of Fame. We only had a handful of people who believed in what we could do."[59] The first floor of the museum houses the permanent exhibit "Big Mon," which narrates Bill Monroe's early years in Rosine and his creation of bluegrass and the "high lonesome" sound. The museum's annual River of Music Party (ROMP) prominently features the Monroe legacy and the music of the Blue Grass Boys.

It is, perhaps, at this institutional level, that resources add support to claims of representation, and artifacts circulate in more complex political-economic spheres. Monroe, always one to follow his own vision, inaugurated his own bluegrass museum, in 1984, near Opryland, in Tennessee. The museum, which was later moved to Bean Blossom, Indiana, celebrates the history of bluegrass and Monroe's career after Rosine, and includes a wall highlighting members of the Blue Grass Boys, a Hall of Fame, with members hand-picked by the Father of Bluegrass, himself, and its own artifact-laden Bill Monroe room.[60] Monroe's famed 1923 Gibson Lloyd Loar F-5 mandolin—the relic most intimately associated with its former owner—resides in neither venue, nor in the homestead at Jerusalem Ridge, but, through a complex set of circumstances, in Nashville's prestigious Country Music Hall of Fame's Precious Jewels collection.

But while the artifacts and relics of Monroe's career may be subject to conflicting claims, that struggle for control and definition is focused on objects, not essence. Regardless of how far afield claims to his legacy extend, Jerusalem Ridge, Rosine, is the uncontested point of origin— the epicenter, to return to Mercer's exclamation—the point to which all other contexts and historical moments refer. While relics and artifacts may be collected, bartered, removed from their contexts, held at a distance from the source of their meaning, and reinterpreted, it can be argued that Monroe's songbook is composed of music inextricably bound to place, interwoven with the character and essence of his boyhood home. Competing claims to his legacy, or about the man himself, all begin with a remarkably uncontested relationship of a shy boy and a ridge in the hills of Kentucky. After that, as they say, it gets complicated.

NOTES

I would like to express my deepest gratitude to Marianne Pieper, of the Ohio County Tourism Commission; Sally Pontarelli, of Bluegrass Unlimited; and Campbell and Julie Mercer, of the Jerusalem Ridge Foundation, for their kindness, generosity, and invaluable assistance during my research for this article.

1. Rosine population courtesy of the office of the Ohio County Judge Executive.
2. Robert Cantwell, *Bluegrass Breakdown: The Making of the Old Southern Sound* (Urbana: University of Illinois Press, 2003), 36.
3. Richard D. Smith, *Can't You Hear Me Callin': The Life of Bill Monroe, Father of Bluegrass* (Cambridge, MA: Da Capo Press, 2000), 7.
4. Ibid., 8.
5. Schultz is noted as a major influence in the development of the "thumb style" of guitar playing, which would come to characterize the style of many Kentucky musicians, such as Monroe, Chet Atkins, and Merle Travis. See ibid., 25.

6. Cantwell, *Bluegrass Breakdown*, 31.

7. "Tour of the Monroe Homestead," unpublished document, nd, np.

8. Charles K. Wolfe, *Kentucky Country* (Lexington: University Press of Kentucky, 1982), 101.

9. Nicholas Dawidoff, *In the Country of Country: A Journey to the Roots of American Music* (London: Faber and Faber, 1997), 85–87; Wolfe, *Kentucky Country*, 97.

10. Dawidoff, *In the Country of Country*, 84.

11. Ibid., 86.

12. Tom Ewing, ed., *The Bill Monroe Reader* (Urbana: University of Illinois Press, 2000).

13. Gary P. West, "Bill Monroe's Rosine & Jerusalem Ridge," *Kentucky Living*, September 2008, 26.

14. Smith, *Can't You Hear Me Callin'*, 12.

15. Stuart Englert, "The Birthplace of Bluegrass," *American Profile* (May 2004), http://store .americanprofile.com/spotlights/article/4043.html.

16. Richard D. Smith, "Returning to Rosine," *Bluegrass Unlimited*, November 1996, 29.

17. Washington Irving, "The Early Experiences of Ralph Ringwood," in *The Sketchbook of Geoffrey Crayon, Gent.* [Reissue Edition] (New York: Oxford University Press, 2009).

18. Smith, "Returning to Rosine," 29.

19. "Bits of Rosine History," unpublished document, courtesy of the Ohio County Tourism Commission, nd, np; Smith, *Can't You Hear Me Callin'*, 6–7.

20. *Blue Moon News*. Rosine, KY: Rosine Association, December 2005–March 2006, 9–10.

21. Bobby O. Wallace, "Lady from Rosine," unpublished manuscript, 2004, np.

22. Ibid.

23. Cantwell, *Bluegrass Breakdown*, 28.

24. Ibid, 42.

25. Ewing, *The Bill Monroe Reader*, 276.

26. In 1996, Ohio County unemployment was 8.8 percent, while Kentucky unemployment was 5.6; weekly wages in 2000 were $110 below the state average. Ibid., 277.

27. Ibid.

28. "Bits of Rosine History."

29. Robert Henningsen, "Bill Monroe's birthplace is hallowed ground for bluegrass fans," *St. Louis Post-Dispatch*, July 28, 2002.

30. Juan Eduardo Campo, "American Pilgrimage Landscapes," *Annals of the American Academy of Political and Social Science* 558 (1998): 40–56.

31. Alan Thacker, "Loca Sanctorum: The Significance of Place in the Study of the Saints," in *Local Saints and Local Churches in the Early Medieval West*, ed. Alan Thacker and Richard Sharpe (New York: Oxford University Press, 2002), 1–2.

32. Duncan Cameron, "The Museum, a Temple or the Forum," *Journal of World History* 14, no. 1 (1972): 388.

33. Rick Bragg, "A Balladeer of Bluegrass Is Now Gone, Yet Lives On," *New York Times*, November 4, 1996.

34. Thacker, "Loca Sanctorum."

35. Victor and Edith Turner, *Image and Pilgrimage in Christian Culture* (New York: Columbia University Press, 1985), 6.

36. Thomas Schlereth, *Material Culture: A Research Guide* (Lawrence: University of Kansas Press, 1975); Thomas Schlereth, "History Museums and Material Culture," in *History Museums in the United States: A Critical Assessment*, ed. Warren Leon and Roy Rosensweig (Champaign: University of Illinois Press, 1989), 294–320; John A. Herbst, "Historic Houses," in Leon and Rosensweig, 112.

37 Herbst, "Historic Houses," 98.

38. Stuart Hobbs, "Exhibiting Anti-Modernism: History, Memory, and the Aestheticized Past in Mid-twentieth-century America," *The Public Historian* 23, no. 3 (2001): 39.

39. "Tour of the Monroe Homestead."
40. Stephen Brechter, personal communication.
41. Richard D. Smith, "Monroes of Rosine, Kentucky—A Family History," *Bluegrass Unlimited*, January 1997, 26.
42. "Tour of the Monroe Homestead."
43. Eric P. Olsen, "Long Way Back Home: Bill Monroe and the Making of Bluegrass," *The World and I*, December 2002, 77.
44. Wolfe, *Kentucky Country*, 99.
45. Edward P. Alexander, *Museums in Motion* (Nashville: American Association for State and Local History, 1979), 89.
46. Nancy Cardwell, "I'm On My Way to the Old Home: The Bill Monroe Bluegrass Music Foundation," *Bluegrass Unlimited*, November 2001, 23.
47. "Bits of Rosine History."
48. David McBride, "A Living Legend Dies," *Ohio County Times-News*, September 12, 1995, reprinted in Ewing, *The Bill Monroe Reader*, 244.
49. McBride quoted in Ewing, *The Bill Monroe Reader*, 245.
50. Ibid., 245.
51. Ibid., 246.
52. Dawidoff, *In the Country of Country*, 102.
53. Cardwell, "I'm on My Way to the Old Home," 22–24.
54. Don Wilkins, "Monroe Mission," *Ohio County Times-News*, 137, no. 9 (February 2002).
55. Bragg, "A Balladeer of Bluegrass," A14.
56. Quoted in Richard Schechner and Willa Appel, eds., *By Means of Performance* (Cambridge: Cambridge University Press, 1990), 1.
57. "Bits of Rosine History."
58. Cardwell, "I'm on My Way to the Old Home," 24.
59. David McGee, "Carter Family's Dale Jett to Serve on Artistic Advisory Board of Birthplace of Country Music Alliance," *Bristol Herald Courier*, March 3, 2008.
60. Doug Hutchens, "The Bill Monroe Museum and Bluegrass Hall of Fame," *Bluegrass Unlimited*, October 1984, 31.

Meredith Willson leads the Mason City Marching Band to celebrate the 1962 film premier of *The Music Man*. Photo courtesy of the *Mason City Globe Gazette*.

— 8 —

Despite its accomplishments in Bill Monroe's Rosine, birthplace boosterism has had mixed—and, sometimes, deleterious—results in other American towns. Anna Thompson Hajdik makes the point in her lively cultural history of Meredith Willson's birth memory in Mason City, Iowa. Willson immortalized his birthplace as the fictional River City in the runaway stage and screen hit, The Music Man. *Hajdik shows us how, during the 1960s, Mason City's love affair with its fictional counterpart echoed the nation's fantasy of an idealized Midwest as everyone's metaphorical birthplace. Thirty years later, when Cold War Era nationalism succumbed to late-century economic collapse, Mason City repurposed Willson's memory as an engine for community redevelopment. In the process, however, Mason City gave itself so completely to the myth of River City that preservationists restored the home where Willson was born in 1902 to appear as it had in 1912, the year during which* The Music Man *is set! Hajdik challenges us to consider how we draw the line between history and fiction in commemorations of American creativity. By blurring it, she suggests, heritage tourism risks distracting communities from the real complexities of the post-industrial order.*

"Right Here in Mason City"

Meredith Willson and Musical Memory in the American Midwest

ANNA THOMPSON HAJDIK

Iowans marveled at reports of a record-breaking fourteen-pound baby born in Mason City on May 18, 1902.[1] That big baby, otherwise known as Meredith Willson, never stopped grabbing headlines. Grown to be a talented musician and entertainer, the adult Willson penned popular songs, film scores, books, and most notably, several Broadway shows. Willson never forgot his birthplace, which inspired his most enduring work, *The Music Man* (1957). First performed on Broadway and adapted to film in 1962, *The Music Man* tells the story of Harold Hill, a fast-talking con man who descends on a small Iowa town in 1912 to outfit the community with marching band equipment. Hill intends to skip town with the money, but things go awry when he falls in love with the local librarian, Marian Paroo. By the end of the story, Hill has inadvertently enriched the town with a love of music and abandons his scheming ways.[2]

Today, Mason City commemorates Meredith Willson and his most significant work by preserving the home in which he was born and the adjacent Music Man Square. In many ways, the city has reshaped its own cultural identity to reflect Willson's nostalgic portrayal of "River City." The city's tourist appeal hinges on it. Consequently, examining the history of Willson's birthplace commemoration reveals important insights about the crafting of community identity, civic boosterism in both historical and contemporary contexts, and the powerful role popular culture wields on the American landscape. *The Music Man*'s enduring resonance also underscores the significance of the American Midwest's static iconography. Popular representations of this region still hinge on nostalgia rooted in pastoralism, provincialism, and wholesome family values. Willson deployed these themes and his Iowan identity to achieve his professional goals. Mason City's complex relationship with Willson, as this essay demonstrates, has been more challenging, though not without its own achievements and successes.

The Early Years

In 1902, the year Willson was born, Mason City reflected the progressive "booster dreams" of many small Midwest towns.[3] It was a community filled with civic leaders and business owners who truly believed it might someday rival Chicago for the economic and cultural dominance of the region. Named for its Free Masons and a once thriving brick-making industry, the community attracted a wide variety of immigrants with its abundant manufacturing jobs. Plentiful deposits of limestone and clay naturally led to a thriving mining and cement industry, and by 1911, two large cement factories served as the backbone of the town's economy. Brick and tile production became a cornerstone of the town's economy throughout the first half of the twentieth century.[4]

Meredith Willson was born into a prosperous, middle-class family. His father John practiced law, sold real estate, and was by all accounts a well-respected businessman in the community. Rosalie Reiniger Willson, Meredith's mother, graduated from Iowa State Teachers College in Cedar Falls in 1888. She held a progressive outlook toward education, and started the county's first kindergarten program, teaching children on the Willsons' front porch. She was also active in the First Congregational Church and served as the Sunday school instruction superintendent for thirty-two years. Her progressive mindset extended to social causes as well, and she helped found the Mason City chapter of the Humane Society. Most important, Rosalie made sure her children were well-rounded, and she cultivated the creative impulse apparent in Meredith from a young age. After teaching him to play the piano, she encouraged her youngest son to take up a second musical instrument. He chose the flute, a skill he eventually turned to professionally.[5]

Willson's ambitious dreams of a career in music came true when he earned a coveted spot in John Philip Sousa's marching band at the age of nineteen. Only four years later he joined Arturo Toscanini's New York Philharmonic. By 1929, Willson shifted to radio and worked for programs like *The Maxwell House Showboat* and *Good News*. These programs featured a cavalcade of Hollywood stars and provided venues for Willson to showcase his own musical and songwriting abilities. They also allowed him to cultivate a celebrity persona that hinged on a sort of midwestern "aw shucks" naiveté. "Willson's my name; Meredith Willson. I'm from Mason City, Iowa," he proclaimed, during his first appearance on the Burns and Allen radio program.[6] Willson served as the music director for the Armed Forces Radio Service during World War II. Afterward he joined *The Big Show* with Tallulah Bankhead and, throughout the decade, wrote books, composed film scores (Chaplin's *The Great Dictator* and a Bette Davis vehicle, *The Little Foxes*), and wrote songs constantly.

Willson's personal life was more tumultuous. He married his high school girlfriend and Mason City native Elizabeth "Peggy" Wilson shortly after graduating from high school, but the couple divorced in 1947. Their life in Hollywood had been less than perfect, at least according to Peggy. She filed for divorce on grounds of "mental cruelty" and testified that "her husband stayed out late and went on prolonged trips and answered evasively when she tried to learn where he had been."[7] Despite the airing of these grievances during her divorce proceedings, Peggy lived a quiet and comfortable life after their marriage ended. A hefty divorce settlement helped.[8]

Willson meanwhile met and married a Russian opera singer eleven months after the divorce. By many accounts, Willson's second wife, Ralina "Rini" Zarova, seemed a better match for the highly social Willson. She shared his love of music, possessed an extremely vivacious personality, and enthusiastically supported his creative endeavors. A year after the wedding, Rini traveled with her husband to Mason City for the annual North Iowa Band Festival and the *Mason City Globe Gazette* observed that that she was a "stunning brunette in a dark blue spangled dress."[9] Most biographers emphasize that Rini quickly won over Willson's old hometown friends. But Willson himself probably raised more than a few eyebrows by divorcing his hometown sweetheart and marrying an exotic Russian at the onset of the Cold War. He needed to rehabilitate his public image as a solid midwesterner with wholesome American values. He did so, ultimately, by finding personal redemption, public approval, and great creative and financial success in nostalgic portrayals of his own youth.

The Music Man and the American Midwest

With the 1948 publication of Willson's first autobiography, *And There I Stood with My Piccolo*, the Iowa native laid the creative groundwork for what would eventually become *The Music Man*. In this cheery, nostalgic narrative Willson points to the influence of his family and Mason City on his character and musical aspirations. He clearly had begun to think artistically about his childhood experiences, family relationships, and community connections by this point in his life. Years later, he published a follow-up autobiography focusing on his experiences with Broadway. Willson recalled that it had been fellow songwriter and musical composer Frank Loesser who had first suggested he write a musical comedy about Iowa. Even though he knew it was a good idea, Willson was hesitant at first: "I wanted very much to do it but I refused, just to keep my neck bowed . . . Nobody brought it up anymore for some time, and I began to think they thought I couldn't do it. So, of course, I had to give it a try. That's what we call Iowa-arrogance."[10]

It took Willson six years and forty drafts to complete *The Music Man*.[11] By late 1956, he had secured the backing of Broadway producer Kermit Bloomgarden. With a contract signed, the rest of the production slowly began to fall into place from finding a director to locking in the cast.[12] In the fall of 1957, some Broadway observers began to attend early previews. Back in Mason City, the editor of the local paper reprinted excerpts from well-known theater columnist Earl Wilson. Wilson recalled how "I attended an audition of Meredith Willson's first musical . . . and I can assure you that the Mason City, Iowa, genius is going to do for Iowa what Rodgers and Hammerstein did for Oklahoma."[13]

On December 19, 1957, *The Music Man* debuted on Broadway, and it quickly became the smash hit of the 1957–58 season. Running for 1,300 performances, it won the Tony award for best musical, famously (or infamously, depending on the critic) beating *West Side Story* for the honor. Many reviewers noted that the musical's success lay in its wholesome, innocent portrayal of small-town life at a time when stage productions had begun to tackle more controversial topics. The critic for *Time* magazine commented, "In a fat Broadway season whose successes deal so clinically with such subjects as marital frustration, alcoholism, dope addiction, juvenile delinquency and abortion, *The Music Man* is a monument to golden unpretentiousness and wholesome fun."[14] The *Time* review also incorporated an examination of Willson's link to his hometown, displaying key scenes from the musical on its July 21, 1958 cover. "Marvelous," wrote the *New York Times*'s Brooks Atkinson. "If Mark Twain could have collaborated with Vachel Lindsay, they might have devised a rhythmic lark like *The Music Man*, which is as American as apple pie and a Fourth of July oration."[15]

Other reviewers praised the musical's pastoral invocation of a virtuous American Midwest. "It has strength, a strength drawn from the fertile breast of this continent's Middle West," intoned Frank Aston, the theater critic for the *New York World-Telegram and Sun*.[16] Aston's comments demonstrate how and why *The Music Man* has come to be regarded as both a classically "American" musical and as an iconic, idealized representation of midwestern life. As Victoria Johnson argues, the American Midwest is often seen as the most typically "American" region. It is "a preferred place," according to Johnson, the "site of time-bound values of expressed belief in God, pioneering self-sufficiency, "knowable" community and heterosexual/nuclear-familial ideals."[17] Willson's deeply felt nostalgia for his midwestern upbringing conveys these romanticized messages about small-town life, individualism, and community boosterism in early twentieth-century Iowa. At the same time, as Kent Ryden observes, the Midwest "is defined by the absence of past, a sort of temporal emptiness." According to Ryden, midwesterners like Willson who lack "the historical touchstone of identity so readily available to other regions . . . are required to do a different sort of imaginative work."[18]

The Music Man certainly qualifies as an imaginative representation of an idealized slice of midwestern life at the turn of the twentieth century. However, it also does not stand alone in its glorified pastoral portrayal of the region. It is helpful to situate The Music Man within the broader spectrum of twentieth-century popular representations that make use of "middle American" iconography. Much like Willson, the creators of these representations also possessed strong familial and place-bound ties to the American Midwest. In the 1920s and 1930s, the regionalist art of Grant Wood (also an Iowan), John Steuart Curry, and Thomas Hart Benton held powerful artistic connections to midwestern geography and place. The three artists often drew on a regional agrarian heritage, their own childhoods, and family relationships for inspiration in their creative works. Paintings and murals such as American Gothic, Baptism in Kansas, and A Social History of Missouri found receptive, mostly urban audiences willing to consume their nostalgic, pastoral visions of the American Midwest.[19]

Like the regionalist artists, children's author Laura Ingalls Wilder harnessed her midwestern nostalgia for a decidedly earlier time—the late nineteenth century—when she wrote her popular series of Little House books throughout the 1930s and 1940s. Grasshopper plagues, prairie fires, bitterly cold winters, and food scarcity led to some difficult times for the Ingalls family, yet, much like Willson in his crafting of The Music Man, Wilder emphasized the strength of family and the triumph of community in the face of such adversity. Wilder's later books, particularly Little Town on the Prairie, also share the booster spirit of The Music Man, as she chronicles a young frontier railroad town's settlement, development, and budding prosperity.[20]

To understand the musical's popularity within a contextual framework of the 1950s, it is helpful to examine the popularity of another bit of popular culture from the same period that shares many of the same conventions, from the small-town nostalgia consistently on display, to the rather simple aesthetics and wholesome performance styles. *The Lawrence Welk Show* was popular from the 1950s to the 1980s and continues to run in syndication to this day. Born on a windswept, desolate homestead near the small town of Strasburg, North Dakota, Lawrence Welk had a similar career trajectory to Willson's. He built a successful career in musical entertainment after leaving the Midwest behind for the glitz and glamour of Hollywood. Today, much like Mason City, the town of Strasburg commemorates Welk's historic link to the community and offers tours of his family's restored homestead.

Welk's variety show featured him as the bandleader presiding over various musical acts and corny comical skits. The program especially appealed to white, middle-class television viewers, and he positively defined midwestern values and ideals in spite of network television and popular press reservations about appealing to the "typical midwestern" audience. Much like Willson's, Welk's place-bound identity as a midwesterner played a central role in how he crafted his public image for millions of television viewers. Victoria Johnson argues that Welk suggests "residual cultural ideals in the post–World War II American consumer landscape" while program content often featured "folk tunes, historic dance steps and promotes a family atmosphere with rural, Midwestern, and church-going ties."[21] Indeed, as Johnson points out, the program's emphasis on heritage and tradition is prioritized over progress. The program sometimes took contemporary songs and presented them in traditional formats often highlighting quartets or duets between singers. Older generations of artists often used instruments like accordions and honky-tonk piano while musical selections seldom made a "statement." Even technically, the program utilized old-fashioned camera techniques well in to the 1980s.[22] The program's popularity, particularly in the late 1950s and early 1960s, runs in tandem with *The Music Man*'s appeal because it too catered to a nostalgic vision of popular culture closely affiliated with the Midwest.

Hollywood Comes to Mason City

With the massive success of *The Music Man* on Broadway, it was not long before Hollywood film executives approached Willson about a movie version. Negotiations for the film rights began in earnest in 1958 with Willson's stipulations that the movie would be shot on special sets constructed in Mason City. Warner Brothers eventually won the rights, but did not agree to those terms. As the filming wrapped four years later, however, the studio's executives did decide that in order to garner even more publicity for the movie, they would hold the world premiere in Mason City, which would also coincide with the North Iowa Band Festival, an annual musical event held in the community since 1928. The Mason City Chamber of Commerce had its usual $35,000 budget for the festival enhanced substantially by Warner Brothers when it agreed to contribute $175,000. The studio also proposed that the band festival be lengthened to three days instead of the usual one so that the film's stars and other visitors from Hollywood could enjoy the hospitality, sights, and sounds of northern Iowa.[23]

The community response was swift and immediately positive. Soon, however, the reality set in that such an event would require a massive hospitality and public relations undertaking unprecedented in the town's history. Over 75,000 people, three times Mason City's population, were expected to attend the parade alone. Besides the substantial group from Hollywood, the community would be flooded with high school students from 121 marching bands from across the country, key Iowan government officials including the governor and both of the state's senators, as well as curious and star-struck visitors from across the Midwest. One newspaper notice warned that "a few Mason Cityans have called and tried to cancel out their promised housing for visiting band members. This creates a most serious problem." Only dire emergencies such as serious illness or death could be used as valid excuses for not holding to the hospitality commitment.[24]

The centerpiece of the festivities included a 160-unit parade with more than 40 floats. Banners hanging throughout the downtown and along the parade route proclaimed "No Trouble in River City Today!" A total of 190 national guardsmen, state highway patrolmen, and Mason City police were called upon to handle the massive crowds that collected along the parade route.[25] Warner Brothers flew in the film's stars, Robert Preston, Shirley Jones, and a very young Ron Howard, among a variety of other cast members, for a whirlwind of public appearances. Along with the actors came a media entourage, which included such personalities as TV presenter Arthur Godfrey, gossip columnist Hedda

Hopper, and over 150 reporters and Warner Brothers' publicists.[26] The film studio also ran a nationwide press release in a series of major metropolitan newspapers, signed by Jack Warner, the president of Warner Brothers. It emphasized the "heartwarming inspiration" of the film in the face of the seemingly countless "sensational scandals" of Hollywood. When "thousands of American boys and girls . . . march in review before the assembled judges," it continued, "a good hunk of what's wonderful about our country goes marching with them."[27]

Leading up to the festivities, the City Council renamed the town footbridge, a setting for a key scene in the film, the "Meredith Willson Footbridge" in a resolution of appreciation for Willson's service "as a goodwill ambassador for the city." "The composer," it added, "has brought honor and fame to Mason City and continues to do so at every opportunity."[28] The accolades hardly stopped there. Willson received five different plaques and citations from a variety of civic organizations. A "mass band of 8,000 youngsters" serenaded him with "Hometown Boy." And when Willson led the Mason City High School marching band in the parade, it played "76 Trombones." Said one resident of all of the events, "I've been here 15 years, and after all those band festivals, you sometimes wish they'd stop all that noise and let you get down to business. But we love it, really, and this year even more so because it's for Meredith. He has been wonderful to us and he has never forgotten where he came from. I guess *The Music Man* proves that."[29]

Soon enough though, the excitement, glitz, and glamour of the 1962 film premiere faded. After the great success of *The Music Man,* Willson's follow-up shows included the respectable but uneven *The Unsinkable Molly Brown,* and *1491,* an ill-conceived musical based on the explorations of Christopher Columbus. Both failed to capture the interest, momentum, and goodwill that had so galvanized critics and audiences behind *The Music Man.* Willson continued to make periodic public appearances throughout Iowa and the Midwest, and donated money to a variety of charitable causes in the state, including music scholarships and his mother's First Congregational Church. Mason City was slow in providing any lasting monument to Willson, however, and by the 1970s, even the sign welcoming visitors to "River City" had been taken down. The footbridge, which had been so enthusiastically dedicated in Willson's honor, fell into disrepair.

The director of the Kinney Pioneer Museum, the town's only historic attraction at the time, deflected public critiques leveled at the lack of Willson-related material, and noted that a special area had been "dedicated to our most famous booster for many years." In reality, however, the museum possessed few artifacts, including one scrapbook, a wooden sculpture of some marching band musicians, and two trombones used in the movie. The museum's director observed, rather bitterly, "We find it very rewarding to have visitors from other states as well as our own . . . we are however, disappointed in the number of our own friends and neighbors who seem so disinterested in our history and heritage."[30] The landscape of Mason City also reflected this lack of interest. Willson's birthplace had been converted into a shabby apartment building. One journalist sadly noted, "There doesn't seem to be much interest in historic preservation in Mason City. The library of Marian the librarian is for sale; the theater where *The Music Man* premiered is being torn down for a mall."[31]

From River City to Music Man Square

Meredith Willson died on June 16, 1984, and his funeral and interment in his hometown again attracted the public interest of Mason City's residents. The local paper provided lengthy coverage of the funeral and extensive tributes to Willson. But short of the 1962 film premiere and the dedication of the footbridge, the community had done little with regard to lasting memorials. Some observers pointed to Willson's one and only bequest to his hometown—a set of cufflinks—as clear evidence of his disappointment in the lack of gratitude Mason City had shown him in more recent years.[32]

In the weeks following his funeral, a number of letters poured into the *Mason City Globe Gazette* concerning the issue of commemoration. Bill Brissee, the editor of the newspaper at the time, wrote an editorial in which he assembled a large collection of the wide-ranging responses. One popular suggestion involved naming a soon-to-open shopping mall for Willson. "I suggest the name 'River City Mall,'" proposed one reader. "This is easier to say than Meredith Willson Mall . . . and the actors in 'The Music Man' were always joyful and having fun, Meredith would be pleased." Other readers called for the rechristening of the North Iowa Community Auditorium as the Meredith Willson Auditorium, while multiple residents thought that the city park or portions of it could be rededicated in Willson's honor. Other readers held entirely different points of view and questioned their most famous son's commitment to the community. One individual proclaimed, "I don't feel memorialization is needed for Meredith Willson. To name the shopping mall, Central Park, or anything else after him is absurd. We honored him when he was alive. Enough is enough!"[33]

The fortunes of Mason City rose and fell throughout the 1980s. Civic boosters including Mayor Ken Kew were hopeful about a $20 million revitalization effort for downtown, which included the much-discussed shopping mall. It finally opened on May 23, 1985. The farm crisis compounded by a recession hit the region hard, though, and the community's population had declined by over 10 percent from its 1960 high of 30,642 by mid-decade. In a sadly ironic development, state budget cuts led to the closure and sale of the municipal Music Hall. The Mason City school district's music program also suffered difficulties with poorly maintained band uniforms and musical instruments that had not been replaced in decades.[34]

Hard times encouraged enough grassroots philanthropy to sow the seeds of serious commemoration in 1986 with the formation of the Mason City Public Library Foundation and a historical collection fund drive. Members raised $90,000 toward a $200,000 goal for a new facility to house an archival collection.[35] By 1988, the foundation attracted the support of Rosemary Willson, Meredith's third wife. She worked with the organization to select Willson memorabilia for permanent display. The year 1988 also marked the fiftieth anniversary of the North Iowa Band Festival, sparking a fresh re-examination of Willson's legacy. Rosemary Willson attended the festival and received a posthumous Iowa Award on Meredith's behalf, the highest honor given to a private citizen of the state.[36]

Rosemary Willson's visibility and willingness to reach out to the civic boosters of Mason City no doubt contributed to a renewed appreciation of Meredith Willson's link to the community. In 1991, however, the arrival of an energetic newcomer marked a key shift in the focus, organization, and mission of various historic preservation and cultural development efforts. Carl Miller moved to Mason City at the age of 56 to serve as an administrator at a local college.[37] He witnessed how Mason City's strong orientation toward manufacturing had seriously hindered its economy by the early 1990s. The brickyards, which had helped to establish the community as a regional center in the early twentieth century, had closed. The cement factories cut a major portion of their workforce. The local packing plant consolidated with other regional operators, and the hospital served as the largest employer. After learning about Willson's connection to the town, Miller questioned why more had not been done to promote it to the public. Then, he had an epiphany. In the words of one journalist, Miller realized that "Mason City's future was in 1912."[38] Like many small-town boosters living with a now largely postmodern, post-industrial economy, Miller viewed heritage tourism as a sustainable economic alterative to a weakened manufacturing sector.

As numerous scholars have observed, popular interest in heritage tourism has remained steady throughout the United States. Anthropologist Edward Bruner suggests that this form of tourism encourages us to consume nostalgia for a perceived simpler time and place, to buy into the idea of American progress, and to participate in the commemoration of a traditional America closely associated with values like neighborliness and wholesomeness.[39] As the twenty-first century approached, interest in heritage tourist sites seemed to magnify. Anxiety about the approaching millennium and rapid technological change resulted in a wave of collective nostalgia that manifested itself in everything from automobile advertising and fashion to recycled movie and television franchises.

Miller moved quickly. He became involved with the Mason City Foundation and led a feasibility study for an arts and cultural center. A year later, he was elected mayor and began to push for a variety of projects that centered on Willson. In 1994, the Mason City Foundation purchased Willson's birthplace and began restoring the old Victorian home. The house opened to the public a year later.[40] Today, tour guides tell the Willson story through the wholesome lens of family and community, situating the narrative within the historical confines of the early twentieth century. Visitors are shown to the bedroom where Meredith was born and told about his famous birth weight. They learn about the social, cultural, and professional lives of Meredith's parents and siblings. While some of the furniture belonged to the Willson family, the guides also proudly proclaim that many of the period pieces are donated from prominent individuals throughout Mason City and the surrounding area, thus illustrating a community-wide investment in the preservation of the Willson home. Finally, visitors are told that the home is decorated as it might have appeared in 1912, the year *The Music Man* takes place.[41]

At first glance, the home appears to be a preserved time capsule, a window into the actual Mason City of 1912. In reality, however, it symbolizes the labors of a modern, business-savvy organization that has successfully melded historic preservation with popular culture. Unlike the display of community heritage at the Kinney Pioneer Museum, an attraction that contains a hodgepodge of exhibits that span multiple time periods and commemorates Mason City and its surrounding region more broadly, the presentation of history at the birthplace is more narrowly focused around Willson family dynamics and the social, economic, and cultural world of the community at the turn of the twentieth century.

The Foundation also rebuilt the Willson footbridge and, with Miller at the helm, began to develop plans for something even more substantial, Music Man Square.[42] Miller was not the first civic booster with big dreams for *The Music Man* in Mason City. In the flurry of activity surrounding the 1962 film premiere, Luvern Hansen, a member of the Mason City Planning and Zoning Commission, had proposed the building of "River City Land," a memorial to Willson that "could be like Disneyland, the World's Fair, and an introduction to the space age all in one thrilling development." Hansen's description of "River City Land" included an elaborate artistic rendering of the attraction and emphasized a blend of nostalgic features with an amusement aesthetic heavily influenced by Disneyland. Hansen also curiously anticipated several key elements of Music Man Square. "What would a 'River City Land' feature? As a starter, I could suggest an authentic 'River City' Main Street, planned after the Warner Brothers sets for Meredith Willson's *The Music Man*. The show windows in these replicas of bygone days could serve as a museum of early century Mason City and trade area."[43]

Hansen's vision is fascinating for how it anticipates Willson's commemoration during the 1990s. Although he was clearly dreaming big, Hansen's ideas were also rooted in the entertainment and amusement park trends of the twentieth century that often mixed heritage tourism with futuristic displays of technology. Nineteen sixty-two was a particularly significant year for such attractions. In addition to Disneyland's popularity, the Seattle World's Fair captured headlines during the same summer that Mason City basked in the spotlight. Now Carl Miller endeavored to make Hansen's lofty vision a reality. He accepted a position as head of the Mason City Foundation shortly after his term as mayor ended and envisioned Music Man Square as one part museum, one part community center, and one part performance venue. The Square would be a monument to Willson and his most famous work, but not simply a static space or fusty mausoleum. Instead, it would be vibrant and youthful, and would balance the cheery nostalgia originally contained in the musical with the community's present-day cultural arts scene.

Miller contacted Rosemary Willson and persuaded her to pledge $5 million toward the Square's construction, guaranteeing that it would be matched with private donations and grants. With a $10 million dollar price tag, some in the community questioned the soundness of the project, but throughout the late 1990s, Music Man Square seemed like "a shining star" for so many of those volunteers who had worked to keep Willson's memory alive. The editor of the local paper championed the efforts of the Mason City Foundation, but his comments revealed that not everyone in town was excited about the project. "Music Man Square, like all good ideas," he wrote, "has been criticized and chipped away at by those who think it's too grand, too pie in the sky, too much this or not enough that. So it goes for most thinkers and dreamers, the ones who flourish on creating what does not now exist."[44]

Miller and the Foundation had good reason, though, to be optimistic about Music Man Square's chances for success. Throughout the 1990s, popular culture tourism increased throughout the Midwest, helped in part by a wave of films and books that showcased the region. The state of Kansas, for instance, boasted a $2.5 billion tourism industry built on films like *The Wizard of Oz* (1939) and the television program *Gunsmoke,* which had been set in Dodge City. Despite *Gunsmoke's* having gone off the air decades before, Dodge City and its museum still lured over 100,000 tourists a year throughout the 1990s.[45] Similarly, Robert James Waller's bestselling novel *The Bridges of Madison County* (1992) sparked a travel boom to Winterset, Iowa, where Waller set the story. A 1995 film adaptation created even more tourist demand. Dyersville, Iowa, claimed "The Field of Dreams" as a wholesome, family-friendly destination. The 1989 film starring Kevin Costner had been filmed there and a decade later, the setting—an Iowa cornfield transformed into a baseball diamond—was one of the state's top tourist draws, luring 55,000 people annually.[46] Surely, Miller thought, tourists would flock to Music Man Square and want to learn more about Meredith Willson, one of Iowa's most significant cultural producers.

Early promotional literature distributed by the Foundation outlined Music Man Square's central mission:

> The Music Man Square seeks to sustain the spirit of River City, Iowa as portrayed in *The Music Man*. It will preserve the cultural legacy of "the musical"—America's gift to theatre—and will highlight the role of the marching band in the development of American music. Of equal importance, The Music Man Square can aid in the development of creative musical and theatrical talents and create an environment for artistic endeavors throughout the city and state.[47]

Perhaps the most striking element of Music Man Square was its indoor 1912 streetscape, or at least 1912 as envisioned by Hollywood art directors and set designers in 1962. The Mason City Foundation obtained permission from Warner Brothers Studio to replicate the set from *The Music Man* and re-adapt it with twelve storefronts based on actual Mason City stores. The museum designers meticulously studied the film sets before they began construction.[48]

Today as one enters the building, reproductions of early twentieth-century street lamps line a long faux Main Street. A reception hall is located on one side, while a real ice cream parlor and popcorn stand wait for customers on the other side. Mrs. Paroo's cottage has been transformed into a gift shop. The building also includes a museum that houses many of Willson's belongings, and in the exhibition hall, a documentary about the making of *The Music Man* plays constantly in the background. Meanwhile, Willson's birthplace is located right next door, and visitors have the choice of touring just the birthplace or purchasing joint tickets to both the museum and the Willson home.

Music Man Square opened to the public with much fanfare on June 1, 2002. The excitement surrounding the grand opening echoed the enthusiasm of forty years earlier, and although a bit grayer and fewer in number, several Hollywood celebrities returned to Mason City. Shirley Jones, who starred as Marian the Librarian in the 1962 film, and Debbie

Reynolds, who portrayed the title character in the film adaptation of *The Unsinkable Molly Brown,* were the main attractions. They signed autographs at the Square, gave interviews to the local media, and made countless public appearances. Once again, Rosemary Willson proudly served as the public ambassador for her husband's musical legacy. A 1,000-voice barbershop chorus performed songs from *The Music Man,* and all of the festivities again coincided with the North Iowa Band Festival.

Yet, in the wake of success, notes of discord also sounded throughout the community. The dissension began over financing. Although $10.5 million had already been raised, Carl Miller's Mason City Foundation claimed that it needed an additional $12 million to build the next phase of the Square, a performing arts center. Despite earlier promises from the Foundation to target private monies, it nonetheless petitioned for $825,000 in public contributions. While that amount seemed small in comparison to what had already been raised, a vocal group of community leaders and business owners raised concerns about the long-term economic viability of the complex in the face of an ever-changing popular culture landscape, and questioned whether tourism revenue would really trickle down through the rest of Mason City's economy. As one pair of skeptical residents observed, "It's a decent musical, but you can't build a city around it."[49]

Rallying around the White Elephant

As it turns out, they were right. Miller initially estimated that Music Man Square would attract 75,000–100,000 visitors annually with attendance reaching 225,000 by its fifth year of operation.[50] By late 2009, however, the actual number of admissions ran significantly lower, with never more than 65,000 visitors per year since the Square's opening in June of 2002.[51] So, what went wrong in River City? Clearly Mason City risked a great deal by linking its civic and cultural identity so closely to one person. The gamble, of course, was not its citizens' alone. Grand Rapids, Minnesota, just hours north of Mason City, faces a similar dilemma. *The Wizard of Oz* star Judy Garland was born there in 1922 and lived in Grand Rapids for just four years before her family packed up and headed to Hollywood. Like Mason City, Grand Rapids has preserved Garland's birthplace and hosts an annual festival in her honor. A few years ago, the community suffered a very public black eye when an embarrassing lack of museum security enabled a thief to make off with a pair of Garland's celebrated ruby slippers. The real problem facing Grand Rapids, however, is that Judy Garland tourism will continually decline as her fan base ages and disappears.[52] The same reality haunts Mason City.

Then, too, there is the problem in Mason City of Music Man fatigue.[53] Music Man Square had, in a sense, taken over all other facets of Mason City's cultural identity. Some in the community even likened Carl Miller to a modern-day Harold Hill, the fast-talking con man from the musical. Max Weaver, a former city council member, was particularly critical. "For six months of the year, no one wants to come here," Weaver protested. "And how many people care about barbershop quartets and band music or have even heard of Meredith Willson?" Weaver likened Music Man Square to a "white elephant" and predicted that Miller would leave town soon after the Square opened. As it turned out, his predictions came true, at least partly. Miller left Mason City in November 2003 to take a position as the executive director of the historical society in his own hometown of La Crosse, Wisconsin. The board of the Mason City Foundation, initially shocked, moved quickly to find a replacement.[54] But how could Music Man Square survive without the singular determination of its staunchest advocate?

Miller's ardent boosterism, the resistance of some longtime locals to that boosterism, and Weaver's comments raise an important question: who has the right to define a community's landscape of commemoration? As George Lipsitz observes, "What we choose to remember about the past [does] a lot to determine how we live and what decisions we make in the present."[55] Those in Mason City who invested in Miller's vision of the past chose to remember the community as what it never truly was: a nostalgic frozen-in-time utopian incarnation of the fictional River City. Music Man Square, after all, is a simulation of a simulation. It exemplifies Umberto Eco's notion of "hyperreality" wherein "the past must be preserved and celebrated in full-scale authentic copy; a philosophy of immortality as duplication."[56] Blurring the boundaries between fiction and reality, Music Man Square's faux streetscape resembles the most famous miniaturized Main Street of all, Walt Disney's "Main Street, U.S.A." in Disneyland. Portraying Mason City as a place frozen in time, however, and doing it through the lens of fiction, prevents the community's residents from confronting deeper social problems like joblessness, poverty, and, as Iowa becomes more diverse, racial discrimination. Such static imagery might work for a certain brand of tourism, but it can also hinder economic development. And development is what is needed as the community adjusts to a new post-industrial economy.

Fortunately, new preservation efforts seek to broaden Mason City's historical purview beyond *The Music Man*. For example, the chamber of commerce began printing a "Historical Walking Tour" brochure in 2008. While Willson-related sites are noted on a fold-out map, other aspects of the town's history are emphasized as well. These other attractions include an extensive neighborhood of homes designed by Prairie School architect Walter Burley Griffin, a contemporary of Frank Lloyd Wright. On the map too is the imposing structure of the First National Bank, famously robbed by John Dillinger in 1934. A major historic preservation project is also under way. "Wright on the Park" focuses on preserving and maintaining all of the Frank Lloyd Wright–designed structures in downtown Mason City. The Park Inn Hotel, a once grand establishment built and designed by Wright in 1910, housed all of those movie stars and Hollywood celebrities who descended on Mason City back in 1962. It is the only remaining hotel in the world designed by Wright.[57]

It is clear, though, that Willson has become the main attraction in Mason City and Music Man Square the chief rallying point for the community. During the last two presidential elections, the venue took on another intriguing role. The community space has provided the perfect photo backdrop for a wide variety of political candidates who routinely trek through the state during the much-hyped Iowa presidential caucuses. One 2008 campaign observer noted how the now disgraced former candidate John Edwards made the most of his surroundings during one of his many stump speeches:

> More than 500 Iowans crammed themselves into the indoor atrium of Music Man Square, a museum dedicated to Broadway composer Meredith Willson, who fictionalized his hometown as River City in the 1950s musical. Although Edwards never alluded to "The Music Man" in his stump speech, the former trial lawyer is the Democrats' best huckster, and his pitch is a 2008 variant on "We've got trouble in River City . . ." As Edwards railed against the "monied interests," he

was speaking opposite the false-front façade of the "River City Bank," a mythical financial institution unlikely to rival Citicorp.[58]

Against the backdrop of the Square's faux streetscape, Edwards touted the virtues of his candidacy and disarmed the crowd with his charisma and affable charm. His subsequent political scandals only add to the irony of the event and, of course, beg for comparison with the smooth-talking con man Harold Hill. Once again, the lines blur between the fiction and reality of American popular culture.

The well-intentioned preservation and civic heritage efforts in Mason City have resulted in a fascinating blend of history and popular culture. Willson's birthplace and Music Man Square literally stand side by side as tourist attractions tailor-made for a postmodern, post-industrial era. In Mason City, community leaders, through their support of Music Man Square, have willingly merged the identity of their town with Willson's River City, a bright, cheery, but fictional representation, thus illustrating Jean Baudrillard's contention that the perfect definition of simulacra is when the reproduction is "more real" than the original."[59] *The Music Man* is also Willson's most enduring work, perhaps even outstripping its author in its fame and notoriety. There is no doubt that his formative years in Mason City nourished his early musical talents and provided him with the needed inspiration for a work of musical theater that continues to loom large in the American imagination.

And yet, the significance of Meredith Willson's birthplace to American popular culture is only one part of a larger story about communities of memory. As Andrew Ross notes, community is what happens when a group is united around a common cause, or "can identify common concerns and affinities."[60] While Music Man Square has stood as a lightning rod of controversy or a symbol of outside interests for some in Mason City, it also represents the hard work and dedication of many individuals who want to see their community prosper and be recognized far beyond the boundaries of Iowa. As Mason City moves forward, it now needs to broaden the scope of its cultural identity beyond the nostalgia of *The Music Man*. The enthusiastic, energetic members of the Mason City Foundation certainly have a strong track record. They also have the power to use their town's history as a tool of community empowerment in a post-industrial economy that demands honest discourse about an uncertain future.

NOTES

1. This bit of information is one of the first shared with visitors on the Willson birthplace house tour and is also found in John Skipper, *Meredith Willson: The Unsinkable Music Man* (Mason City, IA: Savas Publishing, 2000), 1.

2. Morton DaCosta, Director, *The Music Man,* based on the stage musical written by Meredith Willson, 1962.

3. William Cronon, *Nature's Metropolis: Chicago and the Great West* (New York: W. W. Norton, 1991), 31.

4. Bill Oates, *Meredith Willson: America's Music Man* (Bloomington, IN: AuthorHouse, 2005), 2.

5. Skipper, *Meredith Willson,* 4–23.

6. Ibid., 66–85.

7. Associated Press, *Des Moines Register,* March 5, 1947.

8. Ibid.

9. Skipper, *Meredith Willson,* 87–93.

10. Meredith Willson, *"But He Doesn't Know the Territory:" The Making of Meredith Willson's The Music Man* (New York: G. P. Putnam's Sons, 1959), 16.

11. Roberta Freund Schwartz, "Iowa Stubborn: Meredith Willson's Musical Characterization of His Fellow Iowans," *Studies in Musical Theater* 3, no. 1 (2009): 32.

12. Skipper, *Meredith Willson,* 113.

13. E.A.N., "Straws: Showing Which Way the Wind Blows: The Music Man," *Mason City Globe Gazette,* September 11, 1957.

14. "Pied Piper of Broadway," *Time,* July 21, 1958, 42–46.

15. Brooks Atkinson, "The Music Man," *New York Times,* December 20, 1957.

16. Frank Aston, "Tune Show Has Fun and Style," *New York World-Telegram and Sun,* December 20, 1957.

17. Victoria E. Johnson, "Welcome Home? CBS, PAX-TV, and 'Heartland' Values in a Neo-network Era," in *The Television Studies Reader,* ed. Robert C. Allen and Annette Hill (New York: Routledge, 2004), 43.

18. Kent C. Ryden, "Writing the Midwest: History, Literature, and Regional Identity," *The Geographical Review* 89 (1999): 513.

19. James M. Dennis, *Renegade Regionalists: The Modern Independence of Grant Wood, Thomas Hart Benton, and John Steuart Curry* (Madison: University of Wisconsin Press, 1998).

20. Laura Ingalls Wilder, *Little Town on the Prairie* (New York: Harper and Row, 1941).

21. Victoria E. Johnson, "Citizen Welk: Bubbles, Blue Hair, and Middle America," in *The Revolution Wasn't Televised: Sixties Television and Social Conflict,* ed. Lynn Spigel and Michael Curtin (New York: Routledge, 1997), 264–85.

22. Ibid.

23. Skipper, *Meredith Willson,* 146–51.

24. "No cancellation of housing facilities now, Please!" *Mason City Globe Gazette,* June 14, 1962.

25. Richard Christiansen, "Little Mason City Cheers 'Music Man:' Film Premiere, Bands Salute Native Son Meredith Willson," *Chicago Daily News,* June 19,1962.

26. Ibid.

27. Jack L. Warner, "Tahiti, Mason City, and Rome," *Mason City Globe Gazette,* June 19, 1962.

28. "Footbridge named for Willson," *Mason City Globe Gazette,* June 5, 1962.

29. Christiansen, "Little Mason City Cheers 'Music Man.'"

30. Ralph Peterson, "You're invited to visit Pioneer Museum," *Mason City Globe Gazette,* February 2, 1983.

31. Pete Young, "No more big brass bands . . . Mason City says 'So what?' about 'The Music Man," *St. Louis Post-Dispatch,* 1979.

32. Rick Hampson, "Troubled towns toot heroes' horns: Tourist attractions meant to boost local economy," *USA Today,* June 14, 2002.

33. Bill Brissee, "Readers want to honor Willson," *Mason City Globe Gazette,* July 5, 1984.

34. Douglas Martin, "Downtown projects give Mason City a lot to brag about," *Minneapolis Star Tribune,* June 8, 1985.

35. "Willson memorabilia coming to city library," *Mason City Globe Gazette,* August 28, 1986.

36. Kristin Buehner, "She works for her 'Music Man,'" *Mason City Globe Gazette,* May 28, 1988.

37. Hampson, "Troubled towns toot heroes' horns."

38. Ibid.

39. Edward Bruner, "Abraham Lincoln as Authentic Reproduction: A Critique of Postmodernism," *American Anthropologist* 96, no. 2 (June 1994): 411.

40. "The Music Man Square History and Information," The Mason City Foundation.

41. I have toured the Meredith Willson birthplace on two separate occasions, once in July 2002 shortly after the opening of Music Man Square, and again in March 2010.

42. "Willson landmarks take a new lease on life," *Mason City Globe Gazette,* September 2, 1995.

43. Luvern J. Hansen, "Dream envisions real River City," *Mason City Globe Gazette,* June 15, 1962.

44. John Smalley, "Going from 'thinking' to 'doing,'" *Mason City Globe Gazette,* March 1, 1998.

45. "Movie tourism in America's mid-west: Where bluebirds fly," *The Economist,* October 30, 1999, 97.

46. Ibid.

47. "The Music Man Square . . . Preserving Our Cultural Inheritance," The Mason City Foundation, 1997.

48. Kristin Buehner, "Main Street Revisited," *Mason City Globe Gazette,* October 1, 1999.

49. Louise Roug, "Many are wooed, but few caucus in Mason City," *Los Angeles Times,* November 20, 2007, www.globegazette.com/news/article_0e0e6dc1-3587-5ac7-9460-e1aef3a9ac7a.html.

50. Hampson, "Troubled towns toot heroes' horns."

51. Karry Taylor, Interview with Author, March 16, 2010.

52. Tim Gihring, "Who Stole the Ruby Slippers? Suspicious Munchkins, Hollywood hucksters, and lunatic fans (oh, my)," *Minnesota Monthly,* March 2009, www.minnesotamonthly.com/media/Minnesota-Monthly/March-2009/Who-Stole-the-Ruby-Slippers.

53. Staci Hupp, "Growing 'Music Man' project stirs trouble in Mason City," *Des Moines Sunday Registrar,* February 24, 2002.

54. John Skipper, "Miller heads home to La Crosse," *Mason City Globe Gazette,* November 22, 2003.

55. George Lipsitz, *Time Passages: Collective Memory and American Popular Culture* (Minneapolis: University of Minnesota Press, 1990), 34.

56. Umberto Eco, *Travels in Hyperreality* (San Diego: Harcourt Brace Jovanovich, 1986), 6.

57. Mason City Downtown Association, "Historic Walking Tour," Map Prepared by Tim Moreau, P.E., Veenstra & Kim Inc.; Mason City, Iowa; August 2008.

58. Walter Shapiro, "America's next top democrat: With the Iowa vote nearing, Clinton, Obama and Edwards reveal sharp tonal differences, betting the farm not on policy but on political panache," *Salon.com,* December 18, 2007, www.salon.com/news/feature/2007/12/18/democrats.

59. Jean Baudrillard, *America* (London: Verso, 1988).

60. Andrew Ross, The Celebration Chronicles: Life, Liberty, and the Pursuit of Property Value in Disney's New Town (New York: Ballantine Books, 1999), 219.

Paulsdale, birthplace of Alice Stokes Paul, 128 Hooton Road, Mount Laurel, New Jersey, as it appears today. Photo courtesy of the Alice Paul Institute.

~ 9 ~

Kris Myers leads up a triptych of essays that will conclude our volume by consider-
ing new possibilities for thinking about the past and present at historic birthplaces.
As we've seen, birthplace commemoration garnered renewed interest during the late
twentieth century as more and more communities turned to heritage tourism for
economic relief. They recalled an old model of birthplace reverence that, a century
before, had figured in heated contests over the very nature of American identity. In
recounting the story of Alice Paul's birthplace, however, Myers shows us that new
models and motivations for remembering birth have come to light during the new
century. At Paulsdale, interpreters eschew the customary house museum in favor
of a dynamic learning space that encourages young people, often from disadvan-
taged communities, to emulate Paul's leadership qualities. Past serves present in
Paulsdale's struggle against inequality, which is itself inspired by the home in which
Paul discovered her own commitments to social justice. Paulsdale's success suggests
that community engagement is vital to repurposing old commemorative forms for a
new generation. It also reminds us that doing good public history has always been
about taking risks and remembering Americans whom others would have us forget.

Paulsdale

Adapting Alice Paul's Birthplace for a New Generation of Leaders

KRIS MYERS

A charming historic home sits quietly atop six-and-a-half acres in a suburban New Jersey neighborhood thirteen miles outside Philadelphia.
Inside, however, it is anything but quiet. Twenty-five eighth-grade girls
squeal with delight as they scramble to free themselves from a "human
knot." This teamwork-building exercise is part of the Lens of Leadership

program hosted at Paulsdale, the birthplace and childhood home of Alice Stokes Paul (1885–1977). A Quaker, suffragist, and author of the Equal Rights Amendment, Paul dedicated her life to the cause of advancing equality.

Today, Paulsdale is home to the Alice Paul Institute's (API) women's heritage and girls' leadership center. Inspired by Paul and other female heroes of history, the API's founders purchased Paulsdale in 1990 but made an early decision not to convert the home into a house museum. Instead, with a desire to honor Paul with a living memorial, the API adapted the building for re-use as its center for public programming. In 1995, the Institute launched the Alice Paul Leadership Program, a series of grade 5–12 workshops that teach girls leadership skills like public speaking, teamwork, assertiveness, and creative thinking by focusing on Alice Paul and other historically significant women as role models. In 2002, having rehabilitated Paulsdale, the API added its Women's Heritage Program, which includes history-focused workshops that inspire boys and girls in grades 2–12 with the message that one person can truly make a difference. API hosts tours and events for adults too, and today Paulsdale evokes the power of place by inspiring students and guests to become active citizens and agents of change within their communities.

While Paulsdale's destiny as a leadership and heritage center today seems clear, the organization's decision to preserve the home for a modern purpose perplexed a public that expected a house museum full of women's suffrage banners and sashes. In its founding years, the API faced many challenges with every detail of preservation from purchasing the home to restoring it and defending its national significance. The difficulties continued when historians, preservationists, community leaders, and the public pressured the organization to explain who Alice Paul was, how her story connects to American history, and if she was important enough to warrant the preservation of her birthplace and childhood home. This essay explains how the API responded to those challenges and what its solutions suggest about the commemorative possibilities for historic birthplaces.

Who Is Alice Paul?

When asked by a journalist why she devoted her long life to equal rights advocacy, Alice Paul responded modestly, "I have never doubted that equal rights was the right direction. Most reforms, most problems are complicated. But to me there is nothing complicated about ordinary equality."[1] A brilliant leader dedicated to the notion of "ordinary equality," Paul was willing to endure harassment and imprisonment, and if necessary to give her life for the principles of democracy she felt the United States should model.

Paul's name first emerged in the national consciousness after she left home at sixteen for college and later joined the English women's suffrage movement. Newspapers dubbed her a "window smasher" when she joined the rabble-rousing suffragettes of the Women's Social & Political Union (WSPU) and practiced their motto, "Deeds, not words" by breaking windows, protesting in the streets, sneaking into government meetings, and getting arrested in the name of women's right to vote.[2] In 1910 Paul returned to the U.S. and joined the National American Woman's Suffrage Association (NAWSA). In 1913, she took over the Congressional Committee, a Washington, DC, branch that lobbied for a constitutional amendment to enfranchise women. Within a year, Paul coordinated over 8,000 suffrage marchers in a massive parade, sent four deputations of suffragists to pressure President Wilson to support the amendment, and began a newspaper, *The Suffragist*.[3] When the NAWSA ejected Paul for her daring behavior, she and a small group of suffragists formed what would become the National Woman's Party (NWP) in 1916.[4]

Paul shocked the nation when she sent NWP suffragists in groups to picket the White House beginning in January 1917.[5] Paul's NWP made clear that it was no longer willing to wait politely for President Wilson's support. Lined up with strict orders from Paul to not speak (unless asked a question), the "Iron-Jawed Angels" let their banners ask, "Mr. President, what will you do for woman suffrage?" More daring messages to "Kaiser Wilson" set off a riot in June during which men beat the picketers and tore their banners to shreds. The next day, police arrested the picketing suffragists on the charge of "obstructing the traffic." Police were delighted to arrest Alice Paul in October, and

authorities sent her to the District of Columbia jail, while other suffragists were sent some miles away to the Occoquan workhouse in Virginia.

Harkening back to her days in England, Paul became a "window
smasher" once again. She led fellow suffragists in breaking as many
windows as possible to ventilate the stifling hot prison cells.[6] When
she went on a hunger strike, guards force-fed her three times a day in
an effort to break her spirit. Twenty-nine others of the 168 suffragists
arrested that year struck too and endured the daily torture of brutal
forced-feedings. Authorities attempted to declare Paul insane by ordering her to the prison's psychopathic ward and threatening to lock her
up at St. Elizabeth's, Washington's insane asylum. When a judge determined that moving suffrage prisoners outside the District of Columbia
to Occoquan was unconstitutional, he ordered the release of all the suffragist prisoners.

The NWP's work intensified in January 1918, when a proposal was
brought before the House of Representatives to amend the constitution
in favor of women's suffrage. Having been urged on the previous year by
Paul and her fellow suffragists, President Wilson addressed Congress
and voiced his strong support of the amendment. But although the
House of Representatives passed the amendment on January 10, the
Senate rejected it later that year. In 1918 and 1919, it took another
round of picketing, a watch fire protest, and more arrests before the
Senate passed the Nineteenth Amendment in June 1919 and sent it to
the states for ratification. NWP suffragists waited until August 1920
for the last of thirty-six states to ratify. With the Constitution officially
amended on August 26, American women—one-half of the nation—
went to polls that November to vote in their first national election.

Paul already had her next step in mind as she began to work with
a team of lawyers to develop a new piece of legislation for women. The
Equal Rights Amendment (ERA) she authored in 1923 demands that
"equality of rights under the law shall not be denied or abridged by the
United States or by any state on account of sex."[7] Susan B. Anthony's
nephew introduced the ERA in Congress in 1923, and legislators re-
introduced it during every session until 1972 when it finally passed
both houses. In the meantime, Paul worked for women's rights inter-
nationally and founded the World Woman's Party in 1938 with its headquarters in Geneva, Switzerland. She also succeeded in getting a sexual

discrimination clause written into Title VII of the 1964 Civil Rights Act.[8] Even at the end of her life, Paul lobbied representatives to pass the ERA from her wheelchair in a nursing home just minutes from her childhood home. When she died in July 1977, the ERA was still three states short of ratification.

Alice Paul periodically resurfaces in the nation's historical consciousness. In 2004, for instance, HBO produced *Iron-Jawed Angels* in which actress Hillary Swank portrays Paul in the NWP suffrage campaign leading to the Nineteenth Amendment.[9] Even years later, visitors to Paulsdale recall how the movie intrigued them. Paul's legacy also continues in her second hometown of Washington, DC, where the last headquarters of the National Woman's Party still stands in the Sewall-Belmont House and Museum across from the Supreme Court.[10] In 2008, Senator Hillary Clinton thanked Paul in her concession speech for the Democratic nomination and again a year later when she accepted the Alice Paul Award at the Sewall-Belmont and stated that "Alice Paul was a visionary and a pioneer. She believed that gender equality was a moral imperative as well as a foundation for progress. And her struggle for women's rights was built on the premise that no society or nation can reach its full potential if half of the population is left behind."[11] Paul's Equal Rights Amendment has been reintroduced into every session of Congress since 1982 until today and continues to garner national attention. It is sometimes called the Alice Paul Amendment. U.S. Rep. Carolyn Maloney (D-NY) and U.S. Sen. Robert Menendez (D-NJ) recently re-introduced it to Congress in June 2011.[12] API staff and volunteers agree that if Paul were alive today, in her typical workhorse manner, she would stop the tours of her home and instead put visitors to work advocating for this amendment.

Preserving Paulsdale

Despite her accomplishments, however, Paul remains largely absent in American memory. This absence is precisely what drove the API to preserve her home as a place that might inspire others to take up Paul's legacy. The API's founders perceived during the mid-1980s, and still do today, that the nation's political and social climate remained largely dismissive of women's history despite the hard-won gains of Paul and others. Historic house museums, for instance, typically portrayed American women as fundamentally apolitical despite Paul's example. It was this adverse climate that pushed the Institute's founders to preserve Paul's memory and establish the house as a site for learning and leadership. There was a sense that even though the ERA did not pass, the women who formed this organization were still determined to do something to advance its cause. As conceived, Paulsdale would symbolize all that women had struggled for in the past, and all that remained to be done.

That the possibility of preserving Paul's home existed at all owed much to the stewardship of its late owners. Miriam Feyerherm and her husband Marvin were Quakers who knew Alice Paul's name well. Feyerherm—once a teacher and later a librarian at Paul's alma mater, Moorestown Friends School—created a small shrine of photographs of Paul within the home and developed lessons about her for students. When she decided to retire in the late 1980s, Feyerherm contacted Barbara Irvine. Irvine had helped establish and served as president of the independent nonprofit Alice Paul Centennial Foundation in 1985 (renamed the Alice Paul Institute in 2003) to mark Alice Paul's centennial birthday with an awards dinner.[13] Miriam asked if the API would be interested in purchasing the home. The organization realized the immense task that raising the funds for the purchase would entail, yet also saw the enormous potential in the home for an organization committed to Paul's legacy.

The API's board members gathered in the summer of 1987 to debate their role in the fate of Alice Paul's birthplace, which had been threatened by real estate development.[14] Deciding to purchase Paulsdale would mean that API, which had been principally focused on coordinating events, workshops, and programs, would inherit a steep mortgage, continual costs of property maintenance, and, ultimately, a restoration project. While not fully aware of the difficulty it would have in preserving a women's history site, the API did understand that its task in preserving the home would be to create a center to teach the public about Alice Paul. Preserving the home, before Paul's legacy had national cachet, however, promised to create numerous hurdles. And how would it succeed against detractors who dismissed API as a radical organization given its association with such a radical figure?

The urgency of API's deliberations owed something to its discovery that Paul's memory was literally in jeopardy. Her only nephew, Donald, had packed many of her books and personal papers in hundreds of boxes that he stored away while searching for an appropriate steward. When Donald died, without having found a home for the papers and without a will, the Bryn Mawr Trust Company put them up for auction in 1987. The treasures included a desk once owned by Paul's hero Susan B. Anthony; purple, white, and gold suffrage banners; hundreds of photographs; and drafts of the original Equal Rights Amendment.[15] API made two adroit maneuvers toward purchasing the collection in its entirety. First, it formed a support committee including politicians, historians, and celebrity notables like feminist activist Gloria Steinem and former first ladies Rosalynn Carter and Betty Ford.[16] Second, the organization arranged for Paul's papers to be housed at the Arthur and Elizabeth Schlesinger Library on the History of Women at Radcliffe College. The Smithsonian Institution's National Museum of American History agreed to hold the Susan B. Anthony desk, photographs, and other objects. Allied with noted supporters and institutions, API won the bid for the entire collection at $26,575.

It was the successful acquisition of Paul's things that led Miriam Feyerherm to contact the Institute about purchasing Paulsdale. The API's success with the auction also bolstered its own confidence to undertake the immense task of purchasing the home. Assessments priced the home at $465,000. API coordinated a meeting with seven different banks hoping that the consortium might be willing to collectively shoulder at least a substantial portion of the mortgage. When the New Jersey Economic Development Authority agreed to provide a 90 percent guarantee on bank investments in Paulsdale, a lead bank offered to take on the full loan. Several years later when the bank agreement ended due to a merger, the Authority agreed to take on the remaining loan. In January 1990, API became the proud owners of Alice Paul's birthplace.

Over the preceding two years, the House Subcommittee on National Parks and Public Lands had been reviewing National Historic Landmarks (NHL) and found few associated with women's history.[17] The discovery prompted a women's landmark project, which brought together representatives from the National Park Service, the Organization of American

Historians, and the National Coordinating Committee for the Promotion of History to provide professional services to sites that honored women's contributions to American history and that might qualify for NHL status. New Jersey's State Historic Preservation Office recommended that the project consider Paulsdale among its list of women's history sites.[18]

Historian Page Putnam Miller, who directed the project, called upon women's historians to help with the project, some of whom would come to the API's aid when Paulsdale's initial application for NHL status was rejected. The NPS was not inclined to grant NHL status to a site just because a person was born there, and the review panel noted that another NHL, the Sewall-Belmont House & Museum (the last headquarters of Paul's NWP), might be a sufficient and possibly more appropriate place to commemorate Paul and her work. In its opinion, there was no need for a second NHL in Paul's honor. Edith Mayo, then Curator of Political History at the Smithsonian Institution, strongly defended Paulsdale's nomination, pointing out that male historical figures, like George Washington, often have multiple sites named NHLs in their honor.[19] While Washington fought battles throughout the country, it was to Mount Vernon that he returned home. Alice Paul fought her battles in Washington, DC, but returned to Paulsdale, her home, for rest and recuperation. Additionally, Mayo asserted, Paul was not simply a women's rights leader but a *civil* rights leader equal in respect to leaders like Martin Luther King, Jr. Finally, Mayo argued that because her influence in passing the Nineteenth Amendment impacted one-half of the entire nation, Paul's labors directly benefited proportionately more Americans than any other single constitutional amendment.

When revising its application, the API also emphasized how Paulsdale would serve as a site to help the public learn about and understand Alice Paul. The application highlighted how Paul's work for suffrage and civil rights demonstrated the key themes of civic engagement, justice, and democracy that American history celebrates. It also stressed how the home was crucial to Paul's development as a leader because it nurtured in her the principles of equality instilled by the Quaker upbringing she experienced there. All of these arguments paid off. Paulsdale became a National Historic Landmark in 1991, and API board members, volunteers, and community representatives held a celebration there. Each attendee, including U.S. Senator Frank Lautenberg, and

New Jersey Governor Jim Florio (whose wife Lucinda was a key advocate for preserving the site), joined in a Quaker tradition and signed a certificate recognizing the achievement.

In the process of obtaining NHL status, the API gained significant name recognition in the press and credibility among the state's public history sites. The Institute, however, needed to move quickly into the next phase of historic home ownership. Paulsdale could not accommodate public programs without extensive restoration, but it would take at least ten years to raise the money for the project. And raising the money would require that API effectively communicate its purpose in preserving the home. In other words, the Institute needed to determine exactly what activities would take place within the house.[20] Throughout much of the 1990s, the organization struggled with a dual mission of fundraising for a restoration project while also establishing the living memorial within it. API brought together teachers, activists, elected officials, and representatives from women's organizations across the state. One of these representatives was Mary S. Hartman, then dean of the all-female Douglass College (now the Douglass Residential College of Rutgers–New Brunswick). The API listened closely when Hartman noted that while various leadership programs existed for college and high school women, there were none for middle-school girls.

At the same time, Myra and David Sadker's *Failing at Fairness: How Our Schools Cheat Girls* (1994) also influenced the Institute to consider the case of adolescent girls.[21] The book launched a national discussion about girls and education by sharing data that showed, overwhelmingly, how the American education system discriminates against young girls. As teachers favor boys in the classroom, the Sadkers demonstrated, girls lose self-confidence often just as they begin puberty. Consequently, studies showed that girls' exam scores dropped below boys' during middle school. *Failing at Fairness,* alongside many articles and extensive commentary, called for a comprehensive rethinking of how young girls receive education.

Prompted by Harman and influenced by *Failing at Fairness,* the API ultimately focused its efforts on developing leadership training for middle-school girls. In 1995, API launched the Alice Paul Leadership Program with a workshop called Share Your Voice that brought together 7th- and 8th-grade girls from various school districts for a full day's experience. The program expanded to other one-day and multi-session workshops staged in schools, libraries, community centers, and colleges throughout the state. Noting a lack of strong female role models to inspire girls, API decided to use historic female role models like Alice Paul to teach leadership skills. This unique forward-thinking approach was truly innovative for a historic site at a time when preservationists were still saving old homes primarily as shrines to the past.

The success of the Alice Paul Leadership Program created more demand for the restoration of Paulsdale as a space for these workshops. The notion of turning a historic home into a modern center for public programs was so new, in fact, that it complicated fundraising. The subjects of women's history and girls' leadership development did not immediately appeal to granting agencies and sponsors. How, they wondered, could an old house in southern New Jersey succeed as an active center for students? API argued that the power of place would encourage in young girls the same leadership skills that Alice Paul honed in her very own birthplace. Within her home, girls might really identify with Paul, a shy girl who led a life very similar to their own, yet made a difference in her world because of her adherence to the Quaker values of equality and morally based activism against injustice.

While the organization developed its focus on girls' leadership, it also renewed its commitment to history through the preservation of Paulsdale and a growing conviction that heritage programs should occur alongside leadership programs. At Paulsdale, API could serve as a model of how to connect the abstract concepts of history to the hands-on lessons that students would identify with. API had already created an Alice Paul presentation that traveled to schools, libraries, and other sites throughout the state. And even before its restoration, history enthusiasts came looking for tours of Paulsdale. Public historians at the time understood, thanks in part to Roy Rosenzweig and David Thelen's *The Presence of the Past* (1998), that Americans perceived cultural institutions, particularly museums and historic sites, as sources of authority and trustworthy information.[22] With this in mind, API realized that it could be an authority on Alice Paul by creating a center where visitors would come to learn about her.

With so many exciting programmatic demands at hand, API set about raising funds by carefully following best practices for preservation at historic sites. It commissioned a comprehensive historic structures report that detailed noteworthy architectural details, preservation priorities, and necessary repairs. The report also suggested how the house might be adapted for its modern use by rehabilitating the interior. API used these findings to develop a planning grant for its construction project. Its project plan called for the restoration of Paulsdale's exterior to approximate its turn-of-the century appearance, reflecting Paul's residency there. The interior, however, would be updated with modern lighting, plumbing, and electricity to accommodate public programs.

More hard work earned Paulsdale a place in local and regional press and a stirring of interest in the New Jersey preservation community.[23] The Preserving Paulsdale project received significant grants from the New Jersey Historic Trust alongside additional support from organizations including the Andy Warhol Foundation, the New Jersey Casino Reinvestment Economic Development Authority, the Burlington Country Freeholders, the U.S. Dept. of Housing & Urban Development, and the Heritage Philadelphia Program (a funding initiative of the Pew Charitable Trusts). These grants enabled API to begin its long-anticipated restoration project. By spring 2002, API staff moved into the house and began programming in earnest. Restoring Alice Paul's home had cost an estimated 1.4 million dollars, but the payoffs were worth far more. The Women's Heritage Program, for instance, officially kicked off in 2003 with Paulsdale as its stage. The Paulsdale project became a model for other historic sites looking to adapt historic structures for modern purposes.

The project also served as a prototype for saving historic sites particularly connected with women. These sites face unique challenges that other historic homes do not. The API confronted constant claims that women's history is not significant to American memory, or that women like Alice Paul represented a radical element that the API would encourage in its programming. Consequently, much of its work at Paulsdale went beyond raising funds and carrying out the actual rehabilitation of the home. The API had to first conquer misperceptions about women's history and about Alice Paul herself, and then prove that Alice Paul was worth honoring, that her home was worth saving, and that its innovative rehabilitation project was worth considering as a model for other historic places.[24]

Paulsdale's path to preservation was unique because the API's founders were neither historians by training nor committed preservationists, but rather feminist activists. Their purpose in preserving Paulsdale and, ultimately, their decision not to turn the home into a house museum, was rooted in principles that infuse interpretation there today. Several of those principles rest in the Quaker upbringing Paul remembered fondly at her childhood home. The Institute's property and interpretation committees, for instance, have caused landscapers and technicians to scratch their heads by turning down projects—sometimes offered free of charge—that promise to make the home look more like what the public would expect of an elegant Victorian home. Instead, the API carefully adheres to the principle of Quaker modesty by maintaining the simple landscape and appearance of the home. This conventional atmosphere contrasts with the computers, tables, and whiteboards used in programs that represent the organization's other major tenet: to teach and inspire a new generation of Alice Pauls.

A Visit to Paulsdale

While Paul might have disliked seeing her childhood home preserved in her honor, she might well have enjoyed seeing future leaders being cultivated in the programs that take place within it. Paulsdale demonstrates the "power of place" in the sense that it was here that Paul honed her dedication to equal rights. It was because she was a Quaker and because she grew up in a Quaker community that she would find herself naturally drawn to a campaign for civil rights. Explaining how her religion connected her to activism, Paul observed that "the principle was always there."[25] Even at the end of her life, Paul spoke fondly of her farm upbringing at Paulsdale as a key influence on her serious work ethic. Paul took her mother's advice seriously in her lifetime commitment to equal rights, remembering her words: "when you put your hand to the plow, you can't put it down until you get to the end of the row."

These themes are interpreted throughout Paulsdale today. Although suburban real-estate development surrounds the house now, in Paul's time the three-story, five-bay, stucco-over-brick farmhouse, built circa 1800, was isolated among bucolic farms and small towns like Moorestown where Paul attended the Friends school and Sunday meeting.[26]

API restored the exterior to resemble the childhood home Paul would have remembered when she lived there from her birth in 1885 until the 1920s, when she returned home periodically during her suffrage years. A visitor to the home today encounters it via a long dirt and pebble driveway that was once a farm road on which Paul used to ride her horse to school in Moorestown. With parking in a lot where a peach orchard once thrived, the reverse orientation of the property briefly baffles guests since the entry of the home faces away from the residential street, turning what looks like the back of the house into the front.

This initial confusion, however, gives way to calm awe when visitors notice the handsome exterior of the home and its large quiet lawn. Its primary feature is a wide wrap-around porch that surrounds the house. Trained tour guides walk guests around the wide porch and explain how it extended domestic space into the farm's natural surroundings. A young Paul and her three siblings may have played checkers here or perhaps she curled up on a deck chair to read her beloved Dickens novels.[27] On the porch, guests learn about the farm that once surrounded the house, where geese flocked at the steps of the porch and an old copper beech tree served as a constant companion to the home and as a cool shaded place for Alice to pursue her deep love of reading.

The house reveals a Quaker preference for modesty over materialism and utility over decoration in its play of decorative and functional details. These themes are evident too when guides discuss the Pauls' social class. Alice's father, William Paul, was a gentleman farmer and a banker who worked in Moorestown, where he founded the Burlington County Trust. Her mother, Tacie, came from the well-to-do Parry family, which resided in a much larger estate in nearby Cinnaminson.[28] The Pauls' wealth contrasts with the lives of its domestic servants, which visitors learn about inside. Guides discuss the suffrage movement in the "old kitchen" where modern appliances recall the building's modern purpose. This room would have been the center of the working home where Irish maids, the only non-Quakers Alice encountered during her youth, washed, cleaned, and cooked.[29] On the walls visitors see the NWP's purple, white, and gold logo and yellowing leaflets handed out by suffragists across New Jersey.

Here guests also learn about Paul's admiration for her suffrage predecessor, Susan B. Anthony, who fought unsuccessfully in 1873 to convince a court that the Fourteenth Amendment implied universal suffrage. Anthony's trial serves as a launching point for guides to discuss Paul's knowledge of the law and the protections she envisioned in her Equal Rights Amendment. In this room, they ask guests to consider questions that Paul might put before them if she were alive today: Does the Constitution today truly grant women express rights beyond that of voting? Is there a need today for an Equal Rights Amendment? While visitors do not expect to encounter contemporary debate in a tour of a historic home, the experience exemplifies who Alice Paul was, a shy Quaker who pondered the weighty issues of women's rights here within Paulsdale.

Visitors learn about Paul's family in the dining room where guides discuss dinner conversation and Quaker "plain" language. Although Paul addressed her family members using the terms "thee" and "thou," she did not speak to her friends, NWP members, or other non-Quakers in this manner. This small detail reveals a woman living astride traditional and contemporary worlds. The dining room also features an oversized photograph of Paul taken in 1920 when she toasted (with a glass of grape juice) the ratification banner of purple, white, and gold that represented each of the thirty-six states that ratified the Nineteenth Amendment. Visitors, particularly those with children, delight in being photographed with Paul, whose arm appears outstretched as if in an embrace.

Making their way across a wide hallway, visitors discover that many of the home's architectural details are still intact, including the wood floors, patterned brass doorknobs, iron hardware, wavy window glass, and the oversized carved newel post on a plain yet elegant stairway. In this center hall, guests often notice the spatial logic of the house with its oversized doorways and simple symmetry. Rooms on either side of the hall sit opposite windows and French doors that allow the efficient circulation of air. API rehabilitated the interior of the home with modern lighting, plumbing, and electricity to facilitate its contemporary mission. Limiting offices to the second-floor bedrooms, however, preserves the first floor's connection to history, which is reinforced by the historical documents and photographs that hang on its walls.

In the "double parlor," the largest room in the house, historic documents accompany modern worktables, school supplies, and computers.

In 1919, *Everybody's Magazine* described its "oil lamps and antlers and shells and almanacs, and on the wall any number of blue-grange ribbons for cattle and corn."[30] Today, visitors see Paul's six college degrees, a hand-drawn map of the Paulsdale farm, and her parents' 1881 wedding certificate signed by Quaker families from throughout the region. The only piece of furniture that remains is a wood-and-glass-door bookcase that once held the books that Paul accumulated throughout her life.[31] Restored to its mid-1800s appearance, the bookcase recalls Paul's love of reading and her shrewd intellect.

Although the almanacs, old lamps, and "blue-grange ribbons" are no longer present, in this room visitors learn that Alice's mother kept a desk in the corner and read newspaper accounts of her daughter's screams resounding through an English prison during her latest hunger strike.[32] Paul's mother also added a piano to the room, purchased some time after her husband's death in 1901. Alice disapproved of the piano, citing a Quaker tenet against music that her father would have rigidly enforced. While we're unsure how his death impacted Paul, it is evident from his assurance that "when there is something to be done, I bank on Alice," that Paul's father recognized her resolve even in youth.

Perhaps it was in the parlor or maybe in Paul's bedroom where she and her friend Lucy Burns planned their 1913 Washington campaign. We do know that because of Paul's transient lifestyle, she would have left many of her personal possessions behind, including the framed testimonial on display from Sylvia Pankhurst "to Alice Paul, on behalf of all the women who will win freedom by her bondage, and dignity by her humiliation."[33] In one of the only sepia-toned photographs that show Alice at Paulsdale, she appears as a young woman, standing in front of the porch in a long skirt and buttoned, high-collar shirt. Her hair is in a messy bun. Later, suffragists admitted not knowing that Paul had brown hair since, being so busy, she often forgot to take off her hat. Her frenetic and sometimes volatile work in Washington stood in stark contrast with the peace and solitude she found at Paulsdale.

The API is currently updating its interpretive plan to capture this tension between Paul's political life and her life at Paulsdale. The importance of saving her home will be reaffirmed in portrayals of Paulsdale as the place where Paul honed her principles of equality, but also where she rested so that she could continue her taxing work on behalf of women.

In the meantime, visitors explore their own interest in the building's decorative details, become engrossed in photographs of girls and boys enjoying recent programs, or ask about the "Red Hat" ladies enjoying tea on the porch. Sometimes guests stop to play with the *Pieces of a Leader* puzzle or an interactive photographic timeline of Paul's life. For the API, these interruptions are welcome companions to informal interpretation. Paulsdale's unpretentious atmosphere reflects the household Paul would have remembered and the personality she would have projected in her work.

The Alice Paul Institute: Alice Paul's Legacy

Sweating from a rousing game of soccer on the lawn, fifty young men and women from Philadelphia's J. R. Masterman High School complete their annual spring visit to Paulsdale with a class photograph on the front porch. Having watched *Iron-Jawed Angels* in their classroom, they came to Paulsdale to learn more about Paul. Looking back, one student recalled that "the visit to the Alice Paul house was simply amazing! Learning about her many accomplishments inspired me. It proved to me that anything is possible and to always strive for greatness." Other visitors send thanks for having discovered a sense of activism in their own lives compelling them to vote, defend the environment, fundraise for a good cause, or work for change in schools and communities. These inspiring words reflect the Institute's own hopes for casual visitors and students who come to the home for its educational programs. It is not enough to simply teach Paul's story or to demonstrate how she was an inspiring role model. Instead, the organization strives for the higher mission that Paul would have embraced: to carry that inspiration outside the home and into communities.

Despite Paul's singular example, she is not the only woman who figures in Paulsdale's girls' leadership development programs. Astronaut Ellen Ochoa, environmentalist Rachel Carson, tennis champion Rosie Casals, and journalist Ida B. Wells-Barnett all have their place, for example, in the curriculum of the Girlblazers Summer Camp, a two-week program where fifth-grade girls become inventors, hikers, tennis pros, and investigative reporters just like these female role models. The girls enjoy games like "barnyard bedlam" and "human knot" in between scrapbooking, journaling, and musical activities. As prospective leaders from underserved communities, these girls learn about history in a way that applies to their lives. By looking to women's history for alternatives to the usual pop culture role models, this leadership program gives girls powerful shoulders to stand on as they develop their own leadership identities. For those who worked so hard to preserve Paulsdale, the sight of these young campers sitting in groups in the parlor, or clustered at worktables on the porch, evokes a sense of pride. Not only are these girls learning within this historic home, they will leave it with a new sense of their own roles in society.

The thousands of students, Scouts, teachers, history enthusiasts, and visitors to Paulsdale are a visual testament to the API's tagline: "Preserving her home to develop future leaders." Fulfillment of that goal is evident in a widening appreciation of Paul's legacy. In 2010, when the API celebrated its 25th anniversary alongside the Nineteenth Amendment's 90th anniversary, the New Jersey Hall of Fame inducted Paul into its 2010 class. API celebrated the milestones by hosting over two hundred women and men of all ages and backgrounds in a celebration at Paulsdale of Women's Equality Day. Paul, of course, would have stopped the celebration and put everyone to work on the unfinished business of equal rights in America. In this sense, this birthplace and home is a metaphor for the women's movement as it links the accomplishments of women to the reminder of what remains to be done. And yet, even in its celebrations, Paulsdale continues the thread of activism started by Paul by nurturing it in the young men and women who visit. The home is not simply a birthplace of one American hero, but an incubator for the thousands of men and women who will become the next generation of American citizens. It is API's hope that those students and visitors who come to Paulsdale will remember, at least in some small way, what they learn about Alice Paul and how to identify themselves as agents of change. Perhaps they will think of her when they cast ballots in their first elections. Or maybe her memory will emerge as they volunteer in their communities or speak out in support of a cause. For the API, a visit to Paulsdale will mean so much more if future generations live in a world that is a little closer to the one Alice Paul envisioned.

NOTES

1. Robert S. Gallagher, "I Was Arrested, of course . . ." *American Heritage* 25 (1974): 17–24, 94.

2. "Suffragette Tells of Forcible Feeding," *New York Times,* February 18, 1910. "Two Americans in Guildhall Exploit," *New York Times,* November 12, 1909. "Miss Paul Describes Feeding by Force," *New York Times,* December 10, 1909. "Alice Paul Returns Home," *New York Times,* January 21, 1910. Patricia Greenwood Harrison, *Connecting Links: The British and American Woman Suffrage Movements, 1900–1914* (London: Greenwood Press, 2000), 91–122.

3. Alice Paul, "Report on Congressional Work from January 1 to December 1, 1913," as reported in *The Suffragist,* January 10, 1914. Ida Husted Harper, ed.,*The History of Woman Suffrage,* vol. 5: *1900–1920* (New York: National Woman Suffrage Association, 1922), 378–81.

4. Carrie Chapman Catt and Nettie Rogers Shuler, *Woman Suffrage and Politics: The Inner Story of the Suffrage Movement* (New York: Charles Scribner's Sons, 1923), 245. "Suffragist Rivals Now in the Field," *New York Times,* January 5, 1914. For more on Alice Paul and the NWP, see Mary Walton, *A Woman's Crusade: Alice Paul and the Battle for the Ballot* (New York: Palgrave Macmillan, 2010); Christine Lunardini, *From Equal Suffrage to Equal Rights: Alice Paul and the National Woman's Party, 1910–1928* (San Jose: toExcel Press, 2000); and Inez Haynes Irwin, *The Story of Alice Paul and the National Woman's Party* (Fairfax, VA: Denlinger's Publishers, 1977), originally printed in 1923.

5. For more on the picketing and prison experience, see Doris Stevens, *Jailed for Freedom: American Women Win the Vote,* ed. Carol O'Hare (Troutdale, OR: New Sage Press, 1996), originally printed in 1920; and Linda Ford, *Iron-Jawed Angels: The Suffrage Militancy of the National Woman's Party, 1912–1920* (Lanham, MD: University Press of America, 1991).

6. Gallagher, "I Was Arrested, of course . . . ," 92.

7. In 1923, Paul wrote a slightly different version of the ERA, which stated that "men and women shall have equal rights throughout the United States and every place subject to its jurisdiction." She changed the wording of the amendment in 1943 to reflect the wording of the Nineteenth Amendment which specified rights "under the law" or according to government. For more information on the ERA, visit www.equalrightsamendment.org.

8. An excellent source on Paul is the oral history interview, "Conversations with Alice Paul: Woman Suffrage and the Equal Rights Amendment," conducted by Amelia Fry in 1976. This extensive interview can be accessed online at http://content.cdlib.org/ark:/13030/kt6f59n89c/.

9. *Iron-Jawed Angels,* dir. Katia Von Garnier (HBO, 2004).

10. For more information on the Sewall-Belmont House & Museum, visit their website, www.sewallbelmont.org.

11. Hillary Clinton, "18 Million Cracks in the Glass Ceiling," speech, June 2008. "Receipt of 2009 Alice Paul Award at the Sewall-Belmont House and Museum," Press release, June 8, 2009, www.state.gov/secretary/rm/2009a.

12. "Rep. Maloney, Sen. Menendez Reintroduce Equal Rights Amendment" Press release, June 22, 2011, http://maloney.house.gov.

13. I use "API" throughout to avoid confusion. Sally Friedman, "Keeping Alice Paul's Memory Alive," *Burlington County Times,* January 1985. Doreen Carvajal, "Three women are honored for their courage," *Philadelphia Inquirer,* January 12, 1985.

14. Barbara Irvine (founding member and Board President of the Alice Paul Centennial Foundation, 1984–1999), interview by Kris Myers, April 19, 2011. In addition to Irvine, the founding members of APCF included: Elsie Behmer, Christine Borget, Judith Buckman, Dee O'Neil, Patricia Owens, Jean Perry, Nancy Quinn, Diane Quinton, Janet Tegley, and Patricia Williams.

15. Mary E. Pembleton, "Foundation lands papers of a feminist," *Courier Post*, February 8, 1987. Sari Harrar, "On the block: Feminist history," *Burlington County Times*, February 1, 1987.

16. This impressive committee also included, among others, actor and ERA activist Alan Alda, Amelia Fry (Alice Paul biographer), Irene Natividad, Esther Peterson, Barbara B. Sigmund, Marlo Thomas, C. Delores Tucker, noted historians Gerda Lerner, William Chafe, Sara Evans, Suzanne Lebsock, Anne Firor Scott, Mary Frances Berry, and Nancy F. Cott, and Congresswoman Patricia S. Schroeder, New Jersey governor Thomas Kean, and State Senator Diane Allen. *Minutes of the Alice Paul Centennial Foundation.* Alice Paul Institute, October 15, 1986. API Minutes, 6/84–3/87.

17. Page Putnam Miller, ed., *Reclaiming the Past: Landmarks of Women's History* (Bloomington: Indiana University Press, 1992), 15–23.

18. Other women's history sites in New Jersey can be found on the New Jersey Women's Heritage Trail through the NJ Historic Preservation Office website, www.nj.gov/dep/hpo.

19. Edith Mayo (Curator Emeritus, Division of Politics and Reform, National Museum of American History, Smithsonian Institution), interview by Kris Myers, June 23, 2011.

20. Irvine, interview, April 19, 2011. Lucienne Beard (former Program Director, API, 2000–2007), interview by Kris Myers, June 14, 2011.

21. Myra and David Sadker, *Failing at Fairness: How Our Schools Cheat Girls* (New York: Charles Scribner's Sons, 1994).

22. Roy Rosenzweig and David Thelan, *The Presence of the Past: Popular Uses of History in American Life* (New York: Columbia University Press, 1998).

23. Rhonda DiMascio (former president, API, 2000–2010), interview by Kris Myers, June 14, 2011.

24. In the vein of helping other women's history sites, the API helped to initiate Reclaiming Women's History through Historic Preservation, the first national conference on the preservation of women's sites. API later became a founding member of the National Collaborative for Women's History Sites (NCWHS), a consortium of historic sites dedicated to and/or incorporating women's history in their interpretation.

25. Gallagher, "I Was Arrested, of course . . . ," 17.

26. *Paulsdale: An Historic Structure Report*, August 9, 1999. This HSR was produced by John Bowie Associates (Media, PA) in association with interpretation consultant Sandra Mackenzie Lloyd. Most of the details about the structure and style of the home are from this report.

27. Fry, "Conversations with Alice Paul."

28. Many Paul family members including Alice are buried at the Westfield Friends Meeting in Cinnaminson because of the Parry connection to the area.

29. Fry, "Conversations with Alice Paul."

30. Anne Herendeen, "What the Home Town Thinks of Alice Paul," *Everybody's Magazine* 41 (1919): 45.

31. Alice Paul's book collection, stored in the third-floor archive room, features women's history texts, *The Suffragist* periodicals, poetry, and a collection of Charles Dickens novels.

32. Alice Paul to Tacie Paul (mother), March–December 1909. Letters between Alice and Tacie Paul during Alice's time in England are housed in the Alice Paul Papers at the Arthur and Elizabeth Schlesinger Library on the History of Women in America.

33. Herendeen, "What the Home Town Thinks of Alice Paul," 45.

Promotional photograph of Edgar Allan Poe Square, at the southeast corner of
Boylston Street and Charles Street South across from Boston Common, produced
in conjunction with the 2009 Poe bicentennial celebration. Photo courtesy Media
Technology Services, Boston College.

⁓ 10 ⁓

A key concern of the preceding essays is to understand whose birthplaces we've remembered and why. But what about the birthplaces that we choose to forget? In this essay and in the next, our contributors consider new directions for birthplace commemoration in the possibility of reclaiming forgotten births. Literary scholar and humorist Paul Lewis figured prominently in the Great Poe Debates of 2009, which pitted Boston, Philadelphia, and Richmond against one another in a tongue-in-cheek contest for ownership of Poe's remains. Here he joins with Dan Currie to restate the position and explain why remembering Poe in the city of his birth is more than just a matter of hubris. Recapturing Poe's bond with Boston, we discover, sheds significant light on his life and the motivations for his work. It also recasts his mother's influence and her hope that Poe would remember his birthplace. Most important, however, we learn that Boston's unwillingness to accept Poe is, in part, precisely what encouraged the literary style that has since made him so famous. Lewis and Currie offer the surprising case of Poe's birthplace as a study in the social construction of historical—and literary—(in)significance. Their work in making Poe relevant to a new generation of Bostonians recalls what Poe knew so well: "To be appreciated, you must be read."

The Raven in the Frog Pond

Edgar Allan Poe and the City of Boston

PAUL LEWIS AND DAN CURRIE

One of the best-kept secrets in Boston's literary history concerns the most influential writer qua writer ever born here: Edgar Allan Poe. And the secret is this: he was born here! Over the 200 years leading up to the bicentennial of Poe's birth on January 19, 2009, his connections to other East Coast cities—Richmond, Baltimore, Philadelphia, and New York—have been celebrated and memorialized. While each of these cities hosts a museum or historic house that commemorates Poe's standing as a local author, Boston has made itself conspicuous for its apparent determination to treat the master of mystery—America's first great critic and a foundational figure in the development of popular culture—like an unworthy orphan. Considering the lengths to which American heritage boosters have gone throughout the last century to take advantage of the birthplaces of comparatively undistinguished Americans, Boston's approach to Poe is unusual if not unique. It is also fascinating insofar as it can be traced back to the antebellum period, involves a war of words as snarky as any from that time, and is based on a misunderstanding of the importance of Boston to Poe's development. It turns out that both Poe the baby and Poe the writer and critic were born in the same place.

Remembering Poe today in the city of his birth provides insight into the man, Boston, and the era that bound them together. We learn, for instance, that Poe's identity was not, as critics would have us believe, shaped only by his mother's death, but by her life as well. We discover, too, in the story of his Boston birth evidence of the theater's growing significance to nineteenth-century Americans. Most significantly, however, we learn about Poe's intellectual, critical, and aesthetic engagement with the city's literary establishment. Poe has too often been typecast as a gadfly and opponent: the upstart raven among the swans who dared to insult the area's great authors and call its citizens "Frogpondians." On closer examination, we see that Poe's first and last publications were produced in Boston; that Poe at some point wanted to die and, therefore, be buried in Boston; and that, far from hating the city and its environs, the "Boston" he assailed had little to do with the place and everything to do with a set of literary practices he opposed. Perhaps most remarkably, given his supposed contempt for New England, Poe moved to Boston in 1827 and was seriously thinking about moving back to the area toward the end of his life.

Despite the short time that Poe lived in Boston—11 months in total—his connections to it were formative.[1] For a few years starting in the early 1840s, James Russell Lowell (1819–90), Bostonian par excellence, was arguably his most important literary colleague and "dear friend." In 1845, Poe made literary history by delivering one of the most controversial lectures of the nineteenth century to the Boston Lyceum. And in his last year, he sought out the love and/or friendship of both Annie Richmond of Lowell, Massachusetts, and Sarah Helen Whitman of Providence, Rhode Island. But the deeper story follows Poe's intellectual engagement with "Boston" from the start of his career as an editorial assistant for the *Southern Literary Messenger* in July 1835 through his work on other magazines in Baltimore, Philadelphia, and New York, to the last letter he wrote to his longtime correspondent, F. W. Thomas, in which he defined himself, as usual, in opposition to local writers and critics.

In this essay, we summarize Poe's biographical connections to Boston: what the city meant to him and how it figured in his work as a writer, critic, and literary theorist. We also survey what the city has done so far to celebrate this native, if also wayward, son. Our success in organizing the Poe-Boston project, which staged both a celebration of the bicentennial in January 2009 and an exhibit with the same name as this essay at the Boston Public Library that ran from December 2009 through March 2010, suggests that Bostonians are no longer so reluctant to claim Poe. We conclude by discussing how these events suggest possibilities and challenges for birthplace commemoration.

Poe's Life in Boston

The actual location of Poe's birthplace was not definitively identified until 100 years after his birth, when the preeminent Boston antiquarian Walter K. Watkins determined that the only incontrovertible proof of any Boston address for the family of Edgar Allan Poe—whose local stage appearances were extensively documented in the newspapers— was a record created by municipal assessors who went from house to house in May or June of 1808 to compile a list of taxable Boston residents. This "Taking Book," also known as the "Street Book" (now kept in the Rare Books & Manuscripts Department of the Boston Public Library), documents that "David Poo [*sic*], actor" lived in a house then owned by a "stucco worker" named Henry Haviland. According to contemporaneous records preserved by the Suffolk County Registry of Deeds, and reviewed by independent historian Dan Currie, the only property Haviland owned during the relevant Poe-Boston time frame was located at what would become known as 62 Carver Street, a brick structure he with his wife Hannah had built after purchasing a parcel of land from a Boston distiller named John Haskins on May 16, 1801, for four annual payments totaling $520.[2] Unfortunately, as is the case with many of the Boston buildings originally associated with Poe, the house in which he was born no longer exists—except for a portion of its north wall that abuts the remaining 60 Charles Street South. Number 62 was razed after it was quietly acquired by the Boston Edison Company in 1959. The Poe birthplace is now a parking lot for the electric power plant at 70–74 Charles Street South next to the Milner Hotel in Boston's Bay Village.[3]

Although the birthplace is irretrievable, its story is not. Edgar Allan Poe's mother, Eliza Arnold, and his grandmother, the actress and singer Elizabeth Arnold, arrived at Long Wharf in Boston from their native England aboard the Boston-built brig *Outram* on January 3, 1796. Elizabeth Arnold had been recruited in London by the manager of Boston's new Federal Street Theatre who had seen her perform at the Theatre Royal in Covent Garden. The mother and daughter rented a room in a boardinghouse owned by Mr. and Mrs. William Baylis at 14 State Street. The nearby Federal Street Theatre, designed by the Boston architect Charles Bulfinch and also known as the First Boston Theatre, had opened on the northwest corner of Federal and Franklin Streets two years earlier. It quickly became known as the finest theater in the country. Nine-year-old Eliza made her stage debut there on April 15, 1796, singing a song named "The Market Lass" at the end of a romantic melodrama, *Mysteries of the Castle,* in which her mother had the lead role. Their final performance together in Boston was in the ballroom of the Museum Building on Tremont Street opposite the Granary Burying Ground. Fifty years later, it was the location of Gleason's Publishing Hall, the home of Edgar Poe's last publisher.[4]

The Arnolds departed Boston later in 1796 to tour theaters from Portland, Maine to Charleston, South Carolina. Mrs. Arnold is believed to have died of yellow fever contracted in North Carolina in the summer of 1798. But eleven-year-old Eliza continued singing, dancing and acting, including with a troupe known as the "Charleston Comedians" under the management of a Mr. Edgar in whose honor her second son may have been named after she returned to Boston with David Poe Jr., a Baltimore man she married in Richmond, Virginia, on March 14, 1798.[5] David and Eliza Poe have often been described as "itinerant" actors—as if to diminish the significance of their connections to Boston, and to the Boston stage where three generations of the Poe family would eventually appear, including when Edgar was *in utero,* and in the notorious return of the prodigal son thirty-six years later. But the fact is: Poe's parents were very well established. They performed at the Federal Street Theatre for three complete theatrical seasons, from 1806 to 1809, during which Eliza—by then considered one of the most enchanting actresses on the American stage—had appeared, often to "unbounded applause," in more than seventy roles. During their long engagement in the city, she would give birth not only to Edgar but also to his elder brother, William Henry Leonard, on January 30, 1807.

David Poe, Jr., a former law student who was far less talented as an actor than his spouse, was at least as forthright in addressing Boston critics as his son Edgar would become. On one occasion, according to an 1807 newspaper report, David confronted a disapproving audience in an "obnoxious and insulting way." Another Boston critic described how the actor—who may have also genetically shared a theatrical air and high susceptibility to the volatile effects of alcohol—once showed up at his front door "to chastise my impertinence" in a review.[6]

Edgar Poe was born on the morning of January 19, 1809, in a boardinghouse at 62 Carver Street (today named Charles Street South) in Boston approximately 220 yards south of Boston Common and the intersection of Boylston Street (which was then called Frog Lane). His mother had continued to appear on stage until about ten days before his birth. She resumed her acting schedule three weeks later. Eliza Poe's final performance in Boston, before she embarked with her two infant sons on what was to be her final theatrical tour, occurred on May 16, 1809, at the Boston Exchange Coffee House, which has been described as the nation's first luxury hotel. The venue was located between Congress and Devonshire Streets across from the original Massachusetts State House, one block from where Eliza resided with her mother when they first arrived in America thirteen years earlier. On December 8, 1811, Eliza, then twenty-four years old, died in Richmond before Edgar was three and within a few days of when his father, David, is also believed to have died after abandoning them five months earlier.[7] Upon her death, she left her son a small portrait of herself and a water-color she had painted and entitled "Boston Harbour, Morning, 1808." On the back of the harbor scene—which is now lost after Poe treasured it all his life—Eliza wrote: "For my little son Edgar, who should ever love Boston, the place of his birth, and where his mother found her best, and most sympathetic friends."[8]

The orphaned Edgar was taken in, raised, and afforded a good edu-cation by an industrious, well-to-do merchant named John Allan and his childless wife Frances who had admired Eliza's performances in Richmond. They gave the boy his middle name, Allan, at a baptism in 1812. Poe's younger sister Rosalie was taken in by another unrelated Richmond family, while older brother Henry went to live with their paternal grandparents in Baltimore. In 1827, after withdrawing from the University of Virginia in Charlottesville at age eighteen and upon becoming increasingly estranged from his strict foster father—who never formally adopted him and eventually disinherited him—Poe took flight from the Allans' Richmond home. Perhaps heeding the advice his birth mother inscribed on his cherished painting as he planned the first independent venture of his life, Poe resolved to return to the city of his birth to begin a new life as a poet. There is inconclusive evi-dence he may have intended to follow in his birth parents' footsteps by becoming an actor when he arrived in Boston, probably on board a coal vessel from Virginia on or about April 3, 1827.[9] It is more likely that he worked briefly as a market reporter for a newspaper called *The Boston Weekly Report of Public Sales and Arrivals,* owned and edited by Peter P. F. Degrand at 65 Broad Street, and as a clerk in a wholesale merchan-dise house on the Boston waterfront. According to a supposed acquain-tance from Charlottesville who reportedly had a chance encounter with him on the waterfront, Edgar's Boston landlady had turned him into the street after she became impatient with the way he "sat up nights writing on paper [that is, doing creative work] he couldn't sell."[10]

Discouraged, his resources depleted, Poe enlisted in Battery H of the 1st Artillery of the U.S. Army in Boston on May 26, 1827, using the alias Edgar A. Perry. Military records of his induction describe him as a 5'8", fair-skinned, twenty-two-year-old with brown hair and gray eyes—although he was only eighteen. He was stationed at Fort Independence on Castle Island in Boston Harbor until his army unit was deployed to South Carolina on November 8, 1827. Evidently a fine soldier, he would eventually qualify for a commission to attend West Point.

In the meantime, Poe's first book was published in Boston in June or July 1827 by the nineteen-year-old printer Calvin F. S. Thomas at 70 Washington Street, at the corner of State Street, just feet from where his mother and grandmother had lived in 1796. The Thomas print shop was connected to the Bowles & Dearborn Book Shop at 72 Washington Street, where Poe also may have applied for work that spring. His forty-page paperbound book, *Tamerlane and Other Poems,* was published anonymously with the author seeking to maximize his connections to the city by identifying himself only as "A Bostonian." The slim volume received little notice during Poe's impoverished lifetime. Only twelve of the estimated fifty copies printed are known to have survived. It is so rare today that book specialists refer to it as "the black tulip" and "the Holy Grail of American book collecting." A copy purchased for $15 from a stack of fertilizer catalogs in a New Hampshire antique store in 1998 was sold at auction by Sotheby's in New York for $198,000 in June that year. On December 4, 2009, the only other copy then in private hands went for $662,500 at Christie's in New York, setting the record for any work of American literature.

Poe's first literary supporter was John Neal, the editor of *The Yankee and Boston Literary Gazette,* to whom the poet dedicated his second volume of verse, *Al Aaraaf, Tamerlane and Minor Poems* (1829). A letter from Poe to Neal in October or November 1829 credits the Boston-based editor with giving him "the very first words of encouragement I ever remember to have heard." Neal's article entitled "Unpublished Poetry" in the December 1829 issue of *The Yankee* provided young Poe with his first meaningful exposure as a writer; and it ends with high praise: "What more can we do for the lovers of genuine poetry? Nothing. They who are judges will not need more; and they who are not—Why waste words upon them? We shall not."

James Russell Lowell was the first to publish Poe's short story "The Tell-Tale Heart" in the first issue (January 1843) of *The Pioneer,* the literary journal based at 67 Washington Street in Boston, directly across the street from where Poe's first book was produced in 1827. Poe also originally composed "Eulalie—A Song," a poem about the transformative effect of the love of his wife, Virginia, for publication in *The Pioneer.* But by the time Lowell received it, the journal had ceased publication. Poe described the closure of the Boston journal after just three issues as "a most severe blow to the cause—the cause of a Pure Taste." Lowell later wrote that Poe possessed "that indescribable something which men have agreed to call *genius.*"

From 1843 on, Poe generously befriended Abijah Metcalf Ide, Jr., a young farmer-poet from South Attleboro, Massachusetts, who wrote to him asking for advice. In a correspondence that began in October 1843, Poe praised Ide and tried to enlist him in his quarrel with established Boston writers and editors:

> You are young, enthusiastic, and possess high talents . . . Be bold—read much—write much—publish little—keep aloof from the little wits, and fear nothing . . . In the meantime I may call upon you for aid in . . . an enterprise which shall elevate this true talent upon the throne of the great usurper called Humbug. At present, the Bobby Buttons rule the world of American Letters—but we must change all that—and if no one else will stir effectively in the task, I must and will.

In an August 1843 *Graham's Magazine* essay entitled "Our Amateur Poets," Poe associates Bobby Buttons with "Boston critics, who have a notion that poets are porpoises, (for they are always talking about their running in 'schools')."

The controversial Poe reading known as the "Boston Lyceum Fiasco" took place on October 16, 1845, at the Odeon Theatre, formerly the Federal Street Theatre, the same venue where his mother was a star when he was born. During his return, he stayed at the Pavilion Hotel, which was located on Tremont Street opposite the King's Chapel Burying Ground.[11] Beyond the generational overlap on stage, as we will consider in some detail below, there are striking parallels between Eliza's work in Boston's nascent theater scene and her son's later quarrel with highbrow Bostonian authors.

Poe visited the Boston area on numerous occasions during his final years. Subsequent to the death of his twenty-four-year-old wife, Virginia Clemm, in New York in January 1847, Poe seriously courted at least two daughters of New England: Annie Richmond, with whom he probably experienced the most romantic (even if platonic) passions of the final fifteen months of his life after they met in Lowell, Massachusetts (25 miles north of Boston), when he was lecturing there in July 1848, and Sarah Helen Whitman of Providence, Rhode Island, the poet, avid Poe reader, and former Boston resident to whom Poe was briefly engaged in December 1848. On November 5, 1848, Poe came close to prematurely eternalizing his connection to the city of his birth by purportedly attempting suicide in a Boston hotel (possibly the Pavilion) by ingesting the opiate laudanum in a dosage equivalent to 300 milligrams of morphine. Distraught over his relationship with Annie Richmond, who was a married woman, he hoped she would come to him, even if only on his deathbed as she had promised during his second known visit to Lowell a month earlier.[12] One of the most iconic images in American literary history, an intensely forlorn portrait of Poe was created in Providence four days later. In an allusion to his 1842 short story "The Pit and the Pendulum," Mrs. Whitman later dubbed the daguerreotype the "Ultima Thule"—or the "ultimate limit."

Poe seemed to be yearning to return to his natal home in the months prior to his unexpected death in Baltimore. In a letter to Annie in Lowell dated November 16, 1848, "Eddy" wrote, "It is not much that I ask, sweet sister Annie—my mother [-in-law, Maria Clemm,] & myself would take a small cottage at Westford . . . I would labor day & night, and with industry, I could accomplish so much—Annie! it would be a Paradise beyond my wildest hopes." Another classic portrait of Poe known as the "Annie Daguerreotype" was created while he spent about ten of the happiest days of his life in a third and final visit to Lowell and nearby Westford the following late May or early June. In a letter to Mrs. Clemm dated September 1849—the month before his death—Poe was still questioning whether he and his mother-in-law would be "happier in Richmond or Lowell." But he repeatedly stated his preference: "I *must* be somewhere where I can see Annie," he wrote, "I want to live *near Annie*" (Poe's emphasis). The week following his death, the heartbroken Mrs. Clemm did move to Lowell. And she resided there with Annie and her family for most of the next two years.[13]

The only publication that would print any of Poe's writings during the final year of his life—paying him money he desperately needed for basic expenses—was the Boston weekly newspaper *The Flag of Our Union*. The last four poems and last five short stories published during his lifetime appeared in this popular Boston publication. Poe's next to last poem was "For Annie," dedicated to his beloved in Lowell and published on April 28, 1849. The final piece published before his death was the poem "To My Mother," a sonnet written to his mother-in-law, Maria Clemm, that also pays tribute to Eliza, "My mother—my own mother, who died early." He could not have known that he was closing a circle when this poem was published in the city of his birth on July 7, 1849. If we note that "The Tell-Tale Heart" first appeared in James Russell Lowell's *Pioneer*, then it is fair to say that Poe published his first and last work as well as his most famous short story in the city where his mother had found her "best and most sympathetic friends."

The Inner Life of the Poe-Boston Feud

Despite these facts, which establish Poe's claim to treatment as, if not a local author, then surely an author with significant ties to the area, Boston has for 160 years largely ignored the relationship. Even as Poe's reputation grew decade by decade after his death in 1849, Boston remained aloof. No doubt he has been included in English curriculums as he has everywhere, but the limited effort to celebrate and memorialize the connection is remarkable in the United States. It is particularly striking because both the biographical and literary sides of the Poe-Boston story are fascinating. The former is haunted by the remembrance of a mother too early lost and replete with key moments in Poe's creative and critical development; the latter stands as one of the great turning points in American literature and culture.

On October 16, 1845, at the height of his post-*Raven* fame, Poe addressed the Boston Lyceum, a regular program of readings and lectures open to the public. Months before this, when word of the invitation got out, Boston newspapers started to insult him. After Horace Greeley, writing in the *New York Daily Tribune* on March 1, 1845, praised Poe's then-recent performance at the Society Library in New York and bemoaned the fact that "only three hundred of our four hundred thousand people" attended—the *Boston Daily Atlas* snapped back, "The Tribune may think as it pleases—but we commend the taste of the

399,700 people, as far preferable to that of the 300, in this case." Four days later, on March 5, 1845, Cornelia Wells Walter, the editor of the (Boston) *Evening Transcript* who would become Poe's most relentless opponent, served up this premature epitaph in lieu of welcome:

> There lies, by Death's relentless blow,
> A would-be critic here below;
> His name was Poe
> His life was woe:
> You ask, "what of this Mister Poe?"
> Why nothing of him that I know;
> But echo, answering, saith "Poh!"

Never one to avoid a quarrel, Poe used an essay,"Longfellow's Poems," in the April issue of the *Aristidean* to riposte, describing Boston's "literary circle" as a "knot of rogues and madmen." And so it began: a flaring up of hostilities in the long-smoldering literary war Poe waged throughout his career against the Frogpondians.

The Lyceum lecture took place at a hectic time for Poe, just a few days before he acquired sole ownership of the *Broadway Journal*, which he had been editing for months. Distracted and strung out, he was unable to write a new poem for the occasion as requested. On the fateful evening of the lecture, he was kept waiting for over two hours while the first speaker droned on. After being introduced, he spoke briefly about the nature of poetry and then read the interminable "Al Aaraaf," written in his adolescence. In his own account of the evening—which he included in the "Editorial Miscellany" section of the *Broadway Journal* on November 1, 1845—Poe described his opening comments as follows: "We occupied some fifteen minutes with an apology for not 'delivering,' as is usual in such cases, a didactic poem: a didactic poem, in our opinion, being precisely no poem at all." As the crowd thinned, he was prevailed upon to read "The Raven." The one surviving extended account by an audience member who was not then a reporter or editor was written and published thirty-four years later by the extraordinary Thomas Wentworth Higginson, who had been a student at Harvard Law School at the time of the performance. In addition to calling Poe a "genius" whose "prose-writings had been eagerly read, at least among college-students," Higginson noted that few of those present knew that Poe had been born in Boston, that Poe's opening remarks felt like "nauseous flattery," and that his choice of a poem was "perplexing." Nonetheless, Higginson recalled that at some point the audience became rapt, "hushed, and, as it were, breathless," and that "in walking back to Cambridge my comrades and I felt that we had been under the spell of some wizard."[14]

Reviews the next day, however, were mostly negative. The *Daily Evening Traveller* said that the poem "was hardly adapted to the occasion." The *Yankee Blade* rejected Poe's assertion that didacticism and poetry are incompatible as "outré" and insisted that "the poem [Poe read] proved that its author had not even an incidental connection with the truth." And Cornelia Walter in the *Evening Transcript* decried Poe's lack of tact and noted that, though he "possessed a *raven*-ous desire to be known as the author of a particular piece of poetry on a celebrated croaking bird," he had failed to entertain the rapidly shrinking audience with either his "singularly didactic exordium" or his ill-chosen poem. In response, Poe assailed "Frogpondians" in general, implied that they were chronically asleep, and insisted that he had been trying to hoax and insult them: to make "a fuss."

The response article Poe published on November 1, two weeks after the reading, concludes with his most intemperate remarks on the city of his birth:

> We like Boston [he wrote ironically]. We were born there—and perhaps it is just as well not to mention that we are heartily ashamed of the fact. The Bostonians are very well in their way. Their hotels are bad. Their pumpkin pies are delicious. Their poetry is not so good. Their common is no common thing—and the duck-pond might answer—if its answer could be heard for the frogs. But with all these good qualities the Bostonians have no soul . . . [They] are well-bred— as *very* dull persons very generally are.

In what rapidly became the greatest (or at least most amusing) he-said-she-said exchange of the antebellum period, Walter responded to these insults in the November 4 issue of the *Transcript* as follows: "The editor of the *Journal* probably found himself in a po-kerish po-sition . . . if he had but sent . . . the managers of the Lyceum . . . the fifty dollars which he poked out of them for his childish effort in versification, he would have exhibited the only proof now wanting of his excessive po-liteness."

In the November 22nd issue of the *Journal,* Poe returned fire, delighting in the combat. Biographers have shaken their heads over the seemingly self-destructive gracelessness of his main line of defense: that he deliberately read a "bad" poem because that's all the Frogpondians deserved. But the issue of what made a poem good or bad was at the heart of Poe's quarrel with New England, and his apology was clearly ironic: "a didactic poem, in our opinion, being precisely no poem at all." On a more personal level, Poe returned Walter's serve, in a game of tat-for-tit:

> Miss Walters (the Syren!) has seen cause, we find, to recant all the ill-natured little insinuations she has been making against us . . . She defends our poem on the ground of its being "juvenile," and we think the more of her defense because she herself has been juvenile so long as to be a judge of juvenility. Well, upon the whole we must forgive her—and do. Say no more about it, you little darling! You are a delightful creature and your heart is in the right place—would to Heaven that we could always say the same thing of your wig!

In connection with the lecture, Poe would write five separate comments, while Walter returned nineteen times to the subject.

Other editors, most notably Leander S. Streeter of the *Boston Daily Star,* joined the assault on Poe in the aftermath of the lecture. Writing in the November 3rd issue, Streeter challenged Poe's claim to have "come all the way from New York" to perpetrate a hoax by reading a "baby-born poem;" described the audience as "critical and refined;" and called the speaker a "quizzical buffoon." And to prove that "Al Aaraaf" was "rich in intense twaddle" and therefore unworthy of presentation in Boston, Streeter printed it on three consecutive days. This apparently delighted Poe who responded as follows in the November 22nd issue of the *Broadway Journal:* "To demonstrate its utter worthlessness, 'The Boston Star' (a journal which, we presume, is to be considered as a fair representative of the Frogpondian genius) has copied the poem in full." As Kent P. Ljungquist observes, Streeter's decision allowed Poe to promote the hot-off-the-press edition of *The Raven and Other Poems*.[15] With an enemy like this, who needed friends?

While this story—rich in banter—was animated by pique, wounded pride, and hurt feelings, it also drew power from one of the crucial disagreements of the period.[16] On one side stood the Boston literary establishment: high-minded, committed to using literature to advance an array of social and political causes—including abolitionism, temperance, women's rights, poor relief, Unitarianism, and Transcendentalism; on the other side stood Poe, who was among the first theorists to argue in defense of art for art's sake. As Sidney P. Moss notes, "At a time when American critics, as well as American writers, confused a moralistic intent with literary value, Poe condemned didacticism both as a critical principle and as an aesthetic purpose."[17] Those who wonder why Poe associated the Frog Pond with Boston need go no further than his contempt for didacticism in poetry and fiction. Just as the famous narrator of "The Tell-Tale Heart" (1843) exclaims, "It was the beating of his hideous heart," so when Poe conjured the image of the Frog Pond, he was always thinking about the croaking sound coming from its shallow, murky water: the noise of Boston writers (ab)using literature to inculcate their versions of the truth. The point is not so much that Poe rejected the causes they espoused, though for the most part he did or would have; it was that he found the noisy, repetitive, insistent, and self-congratulatory sound of their preachy—and therefore to him, hideous—voices offensive.

As early as 1831, Poe arrived at a strikingly un-Frogpondian aesthetic principle: "A poem, in my opinion, . . . [has] for its *immediate* object, pleasure, not truth."[18] Throughout his career as a reviewer and literary theorist, he insisted that fiction and poetry should achieve effects by exciting the souls of readers. And his most direct denunciation of what he called "the heresy of the didactic"—included in the posthumously published version of a late lecture, "The Poetic Principle" (1850)—most directly associates this literary folly with the city of his birth: "Every poem, it is said, should inculcate a moral and by this moral is the poetical merit of the work to be adjudged. We Americans especially have patronized this happy idea, and we Bostonians very especially have developed it in full." The alternative, Poe insisted, was "to write a poem simply for the poem's sake."

Fueled by the exchange between Poe and Walter about whether the opening comments and first poem read were didactic enough, the Lyceum blow-up should be seen as the climax of Poe's struggle against Boston area writers in general and a few specific writers in particular. In the course of an ultimately unsatisfying relationship with James Russell Lowell, Poe moved from admiration to contempt. From as early as 1835, Poe kept his vulture eye on the work of Henry Wadsworth Longfellow (1807–82), charging him with plagiarism from 1840 on. And Poe leveled the same accusation against Hawthorne (1804–64) in an otherwise positive 1842 review, and eventually against Lowell and Margaret Fuller (1810–50) too. In his assessments of these and many other contemporaries, one can see Poe developing the view that poetry and fiction should provide deeply moving experiences. This position allowed him to craft stories intended to amuse, intrigue, puzzle, and terrify. It set him free to invent or enhance such popular genres as detective and mock-detective stories, science fiction and sci-fi hoaxes, gothic and mock-gothic fiction. Rejecting the "ranting" of Lowell's political verse, the "moral taint" of Longfellow's poems, Hawthorne's "monotonous" use of allegory, and the "excess of suggested meaning" of the "so called" Transcendentalists, Poe became the writer celebrated everywhere for his ability to make readers laugh and tremble. And it's worth noting that both sides won the Poe-Boston quarrel. Starting, perhaps, with Charles Baudelaire, Charlotte Perkins Gilman, Sir Arthur Conan Doyle, and Jules Verne, popular culture has drawn from and embraced Poe's works. Meanwhile, Boston writers charged into the 1850s undeterred, ready to advance the causes they held dear.

The literary aesthetic Poe decried in the Frogpondians prevails in *The Boston Book* series published in 1836 and 1850. The thesis-driven poems and stories in these volumes suggest that Poe's association of Boston with literary didacticism was anything but arbitrary. Among the works included in the 1836 edition were "The Blind Mother" by H. T. Tuckerman, "The Vision of Liberty" by Henry Ware, Jr., "Mother's Love" by Mrs. Hale, "To the Chanting Cherubs" by R. H. Dana, and, of course, "Truth" by H. W. Longfellow. Even a tale that promises to be descriptive, Andrews Norton's "A Winter Morning," moves from an account of waking up on a snowy day to a moral and religious lesson. At the time this book was in process, Poe was in Baltimore and then Richmond developing a view of popular taste that could support stories as shock-ing as his own "Berenice." In his April 30, 1835, letter to Thomas Willis White, the printer-publisher of the *Southern Literary Messenger,* Poe conceded that "Berenice"—the story of a man who wakes up to dis-cover that while sleepwalking he surgically removed the teeth of his not-as-dead-as-she-had-looked wife—might have been in "bad taste." But he also grappled with the issue of what readers want: "You ask me in what does this nature consist? In the ludicrous heightened into the grotesque: the fearful coloured into the horrible: the witty exagger-ated into the burlesque: the singular wrought out into the strange and mystical . . . To be appreciated you must be *read,* and these things are invariably sought after with avidity."

Poe was, by no means, the only writer whose works have endured in part because they rebelled against antebellum didacticism. In their own ways, Hawthorne, Melville, Whitman, Emerson, Dickinson, and Thoreau struggled against the easy truths and smug pieties of the time. Seen in this context, Poe's quarrel with the Frogpondians stands in bold relief as a representative event along with Emerson's decision to leave the ministry in 1832, Thoreau's 1846 night in jail, Dickinson's career-long decision not to publish her work, and the reviews of both Melville's *Pierre: or, The Ambiguities* (1852) and Whitman's *Song of Myself* (1855). While each of these interactions captures something of the middle-class values against which the American romantics labored, Poe's resis-tance led directly to the creation of a popular culture based on what readers would find pleasurable and, thus, "seek out with avidity." These ramifications—the place of the Poe-Boston feud in the development of American literature and culture as well as Poe's role in loosening the grip of New England's stern settlers—justify the effort to celebrate the Raven in the city of his birth.

In addition to highlighting the literary significance of Poe's home-town connection, remembering him in Boston allows us also to reas-sess both his relation to his mother and what her life reveals about the increasing legitimacy of the theater in post-Revolutionary New England. Associating Eliza Poe with Richmond, the city where she died a "linger-ing" death after a "long continuing indisposition," has produced the familiar but partial, horror-haunted version of her connection to her famous son.[19] Biographers and psychoanalytic critics back to Marie

Bonaparte, who have seen Eliza's deathbed as a source of Poe's morbid fascination with dying women, surely have a point. Eliza's struggles with whatever killed her—pneumonia, tuberculosis, or an infectious fever—inspired not only charitable appeals in Richmond newspapers but also Poe's obsessive interest in women who can never be forgotten or escaped even after they die. As Bonaparte put it, Eliza's "diaphanous beauty and . . . mysterious malady . . . were later to be immortalized by her son's genius in the forms of Berenice, Morella, Madeline, Eleonora, and Ligeia."[20] Still, just as the Baltimore-Poe connection has received unmerited attention because he died there, so the focus on Eliza's death in Richmond has made it difficult to see the importance of her life in Boston to Poe's matrilineal identity. Indeed, Bonaparte's claim that Poe never heeded Eliza's admonition to "love Boston"[21] is belied by his return in 1827 and his determination to return again in 1849. Even worse, it reduces Eliza's vital connection to her "little son" to her last, fading days and hours.

Throughout her career Eliza Poe was a talented, sparkling performer who had particular gifts as a singer, dancer, and comic actress. In his exhaustive review of theater records, Quinn notes that "she had to her credit, disregarding mere chorus, vocal, or dancing parts, [at least] two hundred and one different roles."[22] But Quinn also notes that attitudes toward actors in the late 1790s, especially in Boston, were in flux. Insofar as the Massachusetts Bay Colony's puritanical 1750 "Act for Preventing Stage Plays and Other Theatrical Entertainments" was still on the books though rarely enforced by the time the Arnolds arrived in 1796, so Poe's grandmother and mother must have been regarded with admiration by some but with suspicion or contempt by others. "To a large section of the public, especially in New England, the theatre was an immoral institution, the resort of the vicious and the extravagant, and the actors were without the pale."[23] And yet the approximately 1,000-seat capacity of the Boston theater in which both Elizabeth and Eliza Arnold first performed in the United States suggests that, for all the resistance, this was a rising, popular form of entertainment. On the one hand, as late as 1793 John Hancock decried "Evils which might flow from Theatrical exhibitions" especially as performed by "Aliens & Foreigners, [who] have lately entered the state, & in the Metropolis of the Government, under advertisements insulting to the habits, &

education of the Citizens."[24] On the other hand, a foreigner like Mrs. Arnold was welcomed in the press as a "valuable acquisition for the Boston Theatre" and greeted with "bursts of applause."[25]

If Eliza's death in Richmond provided material for Poe's tormented lovers, the conflict between Boston's killjoys and its purveyors of popular entertainment around the turn of the century can be seen as a rehearsal for Poe's quarrel with the highbrow, didactic, and reform-minded Frogpondians of the 1830s and 1840s. In his July 1845 defense of a leading actress, Anna Cora Mowatt, Poe identified himself as the proud "son of an actress,"[26] and emphasized the impact of Mowatt's "natural acting . . . by which she . . . effectively . . . lay bare to the audience the movements of her own passionate heart." Long before this, Poe's grandmother Elizabeth offered a summary of the roles she had played in Portland, Maine, between November 1796 and January 1797 in an "Epilogue" written for her final performance. Like her grandson, she insisted that "to please [had been her] never-ceasing end."[27] Quinn's identification of one of Elizabeth's roles with a character in a play called *The Ghost; or the Dead Man Alive* eerily foreshadows Poe's practice as a writer, as her emphasis on delighting audiences prefigured the aesthetic theory that allowed Poe's works to endure.

Half a Cheer for the Raven: Celebrating Poe in Boston

The significance of Poe's legacy to the cultural heritage of his native Boston has been underestimated ever since his death in 1849. Up to and through the Poe bicentennial only a few have tried to reclaim this native son for the Boston public. In a series of brief notices, the *New York Times* followed the halting effort to celebrate the Poe centenary in Boston in 1909. An article by Charles Marshall Graves that appeared in the *Times* on December 12, 1908, noted that celebrations for the Lincoln and Darwin centenaries were in the works but then asked, "What about Poe?" As far as Graves could tell, "no definite plans had yet been made" in Boston or anywhere else. An anonymous article that ran on January 16, 1909, called "Disappointment Over Plans for a Poe Celebration" said that a dinner had been canceled because only an "absurdly small" number of subscribers had signed up. The reporter was struck by the hypocrisy of letting the occasion pass while "protesting affection, admiration, profound respect, and other nice things" about Poe. And yet, dinner or no dinner, a group of writers led by Julia Ward Howe did celebrate the Poe centenary at Boston University with an aged Thomas Wentworth Higginson in attendance. Perhaps Graves's comment stirred a response, but in any case an article that ran in the January 20, 1909, issue of the *Times* reported that, "while all the country paid homage to the memory of Poe on the occasion of the centenary of his birth, the event was especially observed in Boston, where he was born."

In 1913, the city council named the intersection of Broadway and Carver Street near the site of Poe's birthplace in Bay Village "Edgar Allan Poe Square." But just seven years later city officials renamed the square to honor a veteran named Matthew Emmett Ryan, who was killed in World War I. On January 19, 1924, the Boston Authors Club installed a bronze commemorative tablet honoring Poe near Ryan Square, which again became informally known as Poe Square. But that marker has since been lost. In 1989, Boston actor and Poe impersonator Norman George, together with Michael Moskow, the owner of the building on the southeast corner of Boylston and Charles Street South, and others formed an Edgar Allan Poe Memorial Committee to plan festivities for his 180th birthday. They placed a plaque on Moskow's building facing the Common and convinced the city to rename the remnant of the old Carver Street alongside it "Poe Way." But the new street sign later disappeared and, when it was replaced, the original name was restored. Another small plaque commemorating Poe exists on the face of 15 Fayette Street in the neighborhood where Poe was born, but this marker is believed to have been installed there to signal the fact that the structure is referred to as the "Poe Condominium" building, not to indicate any other connection.

Since 2009, thanks to a group from Boston College, the city has begun to take its connection to Poe to heart.[28] In the run-up to the bicentennial, English professor Paul Lewis made the case for Boston in what came to be known as the Great Poe Debate. Students and staff working with Michael Swanson and Kerry Burke in the college's Media Technology Services department Photoshopped images of Poe into iconic Boston sites. Petitions calling on officials to recognize the approaching anniversary were sent to the State House and City Hall. These efforts were officially commended by the Massachusetts House of Representatives on January 15, 2009, and the City Council of Boston on January 19, 2009. In a proclamation issued in advance of Poe's 200th birthday, Mayor Thomas M. Menino acknowledged both the serious and amusing nature of the Poe-Boston feud even as he sought to achieve an overdue reconciliation:

> It's official. After two centuries of indifference and occasional irritation, Boston has embraced America's literary master. It is time to forgive any little quarrel Edgar Allan Poe may have had with the city of Boston and to forget that he ever called us 'Frogpondians,' said that our hotels were poor and our poetry 'not so good' . . . The city of Boston takes great pride in its literary heritage . . . Edgar Allan Poe is one of the most important figures in American Literature. We are proud to call him a Bostonian.[29]

Accordingly, Mayor Menino declared January 2009 Edgar Allan Poe Appreciation Month in Boston. He officially announced that the intersection of Charles and Boylston streets would henceforth be named Edgar Allan Poe Square with signage erected at the location, and he directed the Boston Art Commission to plan the creation of a work of public art in Poe Square. And on April 27, 2009, he officially dedicated Poe Square near the plaque that was installed in 1989.

A single (perhaps again vulnerable) street sign hangs in the new Poe Square. The bicentennial celebration only began to compensate for the decades of bad feeling left over from a quarrel that occurred fifteen years before the outbreak of the Civil War. Considering the significance of that quarrel beyond the sheer inventiveness of the insults it inspired, considering that 160 years is long enough to hold any grudge—it is surely time for Boston to move on, to embrace its inner Edgar, and to fully acknowledge its connection to its most influential native author. In the January 1809 issue of the *Monthly Anthology and Boston Review* published within days of Poe's birth, the editors lamented the state of American literature, characterizing it as "coarse, insipid fare" and noting the absence of hard-working writers. Over the next forty years, no one did more than Poe to add spice to what could be read and imagined.

At the end of the bicentennial year, an exhibit called "The Raven in the Frog Pond: Edgar Allan Poe and the City of Boston" at the Boston

Public Library drew over 23,000 viewers. For three and a half months a large banner boldly showcasing the words POE and BOSTON and depicting a gigantic raven walking in front of the 1844 Boynton map of Boston hung on the side of the historic McKim building facing Copley Square. Up in the Cheverus Room—drawing on the library's superb Poe collection and on loans from Susan Jaffe Tane, the American Antiquarian Society, and M. Thomas Inge—sections dealing with "Poe's Life in Boston" and "Poe's Quarrel with Boston Writers" made the case developed here: that Boston played a significant role in Poe's development as a writer, theorist, and person. In connection with the exhibit, a brochure called "Poe's Boston: Then and Now" was distributed. With eighteen Poe-related addresses—including the birthplace, the Frog Pond, the Federal Street Theatre, and the new Poe Square—the map it featured made a new walking tour called "The Raven's Trail" possible.[30]

There are signs that the Poe-Boston exhibit and other bicentennial celebrations may have had a long-term impact. In 2010, the Edgar Allan Poe Foundation of Boston was incorporated; shortly after, it was awarded a grant from the city's Edward Ingersoll Browne Trust Fund to develop plans for the installation of a permanent work of art celebrating Poe in his new square. Connected online to the bicentennial exhibition at www.poeboston.org, the foundation issued a national call to artists in 2011, expecting to receive a range of proposals befitting this versatile native author. At some point in the future, pedestrians walking through Poe Square may hear the sound of a beating human heart rising from under the red bricks of the sidewalk. Or they may see silhouettes of Poe characters (for instance, a black cat, a raven, a man being bricked up behind a wall) on lampposts around the square. Only after steps like these have been taken will justice be done to a writer and critic who cared enough about the city of his birth to challenge its least defensible convictions. Only then will the raven return.

NOTES

1. Poe lived in Boston for between 16 and 32 weeks as a newborn and for about 32 weeks in 1827 around the time he enlisted in the army. See Arthur Hobson Quinn, *Edgar Allan Poe: A Critical Biography* (Baltimore: Johns Hopkins University Press, 1998; 1941), 35; 118.

2. Ibid., 727–29.

3. Jack Thomas, "Our Towne: Haunted by Poe," *Boston Globe,* January 5, 1989, 65.

4. Geddeth Smith, *The Brief Career of Eliza Poe* (Cranbury, NJ: Associated University Presses, Inc., 1988), 20–21.

5. Kenneth Silverman, *Edgar A. Poe: Mournful and Never-Ending Remembrance* (New York: HarperCollins, 1991), 5.

6. "Last Night's Insult," *The Repertory,* Boston, April 7, 1807; and Joseph T. Buckingham, *Personal Memoirs and Recollections of Editorial Life* (Boston: Ticknor, Reed & Fields, 1852), 57.

7. Dwight Thomas and David K. Jackson, *The Poe Log: A Documentary Life of Edgar Allan Poe, 1809–1849* (New York: G. K. Hall, 1987), 11–15.

8. Quinn, *Edgar Allan Poe,* 35.

9. Ibid., 118.

10. Theodore Pease Stearns, "A Prohibitionist Shakes Dice with Poe," *Outlook* 126 (September 1, 1920): 25–26.

11. Mary E. Phillips, *Edgar Allan Poe—The Man* (Chicago: John C. Winston Co., 1926), vol. 2, 1052–54.

12. Silverman, *Edgar A. Poe,* 373–74.

13. Frederick W. Coburn, "Poe as Seen by the Brother of 'Annie,'" *New England Quarterly* 16 (1943): 468–76. Also see Brad Parker, *The Saga of Eddie & Annie: Lowell's Greatest Romance* (Lowell, MA: Landmark Printing, 1984), 37; and Silverman, *Edgar A. Poe,* 438.

14. Thomas Wentworth Higginson, "Short Studies of American Authors, II: Poe," *Literary World* 10 (March 15, 1879): 89–90.

15. Kent P. Ljungquist, "Poe's 'Al Aaraaf' and the Boston Lyceum: Contributions to Primary and Secondary Bibliography," *Victorian Periodicals Review* 28 (1995): 199–216.

16. On the personal and critical issues engaged in the Lyceum affair, see Ottavio M. Casale, "The Battle of Boston: A Revaluation of Poe's Lyceum Appearance," *American Literature* 45, no. 3 (1973): 423–28; Katherine Hemple Prowne, "The Cavalier and the Syren: Edgar Allan Poe, Cornelia Wells Walter, and the Boston Lyceum Affair," *New England Quarterly* 66, no. 1 (1993): 110–23; and Kent P. Ljungquist, "'Valdemar' and the 'Frogpondians': The Aftermath of Poe's Lyceum Appearance," in *Emersonian Circles: Essays in Honor of Joel Myerson,* ed. Wesley T. Mott (Rochester: University of Rochester Press, 1997), 181–206.

17. Sidney P. Moss, *Poe's Literary Battles: The Critic in the Context of His Literary Milieu* (Durham, NC: Duke University Press, 1963), ix.

18. "Letter to Mr. — — —," *Poems* (New York: Elam Bliss, 1831), 28.

19. These descriptive phrases appeared in public appeals printed in newspapers on November 29, 1811: "lingering" death in "To the Humane Heart," *Enquirer;* "long continuing indisposition" in "Mrs. Poe's Benefit," *Virginia Patriot.*

20. Marie Bonaparte,*The Life and Works of Edgar Allan Poe: A Psycho-Analytic Interpretation* (London: Hogarth Press, 1971; 1949 [first English edition]), 7.

21. Ibid.

22. Quinn, *Edgar Allan Poe,* 47.

23. Ibid., 1.

24. On efforts to repeal the Massachusetts anti-theater law, see William Dunlap, *History of the American Theatre* (London: Richard Bentley, 1833), 250, and Loren K. Ruff, "Joseph Harper and Boston's Board Alley Theatre, 1792–1793," *Educational Theatre Journal* 26, no. 1 (March 1974): 45–52.

25. Phillips, *Edgar Allan Poe—The Man,* vol. 1, 44–45.

26. *Broadway Journal,* II, July 19, 1845.

27. Quinn, *Edgar Allan Poe,* 6.

28. For a brief discussion of urban legends about Poe in Boston, as well as a prediction that the city would not host bicentennial events, see Kathleen Burge, "Poe," *Boston Globe,* January 28, 2007.

29. From Mayor Menino's Proclamation of "Edgar Allan Poe Appreciation Month" as read by City of Boston Poet Laureate Sam Cornish at "The Raven Returns to Boston: A 200th Birthday Party for Edgar Allan Poe" at Boston College on January 15, 2009.

30. See Phillips, *Edgar Allan Poe—The Man,* vol. 2, 1053, for an earlier, less detailed map of Poe's Boston.

W. E. B. Du Bois, Nina Gomer Du Bois, and James Weldon Johnson in front of the Du Bois home in 1928. Du Bois Papers, Special Collections and University Archives, W.E.B. Du Bois Library, University of Massachusetts Amherst.

In our final case study, historian David Glassberg and archaeologist Robert Paynter portray the site of W. E. B. Du Bois's first years as fiercely contested terrain in long-standing battles over the meaning of American citizenship. Despite Du Bois's own efforts to commemorate his origins in Great Barrington, Massachusetts, residents worked feverishly at times to erase his memory from their community. Glassberg and Paynter demonstrate how this resistance typified Cold War Era anxieties about Communism, race, and the reshaping of American communities during the late twentieth century. Economics figures as well in explaining both threats and encouragements to Du Bois's memory. Recent efforts, however, to protect and interpret his legacy in Great Barrington—a project in which Glassberg and Paynter are deeply involved—have made significant strides, thanks in part to innovative community and university partnerships and a healthy dose of reflexivity. In fact, the Du Bois project models a careful balance between history and memory that public historians should aspire to. Even so, as Glassberg and Paynter point out and as several of our contributors have warned, commemorating any person's origins makes muffling the complexity of later lives all too easy. It is this feature of birthplace commemoration, of course, that explains its persistent appeal and ensures its essential quandary.

Du Bois in Great Barrington

The Promises and Pitfalls of a Boyhood Historic Site

DAVID GLASSBERG AND ROBERT PAYNTER

Two places on the international historical landscape have been set aside to commemorate the remarkable life of W. E. B. Du Bois. One is the W. E. B. Du Bois Memorial Centre for Pan-African Culture in Accra, Ghana, an impressive burial site and research center built by the Republic of

Ghana at the house and compound where Du Bois last resided. The other is the W. E. B. Du Bois Boyhood Homesite in Great Barrington, Massachusetts, a small local park built through the efforts of a few private citizens at one of the places where Du Bois lived as a child. The nearly half century of struggle to keep the memory of Du Bois alive in the town of his birth reveals much about the promises and pitfalls of boyhood sites as well as the political economy of heritage and commemoration in the United States.[1]

Du Bois, born in 1868, died on the eve of the Civil Rights March on Washington in 1963, where Roy Wilkins, the executive secretary of the NAACP, told the 250,000 gathered on the Mall that Du Bois had died the night before in Accra, Ghana, noting "his was the voice that was calling you here today."[2] His ninety-five years were filled with accomplishments. The first African American Ph.D. from Harvard, Du Bois became a pioneering historian and sociologist who by the age of thirty-one had published *The Suppression of the African Slave Trade to the United States of America, 1638–1870,* a prescient study of the Atlantic world system, and *The Philadelphia Negro,* arguably the first urban ethnography in the United States. As a professor at Atlanta University, he oversaw one of the earliest and most systematic studies of African American life, ranging over fifteen volumes, and published the classic *The Souls of Black Folk,* since translated into numerous languages. His *Black Reconstruction,* published in 1935, still stands as a powerful analysis of how the postbellum racialized political economy quashed the Civil War's promises of liberation. *The World and Africa,* published posthumously in 1965, provides the capstone to Du Bois's seventy-year effort to bring Africa its proper recognition in world history.

Alongside his innovative scholarship came path-breaking political work. He confronted Booker T. Washington's strategy for racial uplift as a co-founder of the Niagara Movement, and of its successor organization the National Association for the Advancement of Colored People (NAACP). As editor of the NAACP's influential publication *The Crisis,* Du Bois was the voice of progressive change for thousands of African Americans from the 1910s through the 1930s. In addition he worked tirelessly for the cause of African decolonization, co-founding Pan-Africanist Conferences and mentoring many of the first generation of post-colonial Africa's leadership.[3]

Toward the end of his life Du Bois made two completely consistent and integritous moves that were hard for some people to swallow. He joined the Communist Party USA at age ninety-three and accepted President Kwame Nkrumah's invitation to live in Accra to work on the *Encyclopedia Africana*. The latter, coupled with the U.S. State Department revocation of Du Bois's American passport, was turned against Du Bois by his enemies, with the false claim that he renounced his American citizenship.[4]

Given his accomplishments, it is not surprising that land on two continents has been set aside to commemorate Du Bois's long and productive life. And given the controversial nature of Du Bois's life's work, it is not surprising that the only place that commemorates Du Bois in the USA is a plot of ground where his childhood home once stood, and that the boyhood homesite until very recently has been a poison ivy–choked patch of woodland by the side of the road with no place even to pull off. Before 2008, all that you would have seen if you could have found the homesite at all was an obscured National Historic Landmark plaque and a cellar hole.

History of the Homesite

The homesite property, which is approximately two miles from the center of Great Barrington on Egremont Plain, first came into the hands of the Burghardt family (the B in W. E. B.) possibly as early as 1795 and certainly by 1820. This very small property, between .3 and 1 acre, was part of an African American neighborhood occupied by members of the Burghardt family, including Du Bois himself, for around 150 years. Du Bois referred to the place as the House of the Black Burghardts. He describes it as:

> the first home that I remember. There my mother was born and all her nine brothers and sisters . . . [it was the] center of the world . . . a delectable place—simple, square and low, with the great room of the fireplace, the flagged kitchen, half a step below, and the lower woodshed beyond. Steep, strong stairs led up to Sleep, while without was a brook, a well and a mighty elm.[5]

Du Bois did not live long in this ancestral home. He was born in a house since demolished in the center of town, on Church Street. It was only when his father Alfred left the family when Du Bois was two that he, his mother, and older brother Adelbert moved in with his mother's parents in the small house on Egremont Plain. Three years later, when Du Bois was five, his grandfather died, and Du Bois and his mother, grandmother, and brother moved back into town, living for a time over the former stables of a local estate. As Du Bois grew up poor in Great Barrington, he lived in two other rental residences, on Railroad Street and on Church Street, and worked a remarkable array of part-time jobs until he graduated from Great Barrington High School, the first African American to do so. With the financial help of the local Congregational church, at age seventeen he left Great Barrington for Fisk University in Nashville, embarking on a notable career as a scholar and activist that would take him to Cambridge (Massachusetts), Germany, Ohio, Philadelphia, Atlanta, and New York City.[6]

Although Du Bois did not reside in Great Barrington as an adult, he and his family returned to town on numerous occasions, most poignantly in 1897 for the birth of his son Burghardt, and in 1899 to bury that son in Mahaiwe Cemetery, a passing commemorated in *The Souls of Black Folk*.[7] He sent his wife Nina to Great Barrington for the birth of his daughter, Yolande, in 1900, and had them return there as a safe haven in the aftermath of the Atlanta Race Riots of 1906.[8] He kept up correspondence with his Burghardt relatives, and would return to town in 1950 to bury Nina. His last visit to Great Barrington was in the fall of 1956, though in 1961, shortly before he left for Ghana, he arranged to have his daughter Yolande laid to rest in Mahaiwe Cemetery.[9] During these latter visits, by which time the house was no longer standing, he stayed at the Sunset Inn, a guest house owned by a local African American man named Edward Willoughby.[10] Great Barrington was an emotional center of Du Bois's world long after he and many of the Black Burghardts had left the area. The more places Du Bois moved as an adult, the larger his boyhood home became in his imagination. He never forgot about it, and carried the tongs of its fireplace with him to each of the other places where he lived.

The first effort to turn the boyhood homesite into a place of commemoration occurred in the 1920s, and was initiated by Du Bois himself.

Visiting Great Barrington in July 1925 to address the forty-first reunion of his high school class, he noticed that his former home was up for sale. Du Bois wrote to the owner, Edward Wooster of Springfield: "I have a sentimental desire to keep this place which was the home of my grandfather, the birthplace of my mother, and the place that I remember in my earliest childhood . . . Of course the house is almost fallen down, but I should like to try to restore it."[11] But his funds for acquiring the property were limited by the purchase of an apartment house in New York City, his primary residence while he was editing *The Crisis*. Finally, in 1928, on the occasion of his sixtieth birthday, a group of friends purchased the home and gave it to Du Bois as a gift. With the help of Warren Davis, a local Black entrepreneur, Du Bois immediately set to work, hiring local architect J. McArthur Vance to plan renovations to the "cottage."[12]

Du Bois wanted not the modest cottage of his youth, but a middle-class summer retreat, located as it was in Berkshire County, a region long known for its vacation homes. The Du Bois property was near the summer homes of James Weldon Johnson and co-founder of the NAACP Mary White Ovington.[13] His plans to restore the house entailed expanding it to include a living room, dining room, and kitchen, a spacious library and music room with French doors opening out on to a broad porch, four bedrooms, a garage, plaster walls, and indoor plumbing and central heating.[14] Clearly Du Bois sought to restore the house not only as a retreat for himself but also as an impressive tribute to his family's long history in the region.[15]

But just a few years after he took possession of the home, the nation's economic climate changed dramatically, devastating Du Bois's personal finances along with those of *The Crisis,* the NAACP, and the Black community as a whole. Du Bois hung on to the house for the next twenty-six years, but ultimately was unable to restore it. Financing, time, and advancing age made the realization of his ambitious plans for the house impossible.[16] His relocation from New York to Atlanta between 1934 and 1944 put him at a greater distance from Great Barrington. In 1954, at age eighty-six, Du Bois found it necessary to sell the property.[17] The house, by then in extreme disrepair, was torn down and the property folded into the holdings of the neighbor. In essence, by the time of Du Bois's death in Ghana in 1963, his presence and that of his family and ancestors had been erased from the New England landscape.

Controversy over the Dedication of the Homesite

Four years later, in 1967, Walter Wilson, a local white realtor, heard from local Black contractor Warren Davis that the land where the Du Bois home had stood was again up for sale. He contacted Dr. Edmund W. Gordon, a distinguished African American psychologist who had a summer home in the area, and the two men purchased the small Burghardt homesite along with an additional four acres with the intention of creating a memorial park in honor of Du Bois.[18] They founded a Du Bois Memorial Committee, whose ranks soon included many prominent national figures such as Martin Luther King, Jr., Harry Bellefonte, and Sidney Poitier as well as some Great Barrington residents. In February 1968, on the occasion of the centennial of Du Bois's birth, they wrote to Governor John Volpe proposing unsuccessfully that the Commonwealth of Massachusetts establish a state memorial at the homesite for Du Bois.[19]

Their efforts gained additional import following the death of Martin Luther King, Jr., in April 1968. By October 1969, the committee held a dedication ceremony at their local park in honor of Du Bois, emceed by actor Ossie Davis with a keynote address by national civil rights leader Julian Bond. The ceremony drew an international audience, but also the attention of the Federal Bureau of Investigation and hostile reactions from some local townspeople. The opponents repeatedly used legal tactics to block the dedication. And the opponents issued at least thirty threats to blow up or destroy the memorial after its completion.[20] A local newspaper, the *Berkshire Courier,* captured much of this spirit of opposition when it counseled against violence to people but did recommend vandalizing the memorial park after the ceremony.[21]

Anti-Communism, White Supremacy, and Localism

Why were efforts to commemorate Du Bois met with such hostility in the town of his birth? One reason was Du Bois's affiliation with communism.[22] Even though Du Bois was a member of the Communist Party only in the last few years of his long life, the Cold War hung heavy in Great Barrington as it did in other towns across America in the

1960s. The years when Wilson and Gordon sought to establish the Du Bois Boyhood Homesite memorial park coincided with the years when the United States sent its largest number of troops to fight a communist insurgency in Vietnam. Some of the most vociferous opposition to memorializing Du Bois at the homesite came from veterans' groups. Howard Beckwith, commander of the local Veterans of Foreign Wars post, declared that the planned memorial was "like building a statue to Adolf Hitler . . . The man was a Marxist as far back as 1922," and "we oppose a monument to a Communist any place in the United States."[23] More opposition came from groups such as the American Legion, Daughters of the American Revolution, and the John Birch Society.

Worse than being a Communist sympathizer was being Black and a Communist sympathizer. During the Cold War, civil rights organizations were mercilessly red-baited. In 1946 Arthur Schlesinger, Jr., claimed that the CPUSA was "sinking tentacles into the National Association for the Advancement of Colored People."[24] A letter to the editor of the *Berkshire Eagle* in 1968 manifested this conglomeration of racism and anti-Communism, warning, "Young people know little of the real Du Bois, nor do they understand the special meaning of words in the Communist dialect in which . . . civil rights is the catalyst to destroy representative government in America and install Communist dictatorship."[25]

Dedicating a historic site to honor an African American who questioned the course of American foreign policy during the Cold War posed a particular challenge. During World War II, the National Park Service established the George Washington Carver birthplace in Diamond, Missouri, as a park with the idea that it would contribute to Black morale during the war. By the time it was dedicated in 1953, honoring Carver had a Cold War rationale, to demonstrate to the world that the United States did not merit world criticism for its treatment of Blacks. The Cold War rationale was even more evident in the campaign to establish the Booker T. Washington Birthplace National Monument in 1956. At a time when the world was witnessing Civil Rights demonstrations, the National Park Service advanced the Booker T. Washington site as proof that every American who desires to get ahead can achieve; its initial brochure in 1957 explained that Booker T. Washington's "belief that the Negro should adjust to his social and economic environment led him to advocate a doctrine of race relations which has survived in the South for three generations."[26]

Honoring Du Bois was a different matter. The FBI had long had Du Bois under surveillance. This continued after his death. There was a direct connection between the FBI and opposition to the dedication ceremony. In Du Bois's FBI files is evidence that there was an informer in Great Barrington during this period. The owner of the neighboring house recalled two FBI agents perched in his attic house monitoring the dedication ceremony.[27]

Though not mentioned in the press, local opposition to a Du Bois Boyhood Homesite memorial park was also partially based in anti-Black racism.[28] African Americans have always been a small minority of the town's population, on the order of between 2 and 3 percent. Though they had more economic opportunities there than in the Deep South, the "veil" separating Blacks from whites that Du Bois observed growing up at the turn of the twentieth century was still present.[29] Mrs. Elaine Gunn, a retired teacher and resident of Great Barrington for over fifty years, and a member of the original 1969 Du Bois Memorial Committee, recalls that during the 1940s and '50s, most Blacks lived in one section of town near the Clinton A.M.E. Church and Railroad Street. When she sought to purchase a home elsewhere, Mrs. Gunn was shown a Quonset hut rather than a real house. When asked if controversy would have occurred in 1969 had Du Bois *not* become a Communist, Mrs. Gunn quickly responded "yes." She believed that Communism allowed whites to at least partially mask their prejudices behind Du Bois's supposed lack of patriotism.[30]

There was also the matter that the Du Bois Boyhood Homesite memorial park seemed primarily the work of summer residents and outsiders. Walter Wilson was a transplant from Texas; Edmund Gordon was from New York. Wilson was upset that so few year-round residents, Black or white, were involved in the commemoration. The Du Bois Memorial Committee sought to pull off a civic commemorative event that included few of the town's local institutions and customary self-appointed guardians of tradition.[31]

Despite the forces arrayed against them, the Du Bois Memorial Committee prevailed in October 1969. On what people remember as a glorious New England fall day, buses arrived with nearly 800 people and the ceremony went off without a hitch. A massive memorial boulder was dedicated at the site, with Julian Bond giving a powerful address indicting the racial and economic policies of the Nixon administration. The Memorial Committee designed a plaque declaring "The Problem of the Twentieth Century is the Color Line," but did not attach it to the boulder that day for fear of vandalism.[32]

Over the next ten years the Memorial Committee struggled to maintain the homesite as a local park, building fences and planting trees with volunteer labor. Although federal support for their efforts was nowhere in sight, the committee put up a hand-painted wooden sign proclaiming "W. E. B. Du Bois National Historic Site." Its efforts, recognized by Du Bois's widow, Shirley Graham Du Bois, who visited the site during the early 1970s, finally secured National Historic Landmark status for the homesite from the U.S. Department of Interior in 1976. The committee celebrated the milestone at the Boston Symphony Orchestra's summer home at Tanglewood three years later with an elaborate dedication ceremony featuring Julian Bond, Pete Seeger, Du Bois's stepson David Graham Du Bois, Xie Qime from the Embassy of the People's Republic of China, and Quaison-Sackey, Ambassador to the United States from Ghana.[33]

The Memorial Committee gained a powerful ally in 1983, when the University of Massachusetts Amherst, located only an hour east of Great Barrington, launched early archaeological field excavations directed by Robert Paynter to study the demolished house of the Black Burghardts and the homesite.[34] At the same time, UMass had been fostering the Du Bois legacy by acquiring Du Bois's Papers during the early 1970s, creating a traveling exhibit about Du Bois, and naming its main library for Du Bois. In 1987, with interest in Du Bois growing on campus, it seemed logical for the Memorial Committee in Great Barrington to turn the homesite property over to the university to develop further. Professor William Strickland of the W. E. B. Du Bois Department of Afro American Studies, who was on the platform at Tanglewood in 1979, oversaw the transfer of ownership.

As a result, for a period from the late 1960s to the mid-1980s, it looked as if efforts to erase Du Bois and his family from the landscape had been reversed. The university sponsored two seasons of archaeological research at the homesite and hosted regular Du Bois Day celebrations on his birthday in February. But bad economic conditions accomplished what local political opponents of the site could not. National Historic Landmark status in the U.S. comes without a dime of state or federal funding. When the university plunged into a financial crisis in 1989, only two years after receiving the property, developments at the Du Bois Boyhood Homesite ground to a halt and its proponents had nowhere to turn. While other historic sites across the country in the 1980s increasingly turned to private corporate capital for support—those involved, for example, in the restoration of the Statue of Liberty—Du Bois's reputation as a social activist and communist made this avenue nearly impossible.[35] Conditions at the homesite deteriorated. As the university all but abandoned the orphan property, New England forest succession filled in the open fields that Gordon and Wilson had purchased for a memorial park.

Recent Memorialization Attempts

Although there was no local, state, federal or corporate support forthcoming to develop the boyhood homesite, in the mid-1990s a grass-roots movement arose in Great Barrington to create inexpensive memorials to Du Bois elsewhere in town. In 1994, the Great Barrington Historical Society erected signs where Du Bois was born and where his family was buried. Local historian Bernard Drew wrote a new, voluminous history of Great Barrington that recognized Du Bois as a prominent son of the town.[36] In the early 2000s, under Reverend Esther Dozier, the Clinton AME Zion Church began celebrating Du Bois's birthday each year with speakers and music. Local activist Rachel Fletcher developed the W. E. B. Du Bois River Garden and Walk on the banks of the Housatonic River dedicated to Du Bois. A youth project painted a hip-hop style mural honoring Du Bois on the side of Carr's, a local hardware store. Though local opposition to honoring Du Bois did not disappear—the school committee declined to name a new elementary school after Du Bois in 2005—that same year the town voted 2 to 1 to erect signs on the major thoroughfares into town announcing that Great Barrington was Du Bois's birthplace.[37]

Building on this momentum, Great Barrington residents again turned their attention to the homesite property, forming a Du Bois

Homesite friends group to help the University of Massachusetts care for its neglected property.[38] Over the next five years, the partners sponsored more archaeology and the Du Bois Homesite was included on the Upper Housatonic Valley African American Heritage Trail.[39] In 2008, Thomas Cole, an African American interim chancellor of the University of Massachusetts, allocated $50,000 for a modest parking lot, a large sign, and an interpretive trail through the forest to the memorial boulder. That same year, the UMass President's Office, the National Trust for Historic Preservation, and the Berkshire-Taconic Community Foundation funded a year-long planning process to determine how best to interpret Du Bois at the homesite and throughout Great Barrington. This was a Creative Economy grant to encourage UMass faculty and staff to work with local communities on economic development. Among the participants in the planning workshops were Catherine Turton from the National Park Service's National Historical Landmarks program, Rex Ellis from the Smithsonian's National Museum of African American History and Culture, and Lauri Klefos from the Berkshire Visitors Bureau. Completed in July 2009, "W. E. B. Du Bois in Great Barrington: A Plan for Heritage Conservation and Interpretation" calls for significant upgrades to the boyhood homesite facilities, including interpreting archaeology at the site; a walking tour of Du Bois's Great Barrington; and the creation of a new Du Bois Heritage and Interpretation Center in downtown Great Barrington. Toward that end, in 2011, an exhibit on Du Bois, "Becoming a Son of Great Barrington," opened in the lobby of the Triplex movie theater downtown.[40]

What has brought about the town's apparent change of heart? With the end of the Cold War, the high tide of anti-Communist feelings in town has receded somewhat. Also, many proponents of Du Bois who were outsiders in 1969 had become longtime residents thirty years later, and are better positioned to advance the civic importance of Du Bois. But the difference can also be tied to a shift in the economy of Great Barrington. Though Great Barrington had been a popular summer resort for much of the twentieth century, in recent years the town's economy has come to depend more than ever on tourists. It is significant, and more than a little ironic, that the town, so divided over Du Bois's legacy in the 1960s, could come together under the assumption that promoting Du Bois as part of the region's heritage tourism is good for business.[41] Although those seeking to erase the memory of Du Bois are still around—the signage by the boulder has twice been torn out of the ground and thrown into the woods, and a letter to the *Berkshire Record* in August 2010 decried the town's honoring of Du Bois on the grounds that he was "a first class hater" for whom "any foe of America became his friend"—it appears that those in town interested in commemorating Du Bois are now in the ascendancy.[42]

The Challenging Convenience of Origins

The homesite's status as a boyhood homesite may account for some of this recent success. In memorializing Du Bois's youth, Great Barrington can celebrate its role in nurturing an intellectual giant without really coming to terms with his radicalism as an adult. Du Bois's most controversial actions occurred elsewhere, after he had grown up and moved away. The story of Du Bois's hard-working childhood in Great Barrington, and the assistance he received from the white community to further his education, appeals to the town's liberal sense of itself, as well as to the sensibilities of tourists. Without a standing structure on the property, it will always be a boyhood homesite. Visitors can imagine Du Bois's childhood more easily in the archaeological footprint of the demolished home than if Du Bois had been successful in renovating the house and inhabiting it as an adult in the 1920s.

The challenge in interpreting Du Bois in Great Barrington is how to expand the familiar "local boy makes good" trope into a meaningful collection of stories that will communicate to visitors the ongoing significance of Du Bois's political ideas and actions and provoke civic dialogue on issues of contemporary concern. How can we communicate to the public the local political culture of African American resistance in which Du Bois was raised? What influences led him to pick radical abolitionist and socialist Wendell Phillips as the subject of his high school valedictorian address at age sixteen? Can we remind visitors that Du Bois owned the house—even if he did not live in it—when he wrote *Black Reconstruction* and other radical works, and engaged in political activities that earned the enmity of the federal government, when the State Department refused to issue him a passport and the Justice Department indicted him for being a foreign agent?

Another challenge, one that Du Bois would have recognized, comes from the chronic fiscal crisis of the state, which has made it necessary for the university and the Friends to seek private money to develop the site further. While UMass found the money to build a trail from the parking lot to the commemorative boulder in 2008, it was necessary to go to the 1772 Foundation to pay for an extension of the trail to where the house actually stood. In the United States, where private capital is essential to developing new heritage sites, it remains to be seen if Du Bois's legacy of challenging this very system will, as it has in the past, limit funds for the project.

While the site's status as a boyhood homesite might make it eas-ier for the local community to support, and for tourists to accept, it also limits the scope of what can be said about Du Bois there. Perhaps changing the name to the Du Bois Family Homesite would focus visitor attention on the generations of African Americans who lived at the site and in the neighborhood before Du Bois, and in some ways would be more in keeping with W. E. B. Du Bois's intentions for the place in the 1920s as a monument to his ancestors. Certainly having another place in town to tell the story of Du Bois's adult accomplishments, proposed in the 2009 planning report, will take the pressure off the boyhood homesite to do it all.

Despite these challenges, Du Bois's legacy has had an enduring and inspiring effect on the many people who have worked over the years to recover that legacy at the homesite. The depth of his insights and the breadth of his vision may only now be something that Americans can come to understand and respect. It is our challenge that the homesite become not just a celebration of Du Bois's boyhood, but also a place to reflect on and be inspired by the long career of this most prescient of Americans.

NOTES

Many thanks to the Reverend Esther Dozier, David Du Bois, Mrs. Elaine Gunn, Wray Gunn, Rachel Fletcher, Bernard Drew, Jay Schafer, Bill Strickland, Amilcar Shabazz, Whitney Battle-Baptiste, Robert Cox, Dolores Root, and Michael Singer. We also appreciate the insights we have gained from working with Evelyn Jeffers, John Diffley, and Elizabeth Harlow in previ-ous versions of this essay. Our work would not have been possible but for their generosity, intelligence, and commitment to Du Bois's legacy. And we would like to dedicate this chapter to Chancellor Thomas R. Cole, without whose vision and support so much would be still undone.

1. This chapter is based on the following works: Robert Paynter and David Glassberg, "Conflict and Consensus in Great Barrington: Remembering W. E. B. Du Bois," in the session "Communities: from Conflict to Consensus," for the conference Heritage in Conflict and Consensus: New Approaches to the Social, Political, and Religious Impact of Public Heritage in the 21st Century, UMass Amherst, November 2009. That paper was drawn from Robert Paynter, "The Neglect of Du Bois in His Hometown of Great Barrington, Massachusetts and the Subsequent Efforts to Overcome That Neglect," in the session "Du Bois's Lesser Known Legacies," organized by William Strickland for the Annual Meeting of the Association for the Study of African American Life and History, Cincinnati, OH, October 2009, and Robert Paynter, Elizabeth Harlow, Evelyn Jeffers, John Diffley, and MaryEllen Loan, "Erasing and Commemorating Du Bois: The Politics of an Historic Landscape," in the symposium (Re) Historicizing the Human Landscape: Intersections of Space/Race/Place/Memory organized by Melissa Hargrove for the Annual Meeting of the American Anthropological Association, San Jose, CA, November 19, 2006.

2. *The Seventh Son: The Thought and Writings of W. E. B. Du Bois,* ed. with an introduction by Julius Lester (New York: Vintage Books), vol.1, 147.

3. The most complete biography of Du Bois is David Levering Lewis's two-volume *W. E. B. Du Bois: Biography of a Race, 1868–1919* (New York: Henry Holt, 1993), and *W. E. B. Du Bois: The Fight for Equality and the American Century, 1919–63* (New York: Henry Holt, 2000). Du Bois wrote a number of autobiographical sketches, memoirs, and books; this paper draws on *The Autobiography of W. E. B. Du Bois: A Soliloquy on Viewing My Life from the Last Decade of Its First Century* (New York: International Publishers, 1968).

4. On Du Bois's loss of citizenship, see Lewis, *W. E. B. Du Bois: The Fight for Equality and the American Century, 1919–63,* 567–71; and Mike Forrest Keen, *Stalking the Sociological Imagination: J. Edgar Hoover's FBI Surveillance of American Sociology* (Westport, CT: Greenwood, 1999), 25.

5. W. E. B. Du Bois, "The House of the Black Burghardts," *Crisis* 35 (1928): 133–34.

6. On Du Bois's early years, see Lewis, *W. E. B. Du Bois: Biography of a Race, 1868–1919,* 26–55; and Du Bois, *The Autobiography of W. E. B. Du Bois: A Soliloquy on Viewing My Life from the Last Decade of Its First Century,* 61–276.

7. See W. E. B. Du Bois, "Passing of the First Born," *The Souls of Black Folk* (Chicago: A. C. McClurg & Co., 1903).

8. Lewis, *W. E. B. Du Bois: Biography of a Race,* 345.

9. The 1956 date comes from Bernard Drew, *Great Barrington: Great Town, Great History* (Great Barrington Historical Society, 1999), 378. Yolande's memorial service was in Baltimore. Although she was buried in Mahaiwe Cemetry, the grave remains unmarked. Lewis, *W. E. B. DuBois: The Fight for Equality,* 566.

10. Du Bois to Willoughby, W. E. B. Du Bois Papers. Du Bois stayed at the Sunset Inn for two weeks in 1925; his wife Nina stayed there several other times in the 1920s. Du Bois to Charles E. Bently, September 11, 1925. Du Bois Papers, University of Massachusetts, Amherst (hereafter Du Bois Papers).

11. Du Bois to Edward Wooster, September 1, 1925, Du Bois Papers.

12. See Bernard Drew, "Joseph McArthur Vance, Architect," *Great Barrington,* 39.

13. James Weldon Johnson recommended Vance to Du Bois. The enclave of African Americans from New York City who summered in the Berkshires in the 1920s is worth further study.

14. Du Bois outlined his plans for renovating the house in correspondence with Vance. See the blueprint, "Proposed Alterations, Cottage of W. E. B. Du Bois, Great Barrington, MA,

by J. McArthur Vance, Architect," July or August 1928, Box 46, folder 11, Du Bois Papers.

15. For more on Du Bois's efforts to restore the house, see Bernard Drew, *Dr. Du Bois Rebuilds His Dream House* (Great Barrington: Attic Revivals Press, 2006); and Robert Paynter, Kerry Lynch, Elizabeth Norris and Quentin Lewis, *Archaeology at the W. E. B. Du Bois Boyhood Homesite, Chapter 3 Documentary Background,* http://scholarworks.umass.edu/du_bois_boyhood_survey/04/, 47–54.

16. Du Bois wrote to local contractor Frank Vigezzi, "I had hoped to do more work on the Great Barrington house last summer but the depression scared me." Du Bois to Vigezzi, November 4, 1931, Box 61, folder 7, Du Bois Papers,.

17. Du Bois was the target of several federal probes in the 1950s, including a trial for refusing to register as a "foreign agent" when he chaired the Peace Information Committee that publicized the Stockholm Nuclear Disarmament proposal in the United States. See Lewis, *W. E. B. Du Bois: The Fight for Equality.*

18. Both men understood Du Bois's importance to the Civil Rights Movement and to the larger currents of world history, and sought to preserve his legacy. Wilson was a white man from Tennessee who moved to Texas and became active in the American Civil Liberties Union and its civil rights work in the South. He had later moved to New York State and gone into real estate. Edmund Gordon was a distinguished professor at Columbia Teachers College, one of the foremost African American psychologists and educators of the time. His illustrious academic career included public service as one of the architects of the Head Start Program. Gordon had known Du Bois personally, spending time with him in the 1950s in New York City. For more on Wilson and Gordon, see Amy Bass, *Those About Him Remained Silent: The Battle Over W. E. B. Du Bois* (Minneapolis: University of Minnesota Press, 2009), 48–61.

19. On the letter to Governor John Volpe about creating a state memorial to Du Bois, see ibid., 66.

20 Steve Turner, "Black Sheep of the Native Sons," *Berkshire Week,* August 20–27, 1976, 8.

21. "Keeping Cool," *The Berkshire Courier,* October 16, 1969.

22. We especially thank John Diffley for recovering the evidence of the red-baiting of Du Bois and our previous collaborations on the history of the Du Bois Homesite .

23. Harold J. Beckwith, quoted in Douglas Robinson, "W. E. B. Du Bois Hometown in the Berkshires Angered by Plans for Memorial," *New York Times,* May 16, 1969, 49.

24. Arthur Schlesinger, Jr., "The Communist Party," *Life,* July 29, 1946, 84–96, 90. This quote is also cited in Gerald Horne, *Black and Red: W. E. B. Du Bois and the Afro-American Response to the Cold War, 1944–63* (Albany: State University of New York Press, 1986), 58; as well as in Lewis, *W. E. B. Du Bois: The Fight for Equality and the American Century,* 526. Schlesinger's comments had a profound impact not only on perceptions of the NAACP and its prominent associate, Du Bois, but also on how people viewed the Civil Rights movement. Only weeks later the governor of Michigan cited the Schlesinger article as hard evidence that the NAACP was nothing more than a communist front.

25. John Steele, *Berkshire Eagle,* April 18, 1968. Gerald Horne has closely studied the confluence of the streams of white racism and anti-communism. Noting the often-close ties between Senator Joseph McCarthy and the Dixiecrats, Horne remarks, "The repressors of Blacks and Reds tended to march in lockstep." And, as Horne notes, "Du Bois did not escape their attention." Horne, *Black and Red,* 2.

26. Quoted in Patricia West, *Domesticating History: The Political Origins of America's House Museums* (Washington: Smithsonian, 1999), 156–57. Her chapter is titled "The Bricks of Compromise Settle into Place: Booker T. Washington's Birthplace and the Civil Rights Movement." On the importance of the U.S. during the Cold War demonstrating to other nations of the world that it treated Blacks well, see Mary Dudziak, *Cold War, Civil Rights: Race and the Image of American Democracy* (Princeton: Princeton University Press, 2000).

In 1949 the NPS rejected the inclusion of Frederick Douglass's house, which remained administered by the National Association of Colored Women. The NPS finally incorporated the Douglass property in 1962.

27. Drew, *Great Barrington*, 378. Drew cites Stephen Fay, "FBI Takes Credit for Opposition to Du Bois Barrington Memorial," *Berkshire Eagle*, November 30, 1977. See also Rachel Fletcher, "W. E. B. Du Bois Memorial Committee," and "W. E. B. Du Bois Boyhood Homesite Photo Essay," in *African American Heritage in the Upper Housatonic Valley*, ed. David Levinson (Great Barrington: Berkshire Publishing Group, 2006), 37–44.

28. We especially thank Evelyn Jeffers for interviewing Mrs. Elaine Gunn on this subject and for our previous collaborations on the history of the Du Bois Homesite.

29. Du Bois described this veil in *The Souls of Black Folk*, 45. He also recalled a childhood incident when a white classmate refused to accept his calling card in *The Souls of Black Folk*, 44.

30. Elaine Gunn interview with Evelyn Jeffers, in Robert Paynter, Elizabeth Harlow, Evelyn Jeffers, John Diffley, and MaryEllen Loan, "Erasing and Commemorating Du Bois: The Politics of an Historic Landscape" in the symposium (Re) Historicizing the Human Landscape: Intersections Of Space/Race/Place/Memory, organized by Melissa Hargrove for the Annual Meeting of the American Anthropological Association, San Jose, California, November 19, 2006.

31. On the conflict between local and outsider, see Bass, *Those About Him Remained Silent*.

32. A short film of the 1969 dedication ceremony, including Bond's address, can be found at www.library.umass.edu/spcoll/dubois/?p=858.

33. For the 1979 ceremony in Tanglewood, see Drew, *Great Barrington*, 378; Rachel Fletcher, "W. E. B. Du Bois Memorial Committee," and "W. E. B. Du Bois Boyhood Homesite Photo Essay," in *African American Heritage in the Upper Housatonic Valley*, ed. Levinson, 37–44.

34. The results of the archaeological investigations at the homesite have been published in Nancy Muller, "The House of the Black Burghardts: An Investigation of Race, Gender, and Class at the W. E. B. Du Bois Boyhood Homesite," in *Those of Little Note*, ed. E. M. Scott (Tucson: University of Arizona Press, 1994), 81–94; Muller, "W. E. B. Du Bois and the House of the Black Burghardts: Land, Family and African Americans in New England," Ph.D. diss., University of Massachusetts, 2001; Robert Paynter, "Du Boisian Perspectives on Identities and Material Culture," *Anthropology Newsletter* 38, no. 5 (1997): 11; Paynter, "Afro-Americans in the Massachusetts Historical Landscape," in *The Politics of the Past*, ed. Gathercole and D. Lowenthal (London: Unwin Hyman, 1990), 49–62; Paynter, "The Transformations of the W. E. B. Du Bois Boyhood Homesite: A Consideration of Race, Class and Gender," presented in the Symposium on the Archaeology of the Cultural Landscape, organized by E. Hood and J. Garman for the Annual Meeting of the Society for American Archaeology, Las Vegas, NV, 1990; Paynter, "W. E. B. Du Bois and the Material World of African-Americans in Great Barrington, Massachusetts," *Critique of Anthropology* 12, no. 3 (1992): 277–91; Paynter, "The Cult of Whiteness in Western New England," in *Race and the Archaeology of Identity*, ed. C. E. Orser (Salt Lake City: University of Utah Press, 2001), 125–42. Paynter, Susan Hautaniemi, and Nancy Muller, "The Landscapes of the W. E. B. Du Bois Boyhood Homesite: An Agenda for an Archaeology of the Color Line," in *Race*, ed. S. Gregory and R. Sanjek (New Brunswick, NJ: Rutgers University Press 1994), 285–318; Paynter et al., "The Burghardts of Great Barrington: The View from the W. E. B. Du Bois Boyhood Homesite." Presented in the Symposium African American Archaeology in the North, at the Society of Historical Archaeology Annual Conference on Historical and Underwater Archaeology, York, England, 2005.

35. On the distinctive political economy of heritage in the United States relying so heavily on private capital, see David Glassberg, "What's 'American' about American Lieux de Mémoire?" in *The Merits of Memory: Concepts, Contexts, Debates*, ed. Hans-Jürgen

Grabbe and Sabine Schindler (American Studies—A Monograph Series) (Heidelberg: Universitaetsverlag Winter, 2008), 63–77.

36. Drew, *Great Barrington*, 375–79.
37. On the school-naming controversy, see Bass, *Those About Him Remained Silent*, 145–52.
38. See www.duboishomesite.org.
39. Levinson, ed., *African American Heritage in the Upper Housatonic Valley*.
40. "W. E. B. Du Bois in Great Barrington: A Plan for Heritage Conservation and Interpretation," prepared by Michael Singer Studio, July 2009.
41. A similar irony was noted by Manning Marable in his account of the 100th anniversary celebration of *The Souls of Black Folk* in Detroit in 2003. Marable, *Living Black History: How Reimagining the African American Past Can Remake America's Racial Future* (New York: Basic Books, 2006), 67–78.
42. Letter to Editor from Dave Brubriski, *Berkshire Record*, August 13–19, 2010.

CONCLUSION
Of Babies and Bathwater—Birthplace "Shrines" and the Future of the Historic House Museum

PATRICIA WEST

I write the concluding essay of this volume at a time when the viability of the historic house museum is in doubt. So it is with great concern that I approach the question of what the nature of the birthplace site can tell us about the meaning and future of the house museum. Seth Bruggeman has challenged us to ask "how can institutions that interpret birthplace monuments remain vital even as museum professionals openly debate whether house museums are still a worthwhile enterprise?"

Our generation's struggle to locate a current, culturally vital role for the house museum has been the subject of numerous anxious conference panels and professional conversations in recent years. Addressing what Gerald George called the "historic house malaise," a 2004 article inquired, "Does America Need Another House Museum?" The authors stated flatly that "the noble objective of interpretation for the public good may in fact be ill served when a building becomes a museum." Compounding generic troubles such as aging boards, maintenance backlogs, funding deficiencies, and problems with collections care, we have been asking ourselves why house museum visitation has dropped despite the apparent popularity of history. Standards for ethically closing house museums have been produced, and a recent book outlines several practical methods for de-museumizing historic houses as a means to assure their long-term preservation.[1]

Various explanations have been posited for this decline, among them the lure of electronic entertainment and the diminution of leisure time. But maybe the house museum is just entering a period of retooling and there is the possibility that it will evolve from earlier purposes that are no longer useful or engaging. If we want to reformulate the house museum to meet current needs, we might begin by recalling its roots as a "social instrument."[2] The American house museum was established in response to political and social issues of urgent concern. Although the goals and rhetoric from the house museum's early years may seem to us to range somewhere between quaint and offensive, this history helps us to realize that any house museum, even the seemingly inviolable birthplace "shrine," must be useful or risk becoming moribund. Questions before us as we contemplate the meaning of the birthplace in the new century include: what meaningful purpose can it serve? What content can underpin an interpretive approach that will raise salient questions and provide historical perspective for our time?

As we learned from the research of Thelen and Rosenzweig, history is most alive to people when they can find a personal connection to it, and people trust the history they learn at historic sites more than from any other institutional source.[3] Therefore our responsibility is a substantial one. If history has the power to shape culture, inform decisions, and inspire or inhibit social action, then the civic role of the house museum is clear. But this becomes trickier as we acknowledge the more problematical dimensions of the house museum in general and the birthplace in particular, or, as the introduction to this volume so cogently asks, "Will we always, as Henry James suggested over a century ago, be duped by commemorative hyperbole, or is there an opportunity in birthplace commemoration to do serious history?" But if we police against popular "commemorative hyperbole" in our efforts to do "serious history" at birthplaces, do we risk throwing the baby out with the bathwater?

Bruggeman refers above to the 1903 Henry James story "The Birthplace," in which Morris Gedge and his wife are hired as caretakers for a thinly disguised Stratford-upon-Avon birthplace "shrine." Although Mrs. Gedge embraces their genteel though remunerated task of giving tours of the birthplace of "Him," a crisis slowly brews as Mr. Gedge realizes that the entire tour is based on almost no evidence. The story follows his struggle with the problem of what this essay calls "the bathwater," the fact that birthplaces often have substantial dimensions that are pretty much fabricated. Morris Gedge, like Seth Bruggeman, dares to raise the plot-thickening question "what if he wasn't born here?"[4]

The story is more than just a parody of birthplace "shrines." Gedge's dilemma, in particular its denouement, highlights the Pragmatism of Henry's famous brother. William James would propose that truth can be a matter of utility; the "cash value" of ideas needs to be assessed. So when Mrs. Gedge urges her husband to suppress his doubts so that they can keep their jobs, to just accept the birthplace tale and convey it enthusiastically to the daily "pilgrims," she is a Pragmatist. Interestingly, it is Mrs. Gedge's romance with the "shrine" that emerges as the utilitarian approach, literalizing "the cash value" of truth, while Mr. Gedge's yearning for evidence-based objective truth threatens to undermine her practical goals. We may not be quite accustomed to thinking of house museum tours as illuminating scholarly trends, but if we consider the way Henry James parodied them in 1903, it seems that one of the great intellectual issues of the twentieth century could be understood through the problem of the birthplace "shrine." We may reflect on Gedge's internal conflict, and our own, in the context of the way William James described Pragmatism:

> The pragmatic method is primarily a method of settling metaphysical disputes that otherwise might be interminable. Is the world one or many?—fated or free?—material or spiritual?—here are notions either of which may or may not hold good of the world; and disputes over such notions are unending. The pragmatic method in such cases is to try to interpret each notion by tracing its respective practical consequences. What difference would it practically make to any one if this notion rather than that notion were true? If no practical difference whatever can be traced, then the alternatives mean practically the same thing, and all dispute is idle. Whenever a dispute is serious, we ought to be able to show some practical difference that must follow from one side or the other's being right.[5]

In other words, we can frame the task before us as explaining what difference it would practically make to anyone if he was not, in fact, born here. This question is at the heart of our enterprise, whether birthplaces, house museums, historic sites, or monuments. In this respect, it might be argued that the birthplace offers the best way to analyze the prototypical problems of the house museum genre, and the best way to envision its future.

The tension between popular myth and "objective" research in house museums dates to the early twentieth century, when a dynamic conflict between scientized professionalism and voluntarist romance became a hallmark of the American historic house museum. However, while professionalism ascended and claimed legitimacy, the mythological dimension of the genre has retained powerful sway. There is considerable romance in the house tour formula ruthlessly satirized by Henry James:

> It is in this old chimney corner, the quaint inglenook of our ances-tors—just there in the far angle, where His little stool was placed, and where, I dare say, if we could look close enough, we should find the hearthstone scraped with His little feet—that we see the inconceivable child gazing into the blaze of the old oaken logs and making out there pictures and stories, see Him conning, with curly bent head, His well-worn hornbook, or poring over some scrap of an ancient ballad, some page of some such rudely bound volume of chronicles as lay, we may be sure, in His father's window-seat.[6]

The standard house tour draws the visitor into a narrative that climaxes in a happy ending, a satisfying closure that may or may not reflect the facts of biography. This constitutes a quest "seeking in the unfolding of the narrative a line of intention and portent of design that hold the promise of progress toward meaning."[7] The search for meaning at birthplaces frequently represents a powerful enough need to override the constraints of serious history. Here is the fuel for "commemorative hyperbole."

That the formula for the house tour has arisen in the past from time-bound needs and interests explains in large part the fact that the vast majority of birthplace "shrines" memorialize white men. Concerns about particular issues in the political realm dominated the house museum in its first hundred years and onward, casting it in terms that mirrored the culture's exclusion of women and people of color from public places of power. Similarly, this explains the tendency of such places to romanticize domesticity, which has presented formidable challenges to efforts to incorporate the lives of those whose work make domestic life possible.[8] The irony that memorialized domestic settings obscure women's lives makes the entire house museum genre a kind of agent of the "feminine mystique."

Nowhere is this tropism more vivid than in the birthplace. Logically one would assume that birthplaces would have something to do with women, and the fact that their subject is nearly always men is our "problem that has no name," another paradoxical manifestation of women's centrality but invisibility, especially given the fact that women have been so crucial in creating these museums. As Bruggeman has suggested, the birthplace site is typically a sanitized paean to birth, not a place to learn about the history of childbirth. Stylized dimensions of birth may be memorialized, but the actual fact of birth is seen as quite irrelevant and too intimate for the public realm, despite its intense relevance to personal experience. The difficulty of applying the house tour formula cited above to such private matters has been the primary instrument of the ironic exclusion of the history of women from this genre of commemoration.

But before we proceed to a deeper critique of the well-known fact-scouring tendencies of birthplace romance, we should take a moment to reflect on ways of understanding the role of popular legend in constructing connections to the past. As we all know, the house museum is a phantasmagoria: a blend of earnest wish, myth, and metaphor, as well as a product of its own history. Although house museums are also sometimes about serious historical research, our audiences are not often in a position to make these distinctions, and in any case, fact is often rejected in favor of myth.

In this way, as Morris Gedge so painfully discovered, birthplace "shrines" are akin to "haunted houses." And hauntings, explains Judith Richardson, "are about belonging and possessing." In analyzing the meaning of haunted houses, Richardson wonders "how can we resolve the past, especially when that past is obscured by a tangle of myths and contending claims, apparently lost in the shadows of change and neglect, trampled under the feet of restless populations?" These "vexing questions," so similar to our own as we attempt to replace hyperbole with history at historic houses, press us to consider at last how we can "know or adjudicate whose place this is" and whose story will prevail.[9]

It is up to us to assert that there is no tale as compelling as one based on a true story. To make this case we should seek content that resonates and create environments that engage imaginative capacities. This approach rejects a dry search for debunking facts in favor of an explicit search for meaning. It challenges the ethos of what Eric Gable and Richard Handler called "mimetic realism," the idea that the past can somehow be authentically recreated.[10] If we let go of authority by admitting the constructed nature of historic houses, we can align with our audiences in a shared journey toward connection with the past through physical experience of its material remains, a task less scientific than spiritual. Professionals are important members of this choir, providing evidence here, replica there, but they are not the entire choir. In the end "objective facts" alone are not capable of generating the desired end of a historic house museum, an environment in which imaginative contact with the past is possible, through what might be called the metaphysics of the place. This experience is not authentic in the mimetic sense, but is authentic in its facilitation of an actual (versus virtual) experience. In practical terms, this means creating places that encourage contemplation, an antidote to both the standard fact-glutted house tour and the romance of fabricated tales.

Similarly, that it can be absolutely asserted that someone was once a baby is a basis for considerable consensus. A baby establishes an essential humanness, focusing us on not greatness itself, but the potential for greatness, a tenet of the democratic vision of individual promise at the heart of our civilization's hopes for the future. A baby vivifies the pose of time—we know what the midwife did not know, how the story would blossom, fade, and end, finally reachable only by imagination. In this way, a birthplace can raise life's most profound questions: where do we come from, what makes us who we are?

It is true, as Bruggeman suggests, that birthplaces "always connote a relationship between a person and a place," but another key element in the equation is time. They are, in fact, a matter of life and death, concretizing lives once led and shedding light on our own place in time. House museums have the capacity to put our own mortality in perspective and to remind us of the poignancy of death. They offer a place to consider what we might do with our time on earth, and what will remain to tell our story. This helps to legitimize the "innate religiosity" at birthplace "shrines," negotiating and loosening "the stubborn link forged in recent decades between modernity and disenchantment."[11]

If we use the power of the true story generated by strong research and storytelling, we can make the house museum more evocative, and less informative. In our time information is ubiquitous, but the opportunity for reflection and genuine experience is not. Imagine a house tour less like Gedge's and more like this:

Former residents recall that they cooked food, ate meals, washed dishes, bathed, sewed, took medicine, played music, churned butter, swept floors, rested and relaxed, washed clothes, and slept. Babies were conceived, and families heard the first cries of the newborn. In 1929, twenty-one-year-old Elizabeth "Mamie" Johnson gave birth to her second son, George, in the upstairs of this house, and in the months afterward rocked him to sleep in a cradle in the side room downstairs. Death visited this house. Around 1917, young Octavia Parker, whose family lived next door, was brought here by her mother to view the first dead person she ever saw—a small baby, the daughter of the Wilson family, laid out on a cooling board between two chairs in the "front room." She had never forgotten the sight of that tiny, still baby. It resembled a "little doll."[12]

There is rich potential in house museums to tell meaningful stories: childbirth, play, religion, work, worry, the real rhythms of human life, bound by time and place. With "virtual reality" and web "visits" to museums being proposed as viable "experiences," historic houses honor the power real things have to evoke, to inspire, and to raise questions. How may we best make use of time, its passing made palpable by standing in a nursery imagining "the first cries of the newborn" who lived and are now long past.

Just as music is a patterned structure of sound, we can structure the quest for meaning within house museums around the search for the truth, however illusive. But we must be clear that the past cannot be objectively recreated; it must be imagined. Likewise without the search for knowledge the quest devolves into pure fantasy that doesn't engage the need for connection with the reality of the past. The tension between romance and fact can be made conscious and artfully embraced. We can both learn and be awestruck by the metaphysics of the places and objects that affirm the reality of past lives and allow us to pause and reflect on the value of life. In an era proposing that there is such a thing as "virtual reality," the ability of these places to assert the realness of the past is an invaluable counterpoint.

Public history is history as a social act, a "usable past" in the keenest and most current sense, a way of reaching an audience of citizens and energizing them with heightened understanding. Public history is public service; let us be unafraid to claim its heritage as a vehicle for history that ordinary people need. As the great historian Carl Becker said in his 1931 essay "Everyman His Own Historian," our "proper function is not to repeat the past but to make use of it." What better purpose for house museums in a century shaping up to be one of extraordinary hardship than to give us places that, in the words of a psalm, can "teach us to number our days that we may apply our hearts unto wisdom."

NOTES

1. Patricia West, *Domesticating History: The Political Origins of the Historic House Museum* (Washington, DC: Smithsonian Institution Press, 1999); Gerald George, "The Historic House Museum Malaise: A Conference Considers What's Wrong," *History News* 57, no. 4 (2002): 4; Carol B. Stapp and Kenneth C. Turino, "Does America Need Another House Museum?" *History News* 59, no. 3 (2004): 7–11; Donna Ann Harris, *New Solutions for Historic House Museums* (Lanham, MD: Alta Mira, 2007). Cary Carson, in an essay first presented in September 2007 as a lecture addressed to the symposium "New Audiences for Old Houses," sponsored by the Nichols House Museum, Boston University, and the Boston Athenaeum, acknowledges the crisis but holds an optimistic view if history museums can creatively embrace a dynamic new form of storytelling using technology. Cary Carson, "The End of History Museums: What's Plan B?" *The Public Historian* 30 (Fall 2008): 9–27. See also "How Sustainable Is Your Historic House Museum?" AASLH Technical Leaflet 244 in *History News* 63, no. 4 (Autumn 2008).
2. Theodore Low, *The Museum as a Social Instrument* (New York: Metropolitan Museum of Art, 1942).
3. Roy Rosenzweig and David Thelen, *The Presence of the Past: Popular Uses of History in American Life* (New York: Columbia University Press, 1998).
4. Seth C. Bruggeman, *Here, George Washington Was Born: Memory, Material Culture, and the Public History of a National Monument* (Athens: University of Georgia Press, 2008), 199.
5. William James, *Pragmatism: A New Name for Some Old Ways of Thinking* (New York: Longmans, Green, 1907), 45–46.
6. Henry James, *The Birthplace* (1903; Reprint Whitefish, MT: Kessinger Publishing, 2010), 41.
7. Peter Brooks, *Reading for the Plot: Design and Intention in Narrative* (New York: Vintage, 1984), xiii.
8. See Jennifer Pustz, *Voices from the Back Stairs: Interpreting Servants' Lives at Historic House Museums* (DeKalb, IL: Northern Illinois University Press), 2010.
9. Judith Richardson, *Possessions: The History and Uses of Haunting in the Hudson Valley* (Cambridge: Harvard University Press, 2003), 8, 209.
10. Richard Handler and Eric Gable, *The New History in an Old Museum: Creating the Past at Colonial Williamsburg* (Durham, NC: Duke University Press, 1997).
11. Bruggeman, *Here, George Washington Was Born*, 15, 18.
12. George McDaniel, *Hearth and Home: Preserving a People's Culture* (Philadelphia: Temple University Press, 1982), 23.

About the Contributors

CHRISTINE ARATO is the chief historian and National Historic Landmarks program manager for the Southeast Region of the National Park Service. She is currently at work on planning and documentation projects for the Blue Ridge Parkway, Natchez National Historical Park, and a new park area that will interpret Reconstruction.

SETH C. BRUGGEMAN is an assistant professor of history and American studies at Temple University, where he also directs the Center for Public History. He is the author of *Here, George Washington Was Born: Memory, Material Culture, and the Public History of a National Monument* (2008).

DAN CURRIE is an education consultant at Admission Strategies in Boston and an independent historian and founding director of the Edgar Allan Poe Foundation of Boston.

KEITH A. EREKSON is an assistant professor of history at the University of Texas at El Paso, where he directs the university's Center for History Teaching & Learning. He is the author of *Everybody's History: Indiana's Lincoln Inquiry and the Quest to Reclaim a President's Past* (2012).

DAVID GLASSBERG is a professor of history at the University of Massachusetts Amherst. His research concerns the history of popular historical consciousness in America as represented in politics, culture, and the environment. Among his publications are *American Historical Pageantry: The Uses of Tradition in the Early Twentieth Century* (1990), and *Sense of History: The Place of the Past in American Life* (2001).

ANNA THOMPSON HAJDIK holds a Ph.D. in American studies from the University of Texas at Austin, where she has taught courses on rural America, popular culture, and Walt Disney. Her dissertation examines how rural life has been commodified and commercialized in an increasingly urbanized society and considers such topics as Laura Ingalls Wilder tourism, gentleman farming as a form of conspicuous consumption, and the countrified appeal of domestic diva Martha Stewart.

LAURA LAWFER ORR is the special events coordinator and educator at Hampton Roads Naval Museum in Norfolk, Virginia. She served previously as the director of Interpretation and Education at Stratford Hall and has worked with a number of public history organizations including Gettysburg National Military Park, the National Parks Conservation Association, the Greensboro Historical Museum, and the National Endowment for the Humanities.

ZACHARY J. LECHNER is a Ph.D. candidate in history at Temple University. His dissertation investigates Americans' political and cultural imaginings of the South in the 1960s and 1970s. He is the author of "'Are We Ready for the Conflict?': Black Abolitionist Response to the Kansas Crisis, 1854–1856," in *Kansas History: A Journal of the Central Plains* 31 (Spring 2008): 14–31.

PAUL LEWIS, professor of English at Boston College, is the author of two books—*Cracking Up: American Humor in a Time of Conflict* (2006) and *Comic Effects: Interdisciplinary Approaches to Humor in Literature* (1989)—and of articles on gothic fiction, dark humor, and American fiction and culture before the Civil War.

HILARY IRIS LOWE is assistant director of Corporate and Foundation Relations at Drexel University. She writes about literary and historic tourism at http://losthouses.blogspot.com and is the author of *Literary Destinations: Mark Twain's Houses and Literary Tourism* (2012).

CYNTHIA MILLER is a cultural anthropologist, specializing in popular culture and visual media. She is currently Scholar-in-Residence at Emerson College, and is a Kansas Humanities Council Scholar, a Research Fellow of the Will Rogers Memorial, and former Fellow of the Boston Historical Society. Her work has appeared in numerous edited volumes and journals, including *Film & History, Women's Studies Quarterly, Post Script, Social Justice,* and *The Journal of Popular Film and Television*.

ROBERT PAYNTER is a professor of anthropology at the University of Massachusetts Amherst, where his fields of specialization include historical archaeology and the philosophy and history of anthropology. Beyond his work with the W. E. B. Du Bois homesite in Great Barrington, current projects include an architectural history of the Sojourner Truth House. He is the author of numerous reports, journal essays, and *Models of Spatial Inequality: Settlement Pattern and Social Process* (1982).

ANGELA PHELPS is associate lecturer at The Open University, previously principal lecturer in heritage studies at the School of Arts and Humanities, Nottingham Trent University, both in the United Kingdom. Her interests include environmental history, cultural landscapes, and tourism. She has published academic research in heritage and tourism, and also works as a consultant in visitor management for local and national heritage attractions in England.

PAUL REBER is the executive director of Stratford Hall in Stratford, Virginia, and a Historian-in-Residence at American University. He has taught in the public history graduate programs at the University of North Carolina at Greensboro; is a past president of Old Salem, Inc., in Winston-Salem, North Carolina; and has worked with a number of other public historical organizations including the National Trust for Historic Preservation and Historic Mount Vernon.

PATRICIA WEST is a curator for the National Park Service at Martin Van Buren National Historic Site in Kinderhook, New York. She is co-director of the Center for Applied Historical Research at the University at Albany, where she has also taught in the public history graduate program. She is the author of *Domesticating History: The Political Origins of America's Historic House Museums* (1999).

Index